1987

THE CONVE
OF THE PEN

THE CONVERSE
OF THE PEN

*Acts of Intimacy
in the Eighteenth-Century
Familiar Letter*

BRUCE REDFORD

THE UNIVERSITY OF CHICAGO PRESS
Chicago and London

BRUCE REDFORD, associate professor of English at the University of Chicago, is preparing a four-volume edition of the letters of Samuel Johnson.

THE UNIVERSITY OF CHICAGO PRESS, CHICAGO 60637
THE UNIVERSITY OF CHICAGO PRESS, LTD., LONDON

© 1986 by The University of Chicago
All rights reserved. Published 1986
Printed in the United States of America

95 94 93 92 91 90 89 88 87 86   54321

LIBRARY OF CONGRESS CATALOGING-IN-PUBLICATION DATA

Redford, Bruce.
The converse of the pen.

Includes index.
1. English letters—18th century—History and criticism. 2. Authors, English—18th century—Correspondence. 3. Conversation—History—18th century. 4. Intimacy (Psychology) in literature.
5. Friendship—Great Britain—History—18th century.
I. Title.
PR915.R4 1986   826'.6'09   86-11237
ISBN 0-226-70678-8
ISBN 0-226-70679-6 (pbk.)

For my parents
and for
William Feay Shellman

To the extent that we bound our thinking by the so-called imaginative genres canonized in nineteenth-century criticism, we are cut off from a proper judgment of the so-called nonimaginative masterpieces. We neglect Gibbon for Goldsmith. Not our taste but our narrow critical method has sealed us in; and many who must be academic critics condemn themselves to the minute examination of tedious novels, motionless tragedies, icy pentameters, and frivolous essays sooner than confront the fascination of a Walpole or a Hume.

—Irvin Ehrenpreis, "Swift's Letters"

Contents

Acknowledgments

"Letters mingle Soules," and in more ways than Donne could have foreseen. My cherishable obligations reach far and deep, my ability to pay adequate tribute lags painfully behind. A bare chronicle of indebtedness must suffice.

Lora Clarice Bryning Redford first taught me what *the converse of the pen* could be and do. Most of the book she prepared me to write took shape at the Institute for Research in the Humanities, University of Wisconsin, Madison—a scholarly *locus amoenus* beyond compare. To the permanent fellows of the Institute I am deeply grateful for the privilege of spending a year in their midst. Phillip Harth in particular was indispensable.

The following people also made an important difference: Edward Bloom, Frank Brady, Robert Ferguson, Stephen Fix, Loretta Freiling, Barbara Hanrahan, Gwin Kolb, Thomas Palaima, Stephen Parks, John Riely, Edward Rosenheim, Charles Ryskamp, Pamela Schwandt, Sanford Schwartz, Ronald Thomas, Howard Weinbrot, Karl Weintraub. Finally, I must thank my two readers for The University of Chicago Press, both of whom made suggestions that improved the manuscript.

Most of chapter five appeared originally in *Philological Quarterly* 63 (Winter 1984): 55–73. I am gratetul to the editor for permission to reprint in book form.

Introduction

I make no scruple to aver, that a correspondence by letters, written on occasions of necessary absence, and which leaves a higher joy still in hope, which presence takes away, gives the most desirable opportunities of displaying the force of friendship, that can be wished for by a friendly heart. This correspondence is, indeed, the cement of friendship: it is friendship avowed under hand and seal: friendship upon bond, as I may say: more pure, yet more ardent, and less broken in upon, than personal conversation can be even amongst the most pure, because of the deliberation it allows, from the very preparation to, and action of writing. . . . Who then shall decline the converse of the pen? The pen that makes distance, presence; and brings back to sweet remembrance all the delights of presence; which makes even presence but body, while absence becomes the soul . . .

—*Richardson to Sophia Westcomb, 1746(?)*

S AMUEL RICHARDSON takes us to the heart of the matter—to the *cor* of *correspondence*—and thereby addresses the principal subject of this book, the familiar letter as intimate conversation.[1] For all their diversity of background

1. The etymology is inaccurate but suggestive, as Richardson (speaking through Lovelace) fully realized: "I loved familiar letter-writing, as I had more than once told her, above all the species of writing: it was writing from the heart (without the fetters prescribed by method or study), as the very word *correspondence* implied." See *Clarissa* (London and New York: Everyman's Library, 1962), 2.431. For a subtle commentary on the implications of this passage, see William Beatty Warner, *Reading* Clarissa: *The Struggles of Interpretation* (New Haven: Yale University Press, 1979), pp. 97–101.

and technique, the six letter-writers under consideration here were accomplished practitioners of "the humane art," the art "which owes its origin to the love of friends" and its texture to the primacy of a conversational paradigm.[2] All six share with Richardson a sense of the epistolary enterprise that favors voice, the speaking *tone* of voice, above all else. Reporting, interpreting, and recreating the outside world, the voice of the letter-writer "makes distance, presence" by virtue of that very "deliberation" and "preparation" the eighteenth century prized in actual conversation. Certainly "the converse of the pen" metaphor is not unique to the period: "what are letters," says Henry James for example, "but talk."[3] Yet the theory that underpins this metaphor, and the ways in which theory influences practice, do indeed define a specifically Augustan epistolary mode. The fundamental premise behind each chapter can be summarized as follows: the eighteenth-century familiar letter, like the eighteenth-century conversation, is a performance—an "act" in the theatrical sense as well as a "speech-act" in the linguistic.[4] Through a variety of techniques, such as masking and impersonation, the letter-writer devises substitutes for gesture, vocal inflection, and physical context.[5] The subtitle of this book—"Acts of Intimacy"—is intended to underscore those constant adjustments of voice and mask, text and subtext, that characterize epistolary performance.

2. Virginia Woolf, *The Death of the Moth and Other Essays* (New York: Harcourt, Brace and Co., 1942), p. 58.

3. *Selected Letters of Henry James*, ed. Leon Edel (London: Rupert Hart-Davis, 1956), epigraph.

4. For a helpful account of speech-act theory and its implications for literary criticism, see Mary Louise Pratt, *Toward a Speech Act Theory of Literary Discourse* (Bloomington and London: Indiana University Press, 1977), especially chap. 3.

5. Compare Barbara Herrnstein Smith's remarks on this subject in chap. 2 of *On the Margins of Discourse* (Chicago and London: University of Chicago Press, 1978), especially pp. 23, 35. Howard Anderson and Irvin Ehrenpreis make a similar point in their conclusion to *The Familiar Letter in the Eighteenth Century*: "If a good letter-writer had to appear candid and spontaneous, if he had to reveal his character in his manner, he was nevertheless expected to supply a substitute for the courtesy of visible gesture through the courtesy of his style . . ." (Lawrence: University of Kansas Press, 1966), pp. 274–75.

I

In eighteenth-century England conversation and letter-writing alike exemplified the paradox that informs the aesthetic theory of the period: "Nature" takes precedence over "Art," but it is "Nature *methodiz'd*." Dr. Johnson reminds us that face-to-face exchange among the élite was not random utterance but virtuoso exercise:

> Talking of conversation, he said, "There must, in the first place, be knowledge, there must be materials;—in the second place, there must be a command of words;—in the third place, there must be imagination, to place things in such views as they are not commonly seen in;—and in the fourth place, there must be presence of mind, and a resolution that is not to be overcome by failures . . ."[6]

Johnson practiced what his age preached. Swift, Addison, Steele, Shaftesbury, Chesterfield, Fielding, and a host of anonymous courtesy-writers—all exalted "the Art of Conversation." Every writer on the subject emphasized the importance of following rules designed to achieve an ideal of "Civility," an ideal finely poised between impertinent "Freedom" on the one hand and undue "Ceremony" on the other.[7] The theme of conscious yet unobtrusive "Management" prevails. The aim of such management, in the words of one courtesy-writer, is "to gain, conserve, or encrease the esteem and friendship of those we Converse with."[8]

If, as Herbert Davis has claimed, the Augustans regarded conversation as "the chief art of human life," then they accorded almost equal importance to the sister art of letter-writing.[9] William Cowper implies the kinship and defines the ideal when he declares to Lady Hesketh: "I love talking letters

6. *Boswell's Life of Johnson*, 6 vols., ed. G. B. Hill, rev. L. F. Powell (Oxford: Clarendon Press, 1934–50), 4.166.

7. See Henry Knight Miller's commentary in *Essays on Fielding's Miscellanies* (Princeton: Princeton University Press, 1961), pp. 166–80.

8. Quoted in Miller, p. 168, n. 29.

9. Herbert Davis, "The Conversation of the Augustans," in Richard Foster Jones et al., *The Seventeenth Century* (Stanford: Stanford University Press, 1951), p. 194.

3

dearly."[10] Two examples from popular treatises on the arts of language will serve to illustrate the prevalence of this close generic relationship and its implications for epistolary technique. The first treatise, Robert Dodsley's *The Preceptor* (1775), belongs to the popular genre of the courtesy and conduct manual. Its teachings reappear in the more elevated academic context of Hugh Blair's *Lectures on Rhetoric and Belles Lettres* (first edition, 1783).

Part I of *The Preceptor* sets out to give advice on reading, speaking, and letter-writing. "Grace and Propriety," the reader is told, should govern all three activities. The section devoted to letter-writing proper includes model epistles by Temple, Pope, Gay, Cicero, Pliny, Voiture, and Balzac, and concludes with a fictitious treatise, "To a young Gentleman at School," "on the Subject of Writing Letters." *The Preceptor* stresses the importance of "an expressive, genteel, and easy Manner," to be attained by methodizing Nature:

> Set Discourses require a Dignity or Formality of Stile suitable to the Subject; whereas Letter-writing rejects all Pomp of Words, and is most agreeable when most familiar. But, tho' lofty Phrases are here improper, the Stile must not therefore sink into Meanness: And to prevent its doing so, an easy Complaisance, an open Sincerity, and unaffected Good-nature, should appear in every Place. A Letter should wear an honest, chearful Countenance, like one who truly esteems, and is glad to see his Friend; and not look like a Fop admiring his own Dress, and seemingly pleased with nothing but himself.[11]

The writer concludes by extending the ideal of "obliging Manners" from stylistic and social behavior to speech itself: "What I have said of the Stile of your Letters, is intended as a Direction for your Conversation also, of which your Care is necessary, as well as of your Writing."[12]

---

10. *The Letters and Prose Writings of William Cowper*, ed. James King and Charles Ryskamp (Oxford: Clarendon Press, 1979–), 2.526.
11. Robert Dodsley, *The Preceptor*, 6th ed. (London: J. Dodsley, 1775), 1.108.
12. Dodsley, 1.108–9.

Blair's *Lectures* codified what had become one of the century's critical topoi. In Lecture 37, Blair positions his discussion of "epistolary writing" between "dialogue" and "fictitious history." He starts out by distinguishing carefully between philosophical discourses cast in an epistolary mold, as in Seneca and Shaftesbury, and actual letters intended for specific recipients. For Blair, "Epistolary writing becomes a distinct species of composition, subject to the cognizance of Criticism, only, or chiefly, when it is of the easy and familiar kind; when it is conversation carried on upon paper, between two friends at a distance."[13] He goes on to argue that, because "letters from one friend to another make the nearest approach to conversation," they ought to share with it the virtues of simplicity, sprightliness, and wit.[14] Though Blair lays primary stress on a "natural" manner in letter-writing, he contends at the same time "that the ease and simplicity which I have recommended in Epistolary correspondence, are not to be understood as importing entire carelessness."[15] He concludes his theoretical comments by reinforcing the comparison between good manners in social and epistolary intercourse: "The first requisite, both in conversation and correspondence, is to attend to all the proper decorums which our own character, and that of others, demand."[16] Negligence and affectation, too little method and too much art: these are the extremes the letter-writer must shun—just as he would avoid being typed as sloven or fop, babbler or preacher.

How does the eighteenth-century letter-writer—committed to "prattling upon paper," in Johnson's phrase—capture the artful spontaneity of conversation? How does he make himself fully present to his absent interlocutor? The basic challenge is to find satisfactory equivalents to the resources of an actor: the ironic intonation, the raised eyebrow, the rueful smile, the

13. Hugh Blair, *Lectures on Rhetoric and Belles Lettres,* 12th ed. (London: Cadell and Davies, 1812), 3.62.
14. Blair, 3.62.
15. Blair, 3.64.
16. Blair, 3.64.

sudden whisper, the emphatic change of posture, the meaningful glance across the room. Because of their particular literary and social milieu, the letter-writers under scrutiny here have several major advantages. The first and most important of these is a feeling of cultural consensus, which allows them to spin a delicately allusive web. Such a web substitutes for the physical presence that fosters intimacy between actor and audience. When Cowper quotes two words of Milton (p. 91), Gray a line of Horace (p. 105), or Johnson a sentence from Ecclesiasticus (p. 223), he can count on instantaneous recognition and the ability to recover the context of the original. Moreover, allusion is not restricted to literary texts: Lady Mary Wortley Montagu's letters to her sister, or Horace Walpole's to Lady Ossory, gain immeasurably in force and subtlety from the network of shared assumptions, attitudes, and acquaintances that pervades them. Solidarity of this kind promotes a uniquely Augustan union of economy and scope. Time and again meaning is encoded in a subtle shorthand to which the fragmentation of modern society denies us ready access.

Epistolary allusion often consists of resonant literary echoing or telegraphic social reportage. However, it can also expand into sustained impersonation, which delights in elaborate masking or plays off surface meaning against emotional subtext. The public forms of drama and satire supply our six letter-writers with precedents and mechanisms for their performance of private roles; indeed all six were, at one point or another, satirists and dramatists themselves.[17] As they practice it, the familiar letter becomes a form of *repraesentatio*, an exercise in "making present" like the performance of a play.

17. Satire: Lady Mary's *Town Eclogues*, Cowper's *Anti-Thelyphthora*, Gray's "On Lord Holland's Seat near Margate," Walpole's "Verses Addressed to the House of Lords," Boswell's "Ode by Dr. Samuel Johnson to Mrs. Thrale," and Johnson's *London*. Drama: Lady Mary's *Simplicity*, Gray's *Agrippina*, Walpole's *The Mysterious Mother*, Boswell's *The Justiciary Opera*, and Johnson's *Irene*. Cowper is the only one who did not write a play, though his early essays contain several dramatic vignettes, and he is said by Southey to have collaborated on a "burlesque cantata." See Charles Ryskamp, *William Cowper of the Inner Temple, Esq.*, (Cambridge: Cambridge University Press, 1959), p. 110.

Yet the crucial distinction, as Janet Altman reminds us, is that "epistolary language, which is the language of absence, makes present by make-believe."[18] The letter-writer is an actor, but a *magician*-actor who works on his audience by sustaining the illusion of physical presence. Consequently the truest letter, we might say, is the most feigning.

II

My former tutor at Cambridge, the Celtic historian Kathleen Hughes, begins her important study of early Christian Ireland quietly but firmly: "I have written this book because it is needed."[19] My own work, which grows out of a similar conviction, aspires likewise to open up new territory. Although literary historians have for decades been labeling the eighteenth century "the golden age of the familiar letter," no scholar has yet paid more than lip service to the unique craftsmanship of that age. Two books purport to investigate the theory and practice of the genre: William H. Irving's *The Providence of Wit in the English Letter Writers* (Duke University Press, 1955), and the miscellany called *The Familiar Letter in the Eighteenth Century* (University of Kansas Press, 1966). Both are unsatisfactory, albeit for different reasons. Professor Irving provides a general survey, which sprints from Donne to Burns with an introductory glance at classical and Continental models. He conducts a whirlwind tour, not a selective investigation; his procedure is that of the eager cicerone. *The Familiar Letter in the Eighteenth Century* gathers together essays by sixteen different authors. As might be expected, the individual contributions, many of which began life as conference papers, vary sharply in quality. Throughout the collection critical methodology is uncertain, judgments blurred, special pleading much in evidence. Only one essay, the afterword by Howard Anderson and Irvin Ehrenpreis, relates the work of indi-

18. Janet Altman, *Epistolarity: Approaches to a Form* (Columbus: Ohio State University Press, 1982), p. 140.

19. Kathleen Hughes, *Early Christian Ireland: Introduction to the Sources* (Ithaca: Cornell University Press, 1972), p. 11.

vidual letter-writers to a unified conception of the genre's special possibilities. The majority of the contributors to this volume, as well as Professor Irving, treat the letter as a documentary source, a lode of anecdote and observation, not as a verbal construct. The result is to misapprehend, and finally to trivialize, the accomplishment of the finest letter-writers.

In recent years both biography and autobiography—genres which tend to blur the Aristotelian distinction between history and poetry—have shouldered their way into the literary canon. Yet the familiar letter, an equally provocative "marginal" form, continues to suffer from critical neglect. The explanation, I would argue, has much to do with the vexed issue of generic placement: how can we do more than talk impressionistically about the letter until we can fix a category for it and then formulate appropriate aesthetic criteria?

Instead of nurturing an epistolary revival, our wisest contemporary student of such "borderline cases," Barbara Herrnstein Smith, has wedged the letter even more securely into its historical straightjacket. In her influential study, *On the Margins of Discourse,* Smith deploys two categories, "natural discourse" and "fictive discourse," to sort out a welter of "inscribed utterances"—everything from the advertisement to the epic. Examples of "fictive discourse" include poems, tales, dramas, and novels. "Natural discourse" Smith describes as "all utterances . . . that can be taken as someone's saying something, somewhere, sometime, that is, as the verbal acts of real persons on particular occasions in response to particular sets of circumstances."[20] These "particular sets of circumstances" constitute the *raison d'être* of "natural discourse," which "cannot be exclusively identified or described independent of its context, nor can its meaning be understood independent of that context."[21] A given verbal artifact should "be regarded as a *natural utterance* so long as it may be taken as the verbal response of a historically real person, occasioned and determined by a historically real universe."[22]

20. Smith, p. 15.
21. Smith, p. 21.
22. Smith, p. 20.

Though she concedes that "the linguistic features of letters often bear an interesting resemblance to those commonly associated with poetic discourse," Smith nevertheless places the epistolary genre in the category of "natural utterance."[23] Repeatedly she argues that a letter *reflects* a context while a poem *creates* it. For Smith, "what we mean when we speak of *interpreting* a poem is, in large measure, precisely this process of inference, conjecture, and indeed creation of contexts."[24] Certain verbal structures such as proverbs can shift from one camp into the other, but the letter is not one of them.

For all her acuity as theorist of the marginal, Smith manages to ignore the letter-writer's power to create a context as well as to reflect it. When the writer does both, the resulting artifact straddles the barrier between "fictive" and "natural" discourse, between "verbal artwork" and "event in nature."[25] At its most successful, in fact, epistolary discourse accomplishes something even more inventive: it fashions a distinctive world at once internally consistent, vital, and self-supporting. The letters of a master thereby escape from their origins as reservoirs of fact: coherence replaces correspondence as the primary standard of judgment. Such letters achieve, in Northrop Frye's words, "a centripetal structure of meaning" that coexists with a centrifugal movement outward into historical circumstance.[26]

Not all letter-writers achieve this cohesive structure, however. Why do we know in practice that a given writer is an indisputable master of the genre, another irredeemably mediocre? Three tentative criteria come to mind: autonomy, fertility, and versatility. The first of these three has been implicit in our discussion of the letter's potentially "fictive" status. The finest letter-writers project an identity that "stands in for, or memorializes, or replaces, or makes something else" of

---

23. Smith, pp. 23–24, 31.

24. Smith, p. 33.

25. Smith, p. 39.

26. Northrop Frye, *Anatomy of Criticism* (Princeton: Princeton University Press, 1957), pp. 73–74.

the time-bound *I*.[27] This autonomous *I* inhabits a microcosm it seeks to share with the reader—a microcosm that likewise "replaces, or makes something else" of the outside world. It must be emphasized that all great practitioners of the familiar letter are in some sense miniaturists: cultivating squares of ivory, they take infinite pains on a small scale. Their art freezes time by first isolating and then dissecting a tiny portion of experience. Their actual range of subject matter may vary widely, from Lady Mary Wortley Montagu's trans-European adventures to Cowper's cultivation of his tiny garden. Yet the scale of the letter-form minimizes this variation in raw materials: it places an escaped rabbit on a par with trials for treason or visits to a Turkish bath. Miniaturization accompanies and reinforces self-projection. Both in turn promote epistolary autonomy.

The second criterion is sustained fertility of invention. Lytton Strachey, one of the most perceptive connoisseurs of the familiar letter, draws our attention to the importance of a generous oeuvre: "To be a really great letter-writer it is not enough to write an occasional excellent letter; it is necessary to write constantly, indefatigably, with ever-recurring zest."[28] In the case of four of the six writers under consideration here (the exceptions being Boswell and Johnson), both the zest and the conscious commitment to the form lasted a lifetime. Sheer copiousness testifies to a sense of vocation, a feeling that letter-writing is not merely a stopgap enterprise, but rather a campaign for intimacy with the other.

The third criterion is that of versatility. Instead of assuming interest, great letter-writers create it: details are pruned and inflections calibrated according to the identity and interests of the recipient. The finest familiar letters are always correspondent-specific: they play to a particular audience.

27. James Olney, "Autobiography and the Cultural Moment," in *Autobiography: Essays Theoretical and Critical,* ed. James Olney (Princeton: Princeton University Press, 1980), p. 24.

28. Lytton Strachey, *Characters and Commentaries* (New York: Harcourt, Brace and Co., 1933), p. 247.

For example, Horace Walpole takes one event, the Gordon Riots of 1780, and reports it in three very different ways: a sober, factual chronicle to Sir Horace Mann; oratorical cadences to William Mason; and breathy, staccato bulletins to Lady Ossory (see chap. 4, pp. 162–76). Like the Ben Jonson of the court masques, the letter-writer dedicates himself to entertaining, reflecting, and finally inviting the audience through the looking glass.

The rationale for applying these criteria will come into sharper focus if we glance briefly at a letter that obviates Barbara Herrnstein Smith's binary opposition. I have chosen as a representative example Lady Mary's short but incisive account of the coronation of George II, the last of the brilliant series to her sister, Lady Mar:

> *I cannot deny but I was very well diverted the Coronation Day. I saw the procession much at my Ease in a House I fill'd with my own Company, and then got into the Hall without any trouble, where it was very entertaining to Observe the variety of airs that all meant the same thing, the Business of every walker there being to conceal Vanity and gain Admiration. For these purposes some languish'd and others strutted, but a visible Satisfaction was diffused over every countenance as soon as the Coronet was clapp'd on the Head. But she that drew the greatest Number of Eyes was indisputably the Countess of Orkney. She exposed behind a mixture of Fat and Wrinkles, and before a considerable pair of Bubbys a good deal withered, a great Belly that preceeded her; add to this the inimitable roll of her Eyes, and her Grey Hair which by good Fortune stood directly upright, and 'tis impossible to immagine a more Delightfull Spectacle. She had embellish'd all this with a great deal of Magnificence which made her as big again as usual, and I shou'd have thought her one of the largest things of God's making if my Lady St. John had not display'd all her Charms that day. The poor Dutchess of Montross Crep'd along with a Dozen of black Snakes playing round her Face; and my Lady Portland (who is fall'n away since her dismission from Court) represented very finely an Egyptian Mummy embroider'd over with Hieroglyphics. In General I could not perceive*

but the Old were as well pleas'd as the Young, and I (who
dread growing Wise more than any thing in the World) was
overjoy'd to observe one can never outlive one's Vanity.[29]

Approached as natural discourse, this letter leads us back into
the historical context from which it emerged. We experience
the Countess of Orkney, the Duchess of Montrose, and the
Countess of Portland not as self-sufficient characters on the
order of a Lady Booby or a Tabitha Bramble, but as historical
figures whose appearance and behavior can be tested against
other contemporary reports—Hervey's *Some Materials towards
Memoirs of the Reign of King George II* and Walpole's *Memoirs of
King George II.* From this perspective the questions we might
ask include the following. Do other sources confirm or deny
Lady Mary's description of the three women? Why does she
concentrate on them to the exclusion of other participants?
What explains her impulse to caricature, and therefore limits
her reliability as a witness? Does the fact that Lady Mar is
about to lapse into permanent insanity have any bearing on
the matter?

Such questions are valid but constraining. It is undeniable
that Lady Mary's letter constitutes a document in social and
political history, a piece of contingent evidence, an exhibit.
Reportage is part of its purpose and meaning. Yet at the same
time it creates its own context, its own coherent world. To
enjoy the letter we need know nothing outside it; to do it full
justice, in fact, we must curb the impulse to engage in constant "reality-testing." The letter is in large measure its own
sufficient gloss. It tells us, if we look closely, about its author
and its recipient. Diction, syntax, and tone define the narrator. Her emblematic cameos suggest a variety of purposes:
to entertain, to simplify, to minister through irony to both
writer and reader. The letter brings about, as it dramatizes,
an ironic disengagement from the world's foolishness. Although it gains from further knowledge of the series to which

29. *The Complete Letters of Lady Mary Wortley Montagu*, ed. Robert Halsband
(Oxford: Clarendon Press, 1965–67), 2.85–86.

it belongs (indeed I invite the reader to come back to it after completing chapter 1), it does not depend upon such knowledge.

The familiar letter, in sum, belongs exclusively to neither one of Smith's two categories. Instead it turns on the complex interplay between the natural and the fictive—between reflection and creation, history "outside" and artifice "within." The peculiar richness of the genre results from this very ambiguity of status. Like the Japanese poetic diary, we might say, the letter is "at once related to fact and freed by art"; like the diary, it moves between two poles, the historical and the artistic.[30] Certain letters tilt sharply in one direction or the other. The most brilliant, on the other hand, create, sustain, and complicate a mysterious tension between the claims of fact and the possibilities of art. It is invariably the case, however, that letters of every persuasion will only cooperate with an inquirer who is prepared to acknowledge their hybrid nature and adjust his critical stance accordingly. I have tried to be such an inquirer, one who lets the text in question insinuate the most fruitful approach rather than taking the narrow *a priori* road. The fluidity of the genre, in short, demands a corresponding flexibility in the reader. The merit of such a position must depend upon my success in making the rough places plain.

III

The Converse of the Pen presents itself as a group portrait in six panels. The panels are hinged so as to compose three diptychs. These diptychs draw attention to certain underlying similarities in posture, expression, and personal history; their format does not rule out the possibility of other, equally suggestive pairings. In fact all six panels can be viewed in isolation, as one half of a pair, or as part of the whole. The composition *in toto* asks to be apprehended simultaneously, not se-

---

30. *Japanese Poetic Diaries*, trans. Earl Miner (Berkeley, Los Angeles, London: University of California Press, 1969), p. 10.

quentially: instead of telling stories, it probes relationships. From the formal point of view, the portrait belongs to that most engaging of eighteenth-century genres, the conversation piece, which depicts a family as a collective unit without blurring the uniqueness of individual members.

Part I, "Fortifying a Self," traces the ways in which Lady Mary and William Cowper construct designs for living that are also designs for writing. Lady Mary's tenacious stoicism offers her a voice that disciplines sorrow, a style that enacts the virtues of ironical distancing. William Cowper achieves a similar detachment by exploiting the capacity of the familiar letter to reflect and to shrink the outside world. To correspond for both these letter-writers is to sustain a precarious equilibrium between chaotic emotion and lifeless withdrawal. Despite basic differences in style and background, both take strength from an epistolary microcosm that first prefigures and then mirrors a secluded *hortus conclusus* (Gottolengo for Lady Mary, Olney for Cowper).

I have appropriated the title of Henry Fielding's first play, *Love in Several Masques,* as a rubric for Part II, which pairs two letter-writers who simultaneously project and disguise their affection by means of dramatic impersonation. Thomas Gray suggests feelings and tells stories through an assortment of literary masks, often derived from comic drama (Mistress Quickly, Widow Blackacre). His friend Horace Walpole carries epistolary masking to its extreme: so completely does he alter his identity from correspondence to correspondence that the actor often becomes indistinguishable from his role. Both men shape a variety of "implied authors" for a motley crew of "implied readers," but it is Walpole alone who vanishes chameleon-like into his audience.

Part III presents two case studies in the creation and the collapse of epistolary intimacy. The first examines James Boswell's correspondence with two spirited men of affairs, the Earl of Pembroke and John Wilkes. Though he can "chat freely" with Lord Pembroke when they meet, Boswell is unable to sustain an epistolary conversation of sufficient gaiety and ease to overcome the obstacles of absence and social inferiority. In his letters to Wilkes, by contrast, Boswell devises an intimate voice that works through, even makes capital of, the startling discrepancies between correspondents. For all his distrust of the familiar letter, Samuel Johnson displays an alchemical talent similar to Boswell's: against all the odds, the public moralist succeeds in converting young Mrs. Thrale of Streatham Park into "my Mistress." For twenty years he puts into practice all the resources of the eighteenth-century letter-writer: a flexible conversational manner, a repertoire of literary and social allusion, a flair for dramatic impersonation. Johnson's letters to Mrs. Thrale provide a fitting conclusion to this study, for they epitomize both the richness and the fragility of "the converse of the pen."

One final caveat: though it probes certain techniques that might well be considered novelistic, this book does not attempt to trace connections between letter-writing in "real life" and the development of epistolary fiction. To do so would be to stretch the chosen subject irreparably out of shape, and to deny the letter-form both the exclusive attention and the specific methodology that have long been its due. Consequently, research into generic cross-pollination must await another investigator. It is a worthy enterprise; it happens not to be mine.

Throughout my inquiry I have aimed to be suggestive rather than exhaustive: dogmatic and loquacious criticism of texts as concise and tactful as these would betray, at the very least, a culpable tone-deafness. Furthermore, I am convinced that the talents of the miniaturist are as desirable in the critic as they are necessary to the letter-writer. Whether the chapters that follow do satisfactory homage to their subjects is a matter I am least equipped to judge.

Part One

Fortifying a Self

1

Lady Mary Wortley Montagu: The Compass of the Senecan Style

Des sensations trop vives et trop fortes pour sa machine, une activité excessive qui manque d'objet satisfaisans voila la source de tous ses maux. Avec des organes moins sensibles, Zélide eut eu l'âme d'un grand homme, avec moins d'esprit et de raison, elle n'eut été qu'une femme foible.

—*Portrait de Zélide*

LADY MARY WORTLEY MONTAGU professed to despise her great predecessor and namesake, Marie de Rabutin-Chantal, Marquise de Sévigné: "How many readers and admirers has Madame de Sevigny, who only gives us, in a lively manner and fashionable Phrases, mean sentiments, vulgar Prejudices, and endless repetitions! Sometimes the tittle tattle of a fine Lady, sometimes that of an old Nurse, allwaies tittle tattle . . ."[1] Perhaps a feeling of literary rivalry prompted these disparaging remarks: after reading the first edition of the *Lettres* in 1726, Lady Mary asserted "without the least vanity that mine will be full as entertaining 40 years hence" (2.66). Yet something more significant than competitive zeal is at issue here, something Lady Mary's granddaughter Lady Louisa Stuart called "a marked opposition of character between the two women": "The head was the governing power with the one, the heart with the other. If they had lived at the same time, and in the same country and society, they would

1. *The Complete Letters of Lady Mary Wortley Montagu*, 3 vols., ed. Robert Halsband (Oxford: Clarendon Press, 1965–67), 3.62. Subsequent references, all to this edition, will be placed parenthetically in the text.

not have accorded well together."[2] Lady Louisa's astute judgment cannot be faulted: her grandmother's head was undoubtedly "the governing power"—but only because she deliberately and painfully willed it to be so. In fact Lady Mary's letters and other writings chart an unremitting conflict between thinking and feeling. In her early teens she wrote an extravagant pastoral romance, "The Adventurer," which terminates in cynical flippancy.[3] In her forties she turned Perrault's "La Belle au bois dormant" into an autobiographical tale that dramatizes the tension between qualities of judgment, learning, and taste on the one hand and "un grand fond de tendresse" on the other.[4] In her sixties she wept over *Clarissa* and abused it simultaneously as "most miserable stuff" (3.9). Only in her epistolary art did Lady Mary achieve a genuine equilibrium, based on the simultaneous expression and containment of emotion.

Le style est la femme même—or at least the woman as she wished to be. Once again, Lady Louisa speaks to the point:

> As writers also they were dissimilar: Lady Mary wrote admirable letters; *letters*—not dissertations, nor sentimental *effusions*, nor strings of witticisms, but real letters; such as any person of plain sense would be glad to receive. . . . she meant to write well, and was conscious of having succeeded. Madame de Sévigné had no such consciousness; she did not so much *write*, as talk and think upon paper, with no other aim than to make Madame de Grignan present at every incident, and partaker of every feeling, throughout the twenty-four hours of her day.[5]

Plain sense and conscious control: these provide the keys to Lady Mary's epistolary method. Like any dedicated practitioner of the form, she writes in order to communicate with

2. "Biographical Anecdotes of Lady M. W. Montagu," In *Essays and Poems*, ed. Robert Halsband and Isobel Grundy (Oxford: Clarendon Press, 1977), p. 51.

3. See Robert Halsband, "Lady Mary Wortley Montagu and Eighteenth-Century Fiction," *Philological Quarterly* 45 (January 1966): 146.

4. *Essays and Poems*, pp. 153–55.

5. *Essays and Poems*, p. 51.

those she cares for the most. She writes a *particular* kind of letter, however, because of her chosen philosophical outlook and the discipline involved in acting out that philosophy through the medium of language.

Lady Mary found in Stoic teaching and the Senecan style associated with it a design both for living and writing. Her life (fractured within, embattled without) stamps her prose; her prose in turn molds her life. In short, Lady Mary seeks and finds salvation in verbal craftsmanship; she subjects refractory nature to the rigor of art. Madame de Sévigné can afford to let herself go stylistically; her unself-conscious "tattle" reflects a basic security in what Virginia Woolf has called "background": "She is heir to a tradition, which stands guardian and gives proportion. The gaiety, the colour, the chatter, the many movements of the figures in the foreground have a background. . . . But this background, while it gives its scale to the moment, is so well established that she is secure."[6] Lady Mary lacks this security, this external scale, this constructive framework. She feels herself alone: a woman of superior intellect and learning who courts ridicule when she displays either; a wife of tender sensibilities married to an unresponsive husband; a friend mistrusted by most of her circle. Though he overstates his case, Walter Bagehot long ago suspected the truth of the matter: "But it now seems clear that Lady Mary was that most miserable of human beings, an ambitious and wasted woman; that she brought a very cultivated intellect into a very cultivated society; that she gave back to that society what it was most anxious to receive, and received from it all which it had to bestow;—and yet that this all was to her as nothing."[7]

Her letters tell us that pain, frustration, and melancholy must be stoically borne, stoically expressed. Their distinguishing feature, Lady Mary's version of the loose Senecan style,

6. "Madame de Sévigné," in Virginia Woolf, *The Death of the Moth and Other Essays* (New York: Harcourt, Brace and Co., 1942), p. 55.

7. *The Collected Works of Walter Bagehot*, ed. Norman St. John-Stevas (Cambridge, Mass.: Harvard University Press, 1965), 2.209.

itself constitutes a compass—a way of establishing bearings and steering clear of the rocks. The uses of that style are seen to fullest effect in the letters to her sister and her daughter. In these two intimate correspondences, and in them alone, Lady Mary enters what Carroll Smith-Rosenberg has called "the female world of love and ritual," in which "the emotional ties between nonresidential kin were deep and binding and provided one of the fundamental existential realities of women's lives."[8] Because they display Lady Mary's art of intimacy at its finest, this chapter will focus on the letters to Lady Mar and Lady Bute. It begins with a discussion of Lady Mary's personal brand of Stoicism, and concludes with a look at her letters to Francesco Algarotti, in which stoical control is cast to the winds.

Lady Mary referred to her version of Stoicism as "my Philosophy" (3.161, 211). Though she did not expound this philosophy in any detail, she did take care to draw her daughter's attention to a pair of basic maxims: "we ought all to follow the rule of Epicte[t]us, bear and forbear" (3.226), and "What is most in our power (thô little so) is the disposition of our own Minds" (2.480). The most complete application of these Stoic tenets occurs in the context of a letter that concerns the rearing of Lady Bute's children:

> I cannot help adding (out [of] my real affection to you) I wish you would moderate that fondness you have for your children. I do not mean you should abate any part of your Care, or not do your Duty to them in its utmost extent, but I would have you early prepare your selfe for Disapointments, which are heavy in proportion to their being surprizing. It is hardly possible in such a number that none should be unhappy. Prepare your selfe against a misfortune of that kind. I

8. Carroll Smith-Rosenberg, "The Female World of Love and Ritual: Relations between Women in Nineteenth-Century America," *Signs* 1 (Autumn 1975): 11. Though Smith-Rosenberg centers her analysis on middle-class American women of the late eighteenth and the nineteenth centuries, many of her generalizations concerning "female closeness and support networks" (p. 10) apply to Lady Mary's world as well.

> *confess there is hardly any more difficult to support, yet it is*
> *certain Imagination has a great share in the pain of it, and it*
> *is more in our power (than it is commonly beleiv'd) to soften*
> *what ever ills are founded or augmented by Fancy. Strictly*
> *speaking, there is but one real evil; I mean acute pain. All*
> *other Complaints are so considerably diminish'd by Time that it*
> *is plain the Greife is owing to our Passion, since the sensation*
> *of it vanishes when that is over.*

$$(2.451)$$

The emphasis on endurance, emotional detachment, resignation to the inevitable, and the rational assessment of pleasure and pain—all bespeaks a fundamental grounding in and commitment to the doctrines of classical Stoicism. Yet Lady Mary was neither frigid theoretician nor heroic Arria. From bitter experience she knew the difficulties of practicing what she herself recommended. As she makes clear in a letter to her husband about their delinquent son, Stoic teaching defines an ideal to which fallible human beings can only aspire:

> *At my time of Life I ought to be detach'd from a World which*
> *I am soon to leave. To be totally so is a vain Endeavor, and*
> *perhaps there is Vanity in the Endeavor. While we are*
> *Human we must Submit to Human Infirmitys, and suffer*
> *them in Mind as well as Body. All that Reflection and Experi-*
> *ence can do is to mitigate, we can never extinguish, our*
> *passions. I call by that Name every Sentiment that is not*
> *founded upon Reason . . .*

$$(2.482-83)$$

Such rueful understanding makes her continuing struggle for self-mastery all the more admirable.

Lady Mary acquired her Stoic convictions and the style that went with them from a variety of sources. The first of these was undoubtedly her father's richly stocked library, which she ransacked during her solitary youth and adolescence:

> Laeticia had naturally the strongest Inclination for Reading,
> and finding in her Father's house a well furnish'd Library, in-
> stead of the usual diversions of children, made that the seat of

her Pleasures, and had very soon run through the English part of it. Her Appetite for knowledge encreasing with her years, without considering the toilsome task she undertook she begun to learn her selfe the Latin Grammar, and with the help of an uncommon memory and indefatigable Labour made her selfe so far mistrisse of that Language as to be able to understand allmost any Author.[9]

The *Catalogus Bibliothecae Kingstonianae,* now in the British Library, lists five editions and translations of Epictetus and twenty-four of Seneca, including Erasmus's *Flores excerpti* and Sir Roger L'Estrange's *Abstract of Seneca's Morals.*[10] During this same period of intensive reading in the classics, Lady Mary was tutored by Bishop Gilbert Burnet, an admirer of Seneca who both practiced and preached "an easy Simplicity of Stile."[11] When she moved to London she came into close contact with those influential writers, principally Addison and Pope, who admired the Stoic philosophers and formed their prose on the Senecan model.[12]

Most important of all, however, was Lady Mary's own translation of Epictetus's *Enchiridion,* which she prepared from a Latin version (possibly the edition with notes and commentary by Politian and Arrian) during the summer of 1710 and sent to Burnet for his corrections. Her subsequent letters echo many of the *Enchiridion's* central precepts. To quote only those whose influence can be traced directly: "Whoever then

9. *Essays and Poems,* pp. 77–78.
10. British Library 1888.d.7. Information supplied by Professor J. L. Logan. L'Abbe Jean-Bernard Le Blanc described the Duke of Kingston's library as "une Biblioteque tres magnifique.... Elle est composée d'un tres grand nombre de Livres Grecs, Latins, Anglois & François, bien conditionés & avec assés de recherche pour le choix des Editions." See Hélène Monod-Cassidy, *Un Voyageur-Philosophe au XVIIIe Siecle* (Cambridge, Mass.: Harvard University Press, 1941), pp. 266–67.
11. Gilbert Burnet, *A Discourse of the Pastoral Care* (London: Printed for Richard Chiswell, 1692), p. 111.
12. For Lady Mary's literary relations with Addison and Addisonian Stoicism, see in particular her critique of *Cato* in *Essays and Poems,* pp. 62–68. For Seneca's influence on Pope, see W. H. Irving, *The Providence of Wit in the English Letter Writers* (Durham: Duke University Press, 1955), pp. 49–50, 180.

would be free, let him wish nothing, let him decline nothing, which depends on others; else he must necessarily be a slave" (14); "For this is your business, to act well the given part" (17); "When you do anything from a clear judgment that it ought to be done, never shrink from being seen to do it, even though the world should misunderstand it; for if you are not acting rightly, shun the action itself; if you are, why fear those who wrongly censure you?" (35); "The condition and characteristic of a philosopher is, that he looks to himself for all help or harm. . . . He restrains desire, he transfers his aversion to those things only which thwart the proper use of our own will. . . . in a word, he keeps watch over himself as over an enemy and one in ambush" (48).[13]

Not only did Lady Mary's close reading of Epictetus exercise a decisive influence on her philosophical outlook, it also shaped her mature epistolary style. A simple before-and-after comparison establishes the decisive importance of her exposure to the Stoic world of disciplined emotion and laconic expression. In March 1710, three months before undertaking the translation, she writes to Frances Hewet:

> 'Tis so long since I had a letter from dear Mrs. Hewet, I should think her no longer in the land of the living, if Mr. Resingade did not assure me he was happier than I, and had heard of your health from your own hand, which makes me fancy that my last miscarried, and perhaps you are blaming me at the same time that you are thinking me neglectful of you. . . . By long standing on the wall the bricks loosened, and one fatal morning down drops Miss Nelly, and to compleat the misfortune, she fell into a little sink, and bruised her poor—self to that terrible degree, she is forced to have surgeons' plaisters, and God knows what, which discovered the whole intrigue; and their mamma forbade them ever to visit us, but by the door.
>
> (1.22–23)

13. I quote from the Carter-Higginson translation of the *Enchiridion* (Boston: Little, Brown & Co., 1890).

The breathy tone, the rambling syntax, the blandly conventional diction, and the equally conventional sentiments, all contribute to the impression of exclamatory gush. This is the style that characterizes the earliest letters, 1708–10. On the same day that Lady Mary sends her translation to Burnet, however, she abandons the voice of Lydia Melford for that of Epictetus:

> *You speak of losing £20,000. Lose nothing for me. I set you free from any engagement you may think your selfe under. Tis too generous that you take me with nothing; I can never deserve even that Sacrifice. You shall not however have to reproach your selfe or me that I have lessen'd your fortune. You do not know how much I think my selfe oblig'd for what you have allready done. I would make you any return in my power.*
>
> (1.47)

The same clipped, sententious prose marks her next letter to Frances Hewet, which exemplifies a remarkable advance in the handling of irony, the etching of character, and the ability to place the experience of the moment into a larger perspective:

> *For my part I am content my selfe in my humble sphere, am passive in all disputes, and endeavor to study my Italian in peace and quietnesse. But people mistake very much in placeing peace in woods and Shades; I beleive solitude puts folks out of Humour and makes em disposd to quarrel . . .*
>
> (1.50)

Perhaps the most poised and most revealing of her letters to Edward Wortley comes only a month later, during that same "stoic" summer:

> *The dispute I have at present with my selfe is whither I will or will not marry at all. Now in my opinion you are very much obligd to me that it is a dispute. I should not hesitate upon manny proposalls. Was I sure that you would live after a way agreable to me, I should not be long in makeing my Answer. . . . If you expect Passion I am utterly unacquainted*

with any. It may be a fault of my temper. Tis a stupidity I could never justifye, but I do not know I was in my Life ever touch'd with any. I have no Notion of a Transport of Anger, Love, or any other. I here tell you the plain state of my Heart, and more than I shall ever think it worth my while to tell another.

(1.53–54)

Senecan style mirrors Stoic content: tightly controlled feelings express themselves in prose of utter concision and lucidity.

Henceforth Lady Mary commits herself to clear thinking and plain writing. The management of the emotions and of the pen accompany and reinforce each other: "I endeavour to make my Solitude as agreable as I can. Most things of that kind are in the power of the mind; we may make our selves easy if we cannot perfectly happy" (1.107). Throughout her life she finds ease of mind by working toward ease of expression. Her post-*Enchiridion* voice speaks in the deceptively smooth cadences of the later Montaigne. Its qualities are best described by Justus Lipsius, whose praise of Seneca in the *Manuductio ad Stoicam philosophiam* rings true for Lady Mary: "*Verba*, selecta, propria, significantia: imò quae plus aliquid semper dicunt, quam dicunt. Qui proprius quidam ejus Genius videtur, ut in parcimoniâ verborum mira ἐνέργεια atque efficacia sit; in brevitate, claritas et splendor."[14]

The letter to Burnet that accompanies Lady Mary's translation of the *Enchiridion* consists in the main of an apology for the liberal education of women supported by several quotations from Erasmus's "Colloquia Familiaria Abbatis et Eruditae." In this dialogue between a learned lady and a brutish

14. Justus Lipsius, *Opera omnia* (Vesaliae: Apud Andraeam ab Hoogenhuysen et Societatem, 1675), 4.676. Lipsius's encomium is quoted and translated in George Williamson, *The Senecan Amble: A Study in Prose Form from Bacon to Collier* (Chicago: University of Chicago Press, 1951), p. 111: "His words are choice, suitable and significant; they always mean something more than they actually say. And this seems a special genius of his, that in an economy of words he has a wonderful force and efficacy; in brevity he has clearness and brilliance."

abbot, Erasmus maintains that women have the same capacity for learning as men, and that, far from being morally subversive, education actually fortifies the female sex against temptation. Lady Mary founds her defense on Erasmus and on one of the maxims of Epictetus that she had just finished translating:

> Women, after fourteen, are presently called mistresses; afterwards, when they see themselves without any place or employment, except they are married, they begin to dress, and place all their hope in outward ornament. A man ought therefore to do his endeavours to show them they have but one way to be honoured, to behave themselves modestly, soberly, and chastely.[15]

She echoes her own translation in the letter to Burnet, while stiffening and extending the maxim into forthright polemic:

> *We are permitted no Books but such as tend to the weakening and Effeminateing the Mind, our Natural Deffects are every way indulg'd, and tis look'd upon as in a degree Criminal to improve our Reason, or fancy we have any. We are taught to place all our Art in adorning our Outward Forms, and permitted, without reproach, to carry that Custom even to Extravagancy, while our Minds are entirely neglected . . .*
>
> (1.44–45)

Lady Mary was assured of a sympathetic audience, for Gilbert Burnet's position, as she must have known, closely approximated her own: "The ill Methods of Schools and Colleges give the chief Rise to the Irregularities of the Gentry; as the breeding young Women to Vanity, Dressing and a false Appearance of Wit and Behaviour, without proper Work or a due Measure of Knowledge and a serious Sense of Religion, is the Source of the Corruption of that Sex . . ."[16] Lady Mary never ceases to uphold the basic Erasmian position, as expounded in this colloquy, Erasmus's letter to William Bud-

---

15. *The Letters and Works of Lady Mary Wortley Montagu*, ed. Lord Wharncliffe, rev. W. Moy Thomas (London: George Bell and Sons, 1887), 2.420.

16. Gilbert Burnet, *History of his own Time* (London: T. Ward, 1724–34), 2.653.

aeus on Thomas More's scheme of education for his daughter, and the *Christiani Matrimonii Institutio.*

However, Lady Mary is careful, like Erasmus before her, never to depart from Pauline teaching:

> *I am not now arguing for an Equality for the 2 Sexes; I do not doubt God and Nature has thrown us into an Inferior Rank. We are a lower part of the Creation; we owe Obedience and Submission to the Superior Sex; and any Woman who suffers her Vanity and folly to deny this, Rebells against the Law of the Creator and indisputable Order of Nature.*
>
> (1.45)

Robert Halsband, who interprets these sentiments as a mere token profession of orthodoxy, contends that "in advocating learning for women Lady Mary again shows herself a pioneer feminist."[17] In fact she never champions the legal, political, social, or economic equality of women. Quite the contrary: "I do not complain of men for haveing engross'd the Government. In excluding us from all degrees of power, they preserve us from many Fatigues, many Dangers, and perhaps many Crimes" (3.40). The various "feminist" passages in her letters and essays argue instead for the innate *intellectual* potential of women, the passionate conviction that, contrary to what most men believe, "Feminae christianae convenit studium Litterarum."[18] She defends this thesis mainly on pragmatic grounds:

> J'ose avancer hardiment que la Conduitte de la plûspart des Femmes fait plus de mal que du bien. Elles deviennent insensiblement des animaux plus nuisibles qu'utiles. J'attribue cette depravation a la mauvaise education qui éttouffe l'esprit naturel des unes, et augmente la folie des autres. Si les Hommes vouloient seulment nous regarder comme un parti dans l'etat (car je me soumets a l'inferiorité quoyque je pû dire mille qui a écrit comme vous sçavez, pour prouver l'egalite des sexes) ils doivent tacher de mettre a profit tous les Talents.[19]

17. *Essays and Poems,* p. 165.
18. *Essays and Poems,* p. 165.
19. *Essays and Poems,* p. 166.

Her finest poem, the "Epistle from Mrs. Y[onge] to her Husband," moves to the offensive: in the voice of an adulterous wife it attacks the double standard that denies women a substantive education in literature and philosophy, yet holds them to a more stringent code of ethical conduct:[20]

> From whence is this unjust Distinction grown?
> Are we not form'd with Passions like your own?
> Nature with equal Fire our Souls endu'd,
> Our Minds as Haughty, and as warm our blood,
> O're the wide World your pleasures you persue,
> The Change is justify'd by something new;
> But we must sigh in Silence—and be true.
> Our Sexes Weakness you expose and blame
> (Of every Prattling Fop the common Theme),
> Yet from this Weakness you suppose is due
> Sublimer Virtu than your Cato knew.
> Had Heaven design'd us Tryals so severe,
> It would have form'd our Tempers then to bear.
>
> (11.25–37)

It would be a mistake to conclude on the basis of such eloquent passages that Lady Mary was embarked upon a pioneering crusade for female emancipation. In fact she held most women in contempt: "To say Truth, I have never had any great Esteem for the gennerality of the fair Sex, and my only Consolation for being of that Gender has been the assurance it gave me of never being marry'd to any one amongst them" (2.33). Her so-called feminism is rooted not in an altruistic zeal for reform but in loneliness and frustration; it is not a dogmatic credo but a product of her own struggle against those forces that threaten to corrupt and destroy the integrity of the individual. Her letters to Lady Bute, advising on the upbringing of her granddaughters, make it clear that education for women is meant to provide resources for solitude, not a launching pad for social revolution:

20. For a perceptive commentary on the poem and its background, see Isobel Grundy, "Ovid and Eighteenth-Century Divorce: An Unpublished Poem by Lady Mary Wortley Montagu," *Review of English Studies* 23 (November 1972): 417–28.

*I am not now endeavoring to remove the prejudices of Man-
kind. My only Design is to point out to my Grand Daughters
the method of being contented with that retreat to which probably their circumstances will oblige them, and which is perhaps
preferable to all the show of public Life. It has allwaies been
my Inclination.*

(3.27)

In her own retreat, a self-imposed exile of almost twenty-
three years' duration, Lady Mary cultivates the inner strength
that a humanistic education has fostered. In her view, only
such an education can teach women, who are denied the active life open to men, the rationale and the method of for-
bearance: "The use of knowledge in our Sex (beside the
amusement of Solitude) is to moderate the passions and learn
to be contented with a small expence, which are the certain
effects of a studious Life and, it may be, preferable even to
that Fame which Men have engross'd to themselves and will
not suffer us to share" (3.22–23). The female mind should be
its own place, indifferent to the capricious judgments of "the
World," which most women have been taught to fear and to
placate at all costs. Thus Lady Mary's "feminism" issues from
and returns to her guiding stoical philosophy.

The casual reader of Lady Mary's letters to her sister the
Countess of Mar, wife of the exiled Jacobite Earl, might well
consider them sparkling but shallow—the epistolary equivalent of *vers de société,* products of a decorative, brittle sensibility. Careful attention to emotional subtext as well as
biographical context dictates a radically different conclusion.
Herself preoccupied with family troubles and the fear of
aging, Lady Mary writes to a lonely woman who is slowly sink-
ing into insanity. What gives depth and poignancy to the letters, what explains and sustains them, is the strong undertow
of melancholy and the determination to fight against it.
These highly polished bulletins record a dialogue of the mind
with itself: through brilliant social commentary Lady Mary
administers comfort to a troubled sister who represents her
other, darker half. Like La Rochefoucauld in this respect, she
controls a potentially destructive misanthropy through the as-

tringent powers of language: "Tho' after all I am still of
Opinion that 'tis extreamly silly to submit to ill Fortune; one
should pluck up a Spirit, and live upon Cordials when one
can have no other Nourishment. These are my present En-
deavors, and I run about thô I have 5,000 pins and needles
running into my Heart" (2.84). Her letters do indeed function as "Cordials": written from the heart, they administer to
the heart an agreeably bracing medicine.

Throughout the seven-year span of the correspondence,
sorrow is ventilated and contained by wit. Whenever Lady
Mary begins to feel overwhelmed by dark thoughts, she takes
refuge in irony, which consolidates a detached appraisal (of
self, of others) in the act of displaying it:

> *My Lady Stafford set out towards France this morning,*
> *and has carry'd halfe the pleasures of my Life along with her.*
> *I am more stupid than I can describe, and am as full of moral*
> *Refflections as either Cambray or Pascal. I think of nothing*
> *but the nothingness of the good things of this world, the Tran-*
> *sitoryness of its Joys, the pungency of its sorrows, and many*
> *discoverys that have been made this three thousand years and*
> *committed to print ever since the first erecting of Presses.*
>
> (2.73)

This opening paragraph begins in grief and ends in tran-
quility, its focus widening steadily as the writer forsakes
myopic concentration on a specific phenomenon (Lady Stafford's departure and its effect) for a comprehensive panorama. Thinking buffers feeling, irony staunches tears. Every
aspect of the Mar letters, from the small-scale simile to the
design of the whole, works toward this kind of aerial perspective, a stoical vantage point removed from inner turbulence
and outer confusion. Lady Mary describes the achievement of
the desired state as follows: "I now and then peep upon these
things with the same coldness I would do on a moving Picture; I laugh at some of the motions, wonder at others etc.,
and then retire to the elected Few . . ." (2.72–73). Coldness,
spectatorial detachment, laughter, retirement: such hard-
won attributes supply the prerequisites for comic appraisal

and counterpoint the melancholy they have only temporarily displaced.

The first letter to illustrate this distinctive pull toward ironical disengagement comes early in the correspondence:

> *I wish to see you, Dear Sister, more than ever I did in my Life. A thousand things pass before my Eyes that would afford me infinite pleasure in your Conversation and that are lost for want of such a Freind to talk 'em over. Lechmere is to be Lord Hungerford. But the most considerable Incident that has happen'd a good while was the ardent affection that Mrs. Harvey and her dear spouse took to me. They visited me twice or thrice a day, and were perpetually cooing in my rooms. I was complaisant a great while, but (as you know) my Talent has never lain much that way. I grew at last so weary of those Birds of Paradice, I fled to Twictnam as much to avoid their persecution as for my own Health, which is still in a declineing way. I fancy the Bath would be a good Remedy, but my affairs lye so oddly I cannot easily resolve upon it.*
>
> *If you please, Dear Sister, to buy 20 yards of the Lutestring I have bespoke—Black—and send it by the first Oppertunity; I suppose you know we are in mourning for Lady Pierrepont. Lady Loudoun and Lady Stair are in my Neighbourhood. The first of those Ladies is on the brink of Scotland for Life. She says she does not care; to say truth, I see no very lively Reasons why she should.*
>
> (2.8–9)

The letter begins with a frank confession of need: "I wish to see you, Dear Sister, more than ever I did in my Life." The medley of subjects that follows takes its emotional charge from this sentence, which exposes feelings that have been allowed to surface briefly before being channeled underground. There they stay, exerting a subtle pressure on the shape of the letter and preventing its tone from becoming desiccated.

The telegraphic shift into gossip and request ("Lechmere is to be Lord Hungerford") is one measure of Lady Mary's need to control and of her confidence in a total rapport. The abrupt collage of subjects—Lechmere, Hervey, Twictnam,

Lady Pierrepont, Lady Loudoun—is another. As in every truly intimate correspondence, mere facts are made meaningful by the way they are reported and juxtaposed. Here Lady Mary exercises her talent for wry self-awareness and her flair for startling analogies. When the Herveys are metamorphosed into cooing birds of paradise, and Lady Loudoun into a Scotch Mariana, Lady Mary's purpose is not to wound but to give delight. Elsewhere in the Mar letters, making verses is compared to taking snuff, Lord Hillsborough's rakish entertainments to Cardinal Wolsey's charitable foundations. Such unexpected comparisons help to guarantee that her economical quotient of gossip remains playfully free of malice. She takes the creatures of real life and fantasticates them, as did Virginia Woolf:

> *We were at a party at Edith Sitwell's last night, where a good deal of misery was endured. Jews swarmed. It was in honour of Miss Gertrude Stein who was throned on a broken settee (all Ediths furniture is derelict, to make up for which she is stuck about with jewels like a drowned mermaiden.)*[21]

The banderillas both women position so expertly do not draw blood: they are decorated and flung for the pleasure of matador and spectator alike.

While it displays her talent for figurative embellishment, this letter also reflects Lady Mary's preference for brevity and precision. It is deftly streamlined: there is no padding, rambling, or confusion of purpose. The prose is of vintage quality: crisp, direct, guided by an unerring instinct for the right word in the right place.[22] Such *simplex munditiis* perfectly exemplifies Hazlitt's definition of the familiar style, whose hallmarks are "precision" and "purity of expression": "It is not to

21. *The Letters of Virginia Woolf*, ed. Nigel Nicolson and Joanne Trautman (New York and London: Harcourt Brace Jovanovich, 1978), 3.269.

22. Walter Bagehot's description has never been bettered: "She has the highest merit of letter-writing,—she is concise without being affected. . . . She said what she had to say in words that were always graphic and always sufficiently good, but she avoided curious felicity. Her expressions seem choice, but not chosen" (*Collected Works* 2.235).

take the first word that offers, but the best word in common use; it is not to throw words together in any combinations we please, but to follow and avail ourselves of the true idiom of the language."[23]

Each sharply delineated sentence calls attention to itself as a quasi-autonomous artifact rather than as part of a continuous sequence. This combination of leanness, detachment, and surgical articulation of parts assimilates the letter to an extended epigram or character sketch. In other letters actual Theophrastian characters occur, many of them akin to Pope's emblematic portraits in his *Epistle to a Lady*. Lady Mary's remarks on Lady Loudoun, which resemble both an epigram and a condensed anatomy, offer an oblique version of what is developed elsewhere in more graphic detail. For instance, the same letter that begins with the sorrowful news of Lady Stafford's departure goes on to supply an indelible image of a foolish relative:

> *A propos of family affairs, I had allmost forgot our dear and Aimable Cousin Lady Denbiegh, who has blaz'd out all this Winter. She has brought with her from Paris cart loads of Riband, surprizing fashions, and a complexion of the last Edition, which naturally attracts all the she and he fools in London, and accordingly she is surrounded with a little Court of both, and keeps a Sunday Assembly to shew she has learnt to play at cards on that day.*
>
> (2.74)

This letter ends with the news of the improbable love affair between the youthful Lord Sidney Beauclerk and the elderly Duchess of Cleveland:

> *In good earnest, she has turn'd Lady Grace and Family out o'doors to make room for him, and there he lies like leafe Gold upon a pill. There never was so violent and so indiscreet a passion. Lady Stafford says, nothing was ever like it since*

---

23. William Hazlitt, Essay 24, *Table-Talk*, in *The Complete Works*, ed. P. P. Howe (London and Toronto: J. M. Dent & Sons, 1930–34), 8.242.

Phedra and Hipolitus.—Lord ha' mercy upon us; see what we may all come to!

(2.75)

The distance between this brilliant offering of wit and the opening paragraph quoted above exemplifies the emotional poles of the Mar correspondence. As letter after letter testifies, Lady Mary brews her successful cordials from bitter experience.

Lady Mary's introspective account of her unsettled condition in the spring of 1725 can be applied with equal relevance to the spectrum of moods and subjects embodied in the letters to Lady Mar:

> *I have such a complication of things both in my Head and Heart that I do not very well know what I do; and if I can't settle my Brains, your next News of me will be that I am lock'd up by my Relations. In the mean time I lock my selfe up and keep my Distraction as private as possible. The most facetious part of the History is that my Distemper is of such a Nature, I know not whither to laugh or cry at it. I am glad and sorry, and smiling and sad—but this is too long an account of so whimsical a being. I give my selfe sometimes admirable advice but I am incapable of taking it.*

(2.51)

Lady Mary "settles her Brains" not merely by locking herself up, but by locking herself up to write letters.[24] The concern for her sister and the obsession with growing old, both part of the continuing "Distemper," are controlled by laughing and crying together. Typically the Mar letters begin in comparative darkness: "I am heartily sorry (Dear Sister), without any affectation, for any uneasyness that you suffer, let the Cause be what it will, and wish it was in my power to give you some more Essential mark of it than unavailing Pity" (2.42–43). Occasionally Lady Mary links her sister's distress with her own preoccupations: "I wonder with what Conscience you

24. The potent dramatic irony here is that it was Lady Mar who had to be locked up three years later.

36

can talk to me of your being an old Woman; I beg I may hear no more on't. For my part I pretend to be as young as ever, and realy am as young as needs to be, to all Intents and purposes" (2.76). More often, however, Lady Mary will offer a sprightly account of the *beau monde* as the only anodyne at her disposal: "all that remains for me to do to shew my willingness (at least) to divert you, is to send you faithfull Accounts of what passes amongst your Acquaintance in this part of the World" (2.43). She often recurs to this conception of her letters as therapeutic diversion: "I am heartily sorry to have the pleasure of hearing from you lessen'd by your Complaints of uneasyness, which I wish with all my soul I was capable of releiving either by my Letters or any other way" (2.29–30); "If my Letters could be any Consolation to you I should think my time best spent in writeing" (2.48). The diversion consists in the main of tales of sexual intrigue and improbable marriages, selected with an eye to the ridiculous:

> *The first of these Ladys is tenderly attach'd to the polite Mr. Mildmay, and sunk in all the Joys of happy Love notwithstanding she wants the use of her 2 hands by a Rheumatism, and he has an arm that he can't move. I wish I could send you the particulars of this Amour, which seems to me as curious as that between 2 Oysters, and as well worthy the serious Enquiry of Naturalists.*
>
> (2.37)

When melancholy subjects do intrude at the end of a letter, they are handled with a poise attained in the process of writing itself:

> *The Mutability of Sublunary things is the only melancholy Refflection I have to make on my own Account. I am in perfect Health and hear it said I look better than ever I did in my Life, which is one of those Lyes one is allways glad to hear. However, in this dear minute, in this golden Now, I am tenderly touch'd at your Misfortunes, and can never call my selfe quite happy till you are so.*
>
> (2.65–66)

In every letter the writer administers comfort to her reader and to herself by unraveling the "complication of things both in my Head and Heart." The letters to Lady Mar are reports from the arena to the cloister; the correspondence with Lady Bute reverses these locations: "We are both properly scituated according to our different times of Life, she in the Gaitys of a Court, I in a Retirement where my Garden and Dairy are my cheife Diversions" (2.409). Lady Mary's habitual salutation, "My Dear Child," epitomizes the tone of these letters, which express a maternal affection whose relaxed benevolence differs markedly from the urgent claims of Madame de Sévigné. The mere thought of Madame de Grignan's potential ill-health whips her mother into a solicitous frenzy:

> . . . *pensez-vous que votre santé, quoi que vous me puissiez mander, ne soit point un endroit sensible? Il l'est au dernier point. Cette délicatesse, cette maigreur, cette chaleur de poitrine, ces douleurs de jambes, ces coliques, cette fièvre qui vint l'année passée alors que nous y pensions le moins, tout cela me repasse et se représente à moi si tristement que, par cette nouvelle raison, vous devez comprendre que votre absence et notre extrême séparation m'est plus dure que jamais.*[25]

Lady Mary, on the other hand, channels her anxiety into rational admonition: "I am extremely concern'd to hear you complain of ill Health at a Time of Life when you ought to be in the Flower of your strength. I hope I need not recommend to you the care of it. The tenderness you have for your children is sufficient to inforce you to the utmost regard for the preservation of a Life so necessary to their well being" (2.449). Lady Mary cares deeply; to judge otherwise would be a mistake. Several unequivocal declarations of concern make it clear exactly what depth of emotion underlies her prevailing equanimity: "Absence and Distance have not the power to lessen any part of my tenderness for you, which extends to all yours" (2.492); "You have been the Passion of my Life. You need

---

25. Madame de Sévigné, *Correspondance*, ed. Roger Duchêne (Paris: Gallimard, 1972–78), 2.949 (To Madame de Grignan, 27 May 1680).

thank me for nothing; I gratify my selfe whenever I can oblige you" (3.130). Unlike Madame de Sévigné, however, who dramatizes her feelings unrestrainedly, Lady Mary consciously plays them down.

In their understated fashion these letters serve several purposes. They consolidate a relationship that is essentially independent of biological ties: "I take a pleasure in telling you my real thoughts. I would willingly establish the most intimate Freindship between us, and I am sure no proofe of it shall ever be wanting on my Side" (3.36). They allow Lady Mary the opportunity, as she expresses it, to exercise "my Maternal Privelege of being tiresome," to ride her hobbyhorses without embarrassment (3.89). And they permit vicarious participation in the only happy family she has ever known. Relations with grandmother, father, brother, husband, and son have all turned sour. Now, for the first time, she is offered the chance to involve herself—albeit at a distance—with the welfare of dutiful and even grateful kin. As Madame de Sévigné sought in Madame de Grignan a substitute for the mother she had lost at an early age, so Lady Mary, whose mother had died when she was an infant, forges a link that was denied to her as a daughter.[26]

Given her ever-deepening interest in the brood of Butes, Lady Mary's protracted Continental exile becomes even more difficult to explain. Why did she stay away from England after the Algarotti affair had collapsed for good? The letters to Lady Bute suggest at least four possibilities. At one point Lady Mary presents herself whimsically as a latter-day Robinson Crusoe:

My long storys of what passes here can be little entertainment to you, but every thing from England is interesting to me, who live the Life (as I have already told you) of Robinson Crusoe.

26. See Harriet Ray Allentuch, "My Daughter/Myself: Emotional Roots of Madame de Sévigné's Art." *Modern Language Quarterly* 43 (June 1982): 121–37. Allentuch argues persuasively that "her fixation upon her daughter, as evoked in her language, suggests an effort toward a symbolic self-restoring, a repairing of the rent fabric of her subjective life with the substitution of her daughter for her mother" (p. 125).

> *His Goats and kids were as much companions as any of the*
> *people I see here. My Time is wholly dedicated to the care of a*
> *decaying Body, and endeavoring (as the old Song says) to*
> *grow wiser and better as my Strength wears away.*
>
> (3.50)

The playful comparison helps to alert us to the symbolic significance of Lady Mary's Italian "island." Unlike Crusoe, she is a self-appointed castaway: the mysterious references to "that Destiny which confines me" do not disguise the fact that no external circumstances prevented her return to family and friends in England. Like Crusoe, whose geographical isolation makes possible his religious salvation, Lady Mary perpetuates her exile in order "to grow wiser and better." Physical solitude allows her to mesh precept and practice, to preach Stoicism and to live it in a way that would not have been possible at home. When she was fifteen, Lady Mary had projected "an English Monastery" for women: "had I then been mistriss of an Independant fortune, [I] would certainly have executed it and elected my selfe Lady Abbess" (3.97). At Gottolengo, where she can sustain an Epictetan *vita contemplativa*, she fashions a secular equivalent to the monastic state.

It seems clear that Lady Mary chooses to cultivate her eccentricity—quite literally so, if one takes London as the focus of her earlier life—in a country where her learning is not only accepted but prized:

> *I confess I have often been complemented (since I have been*
> *in Italy) on the Books I have given the Public. I us'd at first to*
> *deny it with some Warmth, but finding I persuaded no body, I*
> *have of late contented my selfe with laughing when ever I*
> *heard it mention'd, knowing the character of a learned Wom-*
> *an is far from being ridiculous in this Country, the greatest*
> *Familys being proud of having produce'd female Writers . . .*
>
> (3.39)

Freedom from ridicule allows her to escape her tarnished reputation as Pope's "Sappho," and to create a fresh identity—in

short, to revel in a new life, unimpeded by the past. She speaks
of her Italian self as a disembodied spirit impervious to the
trammels of the past, and discusses her English acquaintances
as if she were Chaucer's Troilus, gazing down from the eighth
sphere to laugh at the "vanite" and "blynde lust" that drive the
world below:

> *By the help of some miserable news papers, with my own
> refflections, I can form such a dimm Telescope as serves As-
> tronomers to survey the moon. I can discern spots and
> inequalitys, but your Beauties (if you have any) are invisible to
> me, your Provinces of Politics, Galantry, and litterature all
> terra Incognita.*
>
> (3.104)

Lady Mary's retirement, her voluminous reading, her philosophical calm, her commitment to a relationship which
could only be perpetuated by mail: all these factors contribute
to the rich expansiveness of the letters to Lady Bute. Her
tight, epigrammatic prose loosens somewhat to accommodate
a procedure she calls "thinking upon paper when I write to
you" (2.457). The brilliantly compressed and heightened vignettes of the Mar letters give way to a leisurely mixture of
reportage and commentary. For the first time Lady Mary sets
out to graph her thoughts and emotions rather than to steer
them; one kind of compass widens as the other is set aside.
The resulting monologues are far from garrulous: in fact
their structure is often more complex and more unified than
many of the letters to Lady Mar. But the canvas is larger:
Lady Mary has given up miniatures for the conversation
piece.

Her letter of 22 June 1752 takes the raw materials of the
Mar letters—the latest in reprehensible goings on among the
English aristocracy—and turns them into a much different
artifact. She centers the letter on a pair of fools and their most
recent pieces of foolishness: Sir John Rawdon, who has accepted an Irish peerage and married a third wife, and Lady
Frances Meadows, who has chosen to live with her brother the

Duke of Kingston and his French mistress. For both she supplies a devastating anatomy of character, from both she extracts a moral. The story of Sir John leads her to conclude: "'Tis realy terrible for a well bred virtuous young Woman to be confin'd to the conversation of the Object of their contempt" (2.458). Lady Frances's history prompts a more somber moral:

> *I do not doubt she has been forc'd to it by Necessity . . . the force of which is never known till it is felt, and it is therefore one of the first Dutys to avoid the Temptation of it. . . . A prudential care of one's affairs, or (to go farther) a desire of being in Circumstances to be usefull to one's Freinds, is not only excusable but highly laudable, never blam'd but by those who would persuade others to throw away their money in hopes to pick up a share of it. The greatest declaimers for disinterestedness I ever knew have been capable of the vilest actions on the least view of profit, and the greatest instances of true Generosity given by those who were regular in their Expences and superiour to the vanitys in Fashion.*
>
> (2.459)

Though she deprecates "my dull moralitys" at the end of the letter, Lady Mary chooses to speak quite unabashedly in her role of philosophical commentator, the actor-turned-spectator who brings past experience to bear on present examples of human folly. The result is not cynicism but an unillusioned summing up. The satirical bite of the Mar letters, a product of emotional involvement, is here replaced by judicial detachment.

Perhaps the most remarkable instance of philosophical calm pervades her response to the news of Sir William Lowther's death (30 May 1756; 3.107–9). Lady Mary offers an understated meditation on human ingratitude, which testifies to the painful experience of a lifetime, a long process of self-discipline, and a total mastery of the Senecan style:

> *The first shocks receiv'd from this conduct of protesting Freinds are felt very severely. I now expect them, and they affect me with no more surprize than Rain after Sunshine. The little good I do is scatter'd with a spareing Hand, against*

*my Inclination, but I now know the necessity of managing
Hopes, as the only links that bind attachment or even secure us
from Injuries.*

(3.108)

Whether or not her daughter recognized the fact, such letters
comprise Lady Mary's private version of the *Enchiridion*—
Epictetus in a maternal key, lessons in the management of
hope. Her own death six years later, of cancer stoically concealed, constitutes the final exemplum. Even Horace Walpole, who had ridiculed everything about her in life, was
obliged to report as she lay dying: "She behaves with great
fortitude, and says she has lived long enough."[27]
To every Madame de Charrière there comes a Benjamin
Constant. Lady Mary's letters to Francesco Algarotti document the passion, all the more violent for its belatedness,
which invaded a resigned middle age. More importantly, they
expose as they contradict the normative practice of a letter-
writer who had made a vocation of restraint. Suddenly, Lady
Mary's ironical, understated mode of reporting and subduing
reality dissolves into the expansive language of the heart. Her
first substantive letter to Algarotti abandons the measured
discourse of Addison's Cato for the tormented monologues of
Racine's Phèdre:

> *Je ne sçai plus de quel façon vous écrire. Mes sentimens
> sont trop vif; je ne sçaurois les expliquer ni les cacher. Il faut
> estre touché d'un entousiasme pareil au mien pour souffrir mes
> Lettres. J'en voye toute la folie sans la possibilité de me
> corriger. La seul Idée de vous revoir m'a donnée un Saissis-
> ment en lisant vostre Lettre, que m'a quasi fait évanouir.
> Qu'est devenu cet Indifference philosophe qui a fait la Gloire
> et la tranquillité de mes jours passée? J'ai l'ai perdu pour le
> retrouver jamais, et si cette passion est guerri, je prevoye rien
> qu'un ennui mortel.—Pardonnez l'extravagance que vous
> avez fait naitre, et venez me voir.*

(2.103)

27. *Horace Walpole's Correspondence*, ed. W. S. Lewis et al. (New Haven:
Yale University Press, 1937–83), 22.56.

This letter, and those that follow in rapid succession, are as unique in epistolary style as they are unprecedented biographically. Casting aside her "Indifference philosophe," Lady Mary turns away from English, the idiom of cerebral control, to a language that will vent her passionate feelings. Grammatical correctness—a form of restraint like any other—matters little in comparison with the psychological freedom and stylistic exuberance to be gained by unmasking in French: "C'est peut estre du mauvais françois que j'écrive, mais comme mes lettres sont entre vos mains de bruler le moment qu'elles vous ennuient, j'écris tout ce que me vient a la tête" (2.105). Her choice of a foreign tongue to express foreign emotions reflects an opinion she had expressed to Pope in a letter containing her version of a Turkish love lyric: "I cannot determine upon the whole how well I have succeeded in the Translation. Neither do I think our English proper to express such violence of passion, which is very seldom felt amongst us" (1.337).

In keeping with her new identity—the passionate lover, clamoring for reciprocity—Lady Mary deliberately jettisons the compass of the Senecan style. She chooses to cast herself linguistically and stylistically adrift, then to position herself in the world of Racine's tragic heroines, whose "enthousiasme," "folie," "passion," and "extravagance" matches her own feverish condition. Like Phèdre in particular, Lady Mary declares herself torn by the conflict between head and heart, convention and inclination. "Ma raison murmure tout bas de sottises de mon coeur sans avoir la force de les detruire" (2.103–4). She dramatizes the struggle more fully in the letter that follows: "Ma raison me fait voir tout l'extravagance, et mon Coeur me fait sentir toute l'importance. Foible Raison! qui choque ma passion et ne le détruit pas, et qui me fait voir inutilement toute la folie d'aimer au point que j'aime sans esperance de retour" (2.105–6). The accents of the despairing heroine, borrowed from seventeenth-century French tragedy, provide the appropriate vehicle for sustained comparisons between her fate and those of Dido and Penelope: "Je suis mille fois plus a plaindre que la triste Didon, et j'ai mille fois plus des raisons de me donner la mort. . . . . J'ai été la Penelope de vostre absence, negligant tous les objets que je voyez pour m'entretenir sans cesse des charmes d'un fugitif dont je ne sçavois pas mesme la demeure, et me doutoit quelque fois de l'existence" (2.104, 116).

What Lady Mary creates in this sequence of letters to Algarotti is her own set of variations on the *Heroides*, as mediated by the Ovidian rhetoric of "Eloisa to Abelard" and Pope's love letters during the Turkish Embassy.[28] Twenty years after she herself was pursued by post, Lady Mary appropriates the extravagant medium favored by her erstwhile courtier, specifically the rhetorical figures of Pope's "Eloisa" and his "Elegy to the Memory of an Unfortunate Lady." At the end of her letter of 10 September 1736, in which she claims to write "tout ce que me vient a la tête," Lady Mary echoes Eloisa's feverish antitheses in a couplet of her own devising: "How much these golden Wishes are in Vain! / I dream to pleasure, but I wake to pain" (2.106). Her verses cap a Popean conceit of blasphemous adoration:

> . . . j'ai une devotion pour vous plus zelé qu'aucun des adorateurs de la Vierge a jamais eû pour elle. Je croi que tous ces messeiurs ont eû un peu de vanité dans leur devoûement, oû ils ont esperé des grandes recompenses de leurs oraisons. Me voici en oraison a vous sans esperance que vous m'en teniez le moindre comte, et je passe des heures entiere en mon Cabinet absorbé dans la contemplation de vos perfections.
>
> (2.105)

Furthermore, she temporarily adopts the approach to letter-

---

28. Robert Halsband proposes Restoration heroic tragedy and seventeenth-century French romances as models for the letters to Algarotti in an essay in *The Familiar Letter in the Eighteenth Century*, ed. Howard Anderson, Philip B. Daghlian, and Irvin Ehrenpreis (Lawrence: University of Kansas Press, 1966), pp. 54–55. I find the parallels with the *Heroides*, Racine, and Pope more persuasive, especially given Lady Mary's well-attested knowledge of Ovid, her taste for classical French drama, and her intimate knowledge of Pope's literary career.

writing the poet had expounded to her in support of his impassioned style:

If Momus his project had taken of having Windows in our breasts, I should be for carrying it further and making those windows Casements: that while a Man showd his Heart to all the world, he might do something more for his friends, e'en take it out, and trust it to their handling.[29]

Accordingly, in her next letter she promises to supply, if only Algarotti will sustain their correspondence, "le fidele portrait d'un Coeur de femme sans detour ou deguisement, peint au naturel, qui se donne pour ce qu'elle est, et qui ne vous cache ni vous farde rien. Mes foiblesses et mes emportemens doivent attirer au moins vostre curiosité en vous presentant la vraie disection d'une Ame femelle" (2.107). The emphasis on artlessness, lack of disguise, and unobstructed revelation (via "vraie disection" rather than a "window in the bosom") underlines the total abandonment of her usual approach to letter-writing in this extraordinary instance, just as it reveals the abyss of feeling into which she had plunged, for the first and last time.[30]

Phaedra, Penelope, Dido—to this Ovidian trio Lady Mary adds another more contemporary role: "Je me recommande a vous dans tous les perils comme Don Quichotte a sa Dulcinée, et je n'ai pas l'imagination moins échauffée que lui" (2.147). For at least five years she tilts pathetically at windmills. Then, seventeen years after the quixotic illusions have finally been discarded, Lady Mary elects to send Algarotti a much different kind of self-portrait:

L'imagination s'échauffe aisement quan on veut traiter de son propre merite, mais Helas! j'ai quelque lueur de sens commun,

---

29. *The Correspondence of Alexander Pope*, ed. George Sherburn (Oxford: Clarendon Press, 1956), 1.353. See also Bruce Redford, "Pope's Epistolary Theory and Practice: Two Probable Sources," *Notes and Queries* 30 (December 1983): 500–502.

30. For Lady Mary's experiments in a newly impassioned poetic mode, which appear to reflect her infatuation with Algarotti, see "Impromptu to a young Lady singing" and "Address'd To—" in *Essays and Poems*, pp. 286, 290–91.

qui me represente impitoyablement telle que je suis. Tout ce j'ai puis dire avec verité, j'etois jeune sans coquetterie, affectation, ou étourderie; je suis vieille sans humeur, superst[it]ion, ou medisance. Voici bien des negatives, miserable resource pour mon Amour propre! Je tache de sauver ses droits en me persuadant que je suis moins sotte qu'une autre, en voiant mes sottises au moment même que je m'ÿ laisse entrainer.

(3.141)

An egoist devoid of vanity, she unflinchingly identifies her own "sottises" without ceasing to practice them. Both the voice and the posture are uncannily reminiscent of Madame de Charrière, who anatomizes herself with equal dispassion:

Tendre a l'excès et non moins delicate, elle ne peut être heureuse ni par l'amour ni sans amour. . . . e voyant trop sensible pour être heureuse, elle a presque cessé de prétendre au bonheur, elle s'attache a la vertu, elle fuit les repentirs et cherche les amusemens. Les plaisirs sont rares pour elle, mais ils sont vifs, elle les saisit et les goute avec ardeur. Connoissant la vanité des projets, et l'incertitude de l'avenir, elle veut surtout rendre heureux le moment qui s'écoule.[31]

The parallels extend beyond those of temperament, vocation, and achievement; indeed once the comparison has been suggested, it seems inevitable. Lady Mary and Zélide are linked by their wit, vivacity, and unflinching candor; by their aristocratic backgrounds, exceptional reading, and prolific writing; by disastrous marriages to cold, phlegmatic older men and passionate involvements with faithless younger writers; by abrupt retreats from society in middle age; by the deification of good sense and the capacity for stoical endurance. Finally, however, this pairing breaks down, and at the point of divergence Lady Mary's distinctive achievement comes most sharply into view. As Frederick Pottle has tellingly observed of Madame de Charrière, "Irony is useful for an author but is perhaps not the best state of mind for happy living."[32] The

31. Isabelle de Charrière, *Oeuvres Complètes*, ed. C. P. Courtney et al. (Amsterdam: G. A. van Oorschot, 1981), 10.37.
32. Frederick A. Pottle, *James Boswell: The Earlier Years, 1740–1769* (London: Heinemann, 1966), p. 386.

rampant exercise of irony not only deprived Zélide of happiness, it sapped her art: ultimately her capacity for detached understanding led away from the cathartic enactments of language into a sterile silence. Lady Mary by contrast turned irony as potential self-torture into irony as effective self-defense. Her emotions found an outlet in the epistolary form as she taught herself to temper and wield it. The result, more often than not, is gaiety—gaiety transfiguring all that dread.

2

William Cowper:
Invitations to the Microcosm

> Within that house secure he hides,
> When danger imminent betides
> Of storm, or other harm besides
>   Of weather.
>
> Give but his horns the slightest touch,
> His self-collecting power is such,
> He shrinks into his house, with much
>   Displeasure.
>
>   — *"The Snail"*

WILLIAM COWPER also tries, through epistolary "Cordials" and geographical seclusion alike, to fortify himself against inner turmoil and outer disturbance. Yet for all his artful endurance, dread finally conquers gaiety. In this second chapter we will be examining strategies equivalent to Lady Mary Wortley Montagu's Senecan voice: Cowper's letters, like Lady Mary's, work both to contain and to communicate, to protect and to nourish an identity under pressure. Because of his peculiar circumstances, however, Cowper is chiefly concerned to objectify his private world. For Lady Mary the converse of the pen is at once an aesthetic and a philosophical exercise; for Cowper it is a psychological necessity.

Like Wemmick in *Great Expectations,* Cowper was "fond of a bit of garden and a summer-house." Like Wemmick's "little wooden cottage," his home was a castle, guarded in all but fact by moat, ramparts, and cannon. And at the back, as at Walworth, "there are fowls and rabbits; then, I knock together my own little frame, you see, and grow cucumbers; and you'll judge at supper what sort of a salad I can raise."[1] Wemmick anticipates an investing army, and stocks his garrison accordingly; Cowper endures a perpetual siege from within, and calculates every aspect of his fortress to keep the enemy at bay. Living in rural isolation, he intensifies the protective qualities latent in his environment. Olney itself distances the threatening macrocosm; Orchardside mutes the clamor of Olney; its garden, slanting away from the marketplace toward the Guinea Field, provides an even securer refuge; and at the furthest reaches of the garden Cowper can take shelter in a tiny summerhouse, the ultimate *sanctum sanctorum*. Within this array of Chinese boxes he fashions even smaller enclosed spaces: greenhouses, squirrel huts, rabbit hutches, birdcages, cucumber frames, flower beds—even poems and letters. For Cowper's total involvement in the topography of his miniature kingdom finds its ideal vehicle of expression and sustenance in the epistolary form, which acts as an equivalent to the *camera obscura:* the familiar letter mirrors, reduces, and composes the outside world, shrinking the unbounded confusions and outsize scale of life-without-the-moat to manageable proportions.

In all of his activities Cowper reenacts the providential care of God—a care he believes has been withheld from him alone. His daily routine, which creates a little Eden *ex vacuo,* acquires the significance of a substitute religion. In his domestic sanctuary this "self-sequestered man" labors to achieve a combination of relative independence (because independence entails immunity) and calm sociability (because solitude is a desert without "Society, friendship, and love"). From Weston, where he finally attains that goal, he invites Lady Hesketh to make a part of his happiness:

> *The Country, this country at least, is pleasant at all times, and when Winter is come, or near at hand, we shall have the better chance for being snug. . . . I have made in the Orchard the*

---

1. Charles Dickens, *Great Expectations*, ed. Angus Calder (Harmondsworth: Penguin English Library, 1965), p. 229 (chap. 25).

*best Winter walk in all the parish, shelter'd from the East and
from the North East, and open to the Sun, except at his rising,
all the day. Then we will have Homer and Don Quixote, and
then we will have saunter and Chat, and one Laugh more
before we die. Our Orchard is alive with creatures of all kinds,
poultry of ev'ry denomination swarms in it, and pigs the drol-
lest in the world.*[2]

Because life in this self-sufficient prelapsarian kingdom requires fit company though few, Cowper uses the letter to
people his microcosm. As he tells William Unwin: "A Letter
written from such a place as this, is a Creation" (2.132). Cata-
lyzing these creative acts is the pressure of a world without
form, and void, whose chaotic darkness he has pushed momentarily into the background.

Letters promote "the luxury of reciprocal endearments,
without which a paradise could afford no comfort" (1.544).
They do so primarily, and somewhat paradoxically, because
of their preoccupation with self: "So far from thinking Ego-
tisms tedious; I think a Letter good for nothing without them.
To hear *from* a friend is little, unless I hear *of* him at the same
time. His Sentiments may be just, but his feelings & his welfare are most to the purpose" (1.494). A satisfactory letter
must therefore do full justice to the claims of "*Ego* and all that
Ego does" (3.292). Cowper claims to prefer spontaneous out-
pourings, self-disclosures of "the true helter-skelter kind"
(3.334); yet at the same time his letters embody the paradox
of artful naturalness that underlies the Augustan theory of
conversation. Keith Stewart has suggested that eighteenth-
century readers looked for three qualities in the familiar letter: substantive content, a sense of character (manifested in

2. *The Letters and Prose Writings of William Cowper*, 4 vols. to date, ed. James
King and Charles Ryskamp (Oxford: Clarendon Press, 1979–), 3.187. All
quotations from Cowper's letters are taken from this edition; references appear parenthetically in the text. Quotations from the poetry come from either *The Poems of William Cowper, 1748–1782*, ed. John D. Baird and Charles
Ryskamp (Oxford: Clarendon Press, 1980), or the fourth edition of H. S.
Milford's *Cowper: Poetical Works*, rev. Norma Russell (London: Oxford University Press, 1967).

"the imaginative capacity of setting things in an uncommon light"), and "the effect of immediacy."[3] Except on very rare occasions, Cowper was incapable of meeting the first of these expectations, a deficiency he laments in phrases such as "frothy matter," "dearth of intelligence," and "sheet full of Trifles."[4] On the other two counts, however, Cowper more than redressed the balance. Because of his peculiar position—geographical isolation necessitated by and compounded with mental pathology—he labors for rhetorical ethos and immediacy with all the resources at his disposal. This chapter will concentrate on the three most important methods by which he renders his private microcosm accessible to the chosen few: mock-heroic transformations of the mundane; emblematic representations of thought and emotion; and painterly descriptions of domestic interiors and neighborhood landscapes. The chapter begins by characterizing the world into which Cowper invited his correspondents.

Cowper habitually called his domestic setting a "nook," as if constant repetition of the word would reinforce its protective connotations. Usually the term helps to point a contrast between the rural sanctuary to which he clung and the tumultuous life from which he had escaped. Accordingly, Cowper presents himself and Mrs. Unwin as "Dormice in a hollow tree" (3.199), secluded observers of the chaotic macrocosm: "Though we Live in a Nook, and the World is quite unconscious that there are any such Beings in it as ourselves, yet we are not unconcern'd about what passes in it" (1.568). Force of habit and fear of change have converted even the nook's deficiencies into a reassuring source of pleasure: "The very Stones in the garden walls are my intimate acquaintance; I should miss almost the minutest object and be disagreeably

3. Keith Stewart, "Towards Defining an Aesthetic for the Familiar Letter in Eighteenth-Century England," *Prose Studies* 5 (1982): 188–89.
4. As Cowper explains to William Unwin: "I assure you faithfully that I do not find the soil of Olney prolific in the growth of such articles as make Letter-writing desireable employment. No place contributes less to the catalogue of incidents, or is more scantily supplied with anecdotes worth notice" (2.194).

affected by its removal, and am persuaded that were it possible I could leave this incommodious and obscure nook for a twelvemonth, I should return to it again with rapture" (2.151). To emphasize the point Cowper quotes Horace's celebration of *his* favorite nook, "ille . . . angulus . . . ubi non Hymetto / mella decedunt viridique certat / baca Venafro."5 When Lady Hesketh visits her "cousin in a corner" (2.511), she comes "to brighten," he tells Earl Cowper, "the obscurest nook in the world with her presence" (2.571).

Because Cowper likes to draw concentric circles of protection about himself, he also constructs nooks within nooks, chief among these his tiny summerhouse—"this comfortable nook, which affords me all that could be found in the most sequester'd hermitage" (1.507). Time and again he underlines its status as ultimate hideaway:

> *Our severest Winter, commonly called the Spring, is now over, and I find myself seated in my favorite recess, the Greenhouse. In such a situation, so silent, so shady, where no human foot is heard, and where only my Myrtles presume to peep in at the window, you may suppose I have no interruption to complain of, and that my thoughts are perfectly at my command.*
>
> (2.139)

Only here, at the point of utmost withdrawal, can Cowper retain complete control ("my thoughts are perfectly at my command"). Only here can he totally discard his role as passive victim and replace it with that of active nurturer. Therefore the summerhouse—surrounded by a profusion of flowers, additional evidence of Cowper's inventive powers—becomes the locus of poetic and epistolary creation:

> *I write in a nook that I call my Bouderie; It is a Summer house not much bigger than a Sedan chair, the door of which opens into the garden that is now crowded with pinks, roses and honey-suckles, and the window into my neighbour's or-*

5. *Odes* 2.6.13–16: "that corner where the honey yields not to Hymettus, and the olive vies with green Venafrum" (trans. C.E. Bennett, Loeb Classical Library).

*chard. . . . Having lined it with garden-mats, and furnished it
with a table and two chairs, here I write all that I write in
summer-time, whether to the Public or to my friends. It is
secure from all noise, and a refuge from all intrusion; for
intrusions sometimes trouble me even at Olney.*

(2.359–60)

Even in wintertime the summerhouse continues to function
as Cowper's "verse-manufactory" (2.397, 569). He pictures
this innermost chamber as a "nutshell" and, even more appropriately, as a nest within a nook:

*As I enter'd the gate a glimpse of something white contained in
a little hole in the gate-post caught my eye. I looked again and
discover'd a bird's nest with two tiney eggs in it. By and by
they will be fledged and tailed and get wing-feathers and fly.
My case is somewhat similar to that of the parent bird. My nest
is in a little nook, here I brood and hatch, and in due time my
progeny takes wing and whistles.*

(2.346)

Unlike the next in "A Fable," this piece of "wicker-work" nur-
tures its occupant safely through the period of gestation.

"Snugness" and "neatness" are the defining attributes of
all Cowper's nooks. These favorite terms of value pinpoint
what he looked for, found, and struggled to maintain in the
Olney-Weston sphere. Describing the new house at Weston to
Lady Hesketh, Cowper emphasized that "the neatness and
snugness of our abode compensates all the dreariness of the
season" (2.599). Inviting his cousin Mrs. Cowper to pay a visit,
he identified himself as dwelling in "a snug corner of a beautiful country" (3.334).

It is only fitting that the hearth—potent symbol of warmth,
security, and domestic comfort—should epitomize the qualities of neatness and snugness. In Book IV of *The Task*, "The
Winter Evening," Cowper celebrates "the glowing hearth"; in
"Conversation" he plays on the Latin to describe a well-told
tale as one that centers "in a focus round and neat" (l.239). In
a prose-equivalent to the opening section of "The Winter
Evening," Cowper exalts the value of the hearth as protection
against stormy blasts:

I see the Winter approaching without much concern,
though a passionate lover of fine weather, and the pleasanter
scenes of Summer. But the long Evenings have their comforts
too, and there is hardly to be found upon the earth, I suppose,
so snug a creature as an Englishman by his fire-side in the
Winter.

(2.172)

To William Unwin he juxtaposes the sterile glitter of Brighton's social life to his own hearth-side rituals: "I cannot envy
you your situation; I even feel myself constrained to prefer
the Silence of this nook, and the snug fire-side in our diminutive parlour to all the splendor and gaiety of Bright-
helmstone" (1.527). As these two passages demonstrate,
whenever Cowper speaks of the hearth, the symbolic implications of its cheer are never far beneath the surface. Inside the
microcosm, its flickering glow focuses the values of compan-
ionship-in-isolation and cosy insulation from the great outdoors. Outside the diminutive domestic context, however, the
same flames are transformed into a terrifying symbol of Cowper's worst fears: "Dream'd that in a state of the most insup-
portable misery I look'd through the window of a strange
room being all alone, and saw preparations making for my
execution. That it was but about 4 days distant, and that then
I was destined to suffer everlasting martyrdom in the fire, my
body being prepared for the purpose and my dissolution
made a thing impossible" (4.237; cf. 4.299).

By taming a force that might otherwise rage out of control,
the hearth illustrates one cogent reason for Cowper's devotion to the small-scale. To miniaturize is to make whatever has
been reduced thoroughly apprehensible, and therefore less
threatening. As Claude Lévi-Strauss has pointed out, the act
of miniaturization diminishes or eliminates the resistance that
reality poses to the ordering instincts of the human mind:

> Quelle vertu s'attache donc à la réduction, que celle-ci soit
> d'échelle, ou qu'elle affecte les propriétés? Elle résulte, semble-
> t-il, d'une sorte de renversement du procès de la connaissance:
> pour connaître l'objet réel dans sa totalité, nous avons toujours
> tendance à opérer depuis ses parties. La résistance qu'il nous

oppose est surmontée en la divisant. La réduction d'échelle renverse cette situation: plus petite, la totalité de l'objet apparaît moins redoutable; du fait d'être quantitativement diminuée, elle nous semble qualitativement simplifiée. Plus exactement, cette transposition quantitative accroît et diversifie notre pouvoir sur un homologue de la chose; à travers lui, celle-ci peut être saisie, soupesée dans la main, appréhendée d'un seul coup d'oeil. La poupée de l'enfant n'est plus un adversaire, un rival ou même un interlocuteur; en elle et par elle, la personne se change en subjet.[6]

And even when the sensation of "knowability" that results is an illusion, "la raison du procédé est de créer ou d'entretenir cette illusion, qui gratifie l'intelligence et la sensibilité d'un plaisir qui, sur cette seule base, peut déjà être appelé esthétique."[7] Cowper's "Aesthetic pleasure" derives from a conception of the beautiful that coincides with Burke's; as a direct result, he can delight only in those things which are naturally diminutive or those which have been miniaturized.[8] He resists overtures to move to Bristol, to visit London, or to write an epic of his own because he senses that only in the microcosm of Olney-Weston can his mental balance and his creative powers be preserved.

The direct relevance of Lévi-Strauss's analysis to Cowper's case is confirmed by the results of the trip to William Hayley's Sussex estate. To this man from Lilliput, the downs seem

6. Claude Lévi-Strauss, *La Pensée Sauvage* (Paris: Librarie Plon, 1962), pp. 34–35.

7. Lévi-Strauss, p. 35.

8. "In the animal creation, out of our own species, it is the small we are inclined to be fond of; little birds, and some of the smaller kinds of beasts. A great beautiful thing, is a manner of expression scarcely ever used; but that of a great ugly thing, is very common. There is a wide difference between admiration and love. The sublime, which is the cause of the former, always dwells on great objects, and terrible; the latter on small ones, and pleasing; we submit to what we admire, but we love what submits to us; in one case we are forced, in the other we are flattered into compliance." See Edmund Burke, *A Philosophical Enquiry into the Origin of Our Ideas of the Sublime and Beautiful*, ed. J.T. Boulton (London: Routledge and Kegan Paul; New York: Columbia University Press, 1958), p. 113 (pt. 3, sec. 13: "Beautiful objects small").

Brobdingnagian in scale: "I indeed myself was a little daunt-
ed by the tremendous height of the Sussex hills in comparison
with which all that I have seen elsewhere are dwarfs; *but I only
was alarm'd*" (4.163, my italics). Cowper fears mountains, as he
fears the sea, because they are not easily dominated and described, because they shrink man to comparative insignificance. Like the ways of God, they are inscrutable and
therefore terrifying. To Lady Hesketh he contrasts the un-
tamed landscape around Eartham with his beloved Weston:
"The Genius of that place suits me better; it has an air of snug
concealment in which a disposition like mine feels itself peculiarly gratified; whereas here I see from ev'ry window woods
like forests and hills like mountains, a wildness in short that
rather encreases my natural melancholy" (4.189). Given Cowper's delicate mental fabric, it is not surprising that the hostile
genius of Eartham should have inhibited the production of
verse: "It [a brief epitaph] is all that I have done since here I
came, and all that I have been able to do. . . . I find, like the
man in the fable who could leap only at Rhodes, that verse is
almost impossible to me, except at Weston" (4.192). The expansive wooded downs of Sussex, converted by his fearful
imagination into forests and mountains, only aggravate the
inner turmoil that the gentle, small-scale topography of Buckinghamshire has been instrumental in controlling.

As Kenneth Maclean has noticed, the threat of the un-
known and the uncontrollable—in short, the threat of the
macrocosm—haunts Cowper's imagination: "Aren't we shut-
ting shutters on winter evenings. . . . Peeping at the world
through the 'loop-holes of retreat'—the newspapers! The
stricken deer is hiding in the shade."[9] Cowper devises ways of
containing this terror in art as well as life, principally by re-
leasing it in controlled doses. His confessional letters to John
Newton and Samuel Teedon provide such an outlet, his
mock-heroic exercises another. Their therapeutic function

9. Kenneth Maclean, "William Cowper," in *The Age of Johnson*, ed. F.W.
Hilles (New Haven and London: Yale University Press, 1949), p. 263.

only intensifies their communicative power: time and again we are impressed by the capacity of an alert and humorous mind to reshape obdurate reality in its own image.

What might be considered separate strands in Cowper's temperament—the playful and the darkly brooding—are interwoven in the mock-heroic idiom he began to perfect from the very beginning of his literary career: the earliest surviving poem, "Verses Written at Bath, in 1748, on Finding the Heel of a Shoe," attempts a Miltonic parody in the tradition of John Phillips's *The Splendid Shilling*. Whether or not one endorses Morris Golden's retrospective interpretation, the poem clearly marks the beginning of Cowper's lifelong interest in exploiting ludicrous disjunctions between style and content—an interest he shared with Thomas Gray, as we will have occasion to observe in the next chapter.[10] In poetry this taste for deliberate violations of stylistic decorum produces "The Colubriad," "On the Death of Mrs. Throckmorton's Bullfinch," the passage on cucumber growing in *The Task,* and the translation of the *Batrachomyomachia.* In Cowper's letters it turns the slim pickings to be gleaned from village affairs into a feast of comic perception.

"John Gilpin and John Calvin," notes Charles Ryskamp of Cowper's early reading, "were part of him from the beginning."[11] John Calvin, we might add, gives birth to John Gilpin:

> *Indeed I wonder that a sportive thought should ever knock at the door of my intellects, and still more that it should gain admittance. It is as if harlequin should intrude himself into the gloomy chamber where a corpse is deposited in state. His antic gesticulations would be unseasonable at any rate, but more especially so if they should distort the features of the*

10. In Golden's view, the "Verses" supply evidence that "at least some of Cowper's mental preoccupations . . . were already well established long before madness, conversion, and the conviction of damnation took place." See Morris Golden, *In Search of Stability: The Poetry of William Cowper* (New York: Bookman Associates, 1960), p. 106.

11. Charles Ryskamp, *William Cowper of the Inner Temple, Esq.* (Cambridge: Cambridge University Press, 1959), p. 56.

> *mournful attendants into laughter. But the mind long wearied*
> *with the sameness of a dull, dreary prospect, will gladly fix its*
> *eyes on any thing that may make a little variety in its con-*
> *templations, though it were but a kitten playing with her tail.*
>
> (1.367)

Cowper's mind turns away from inner nightmare and outer
stultification to the gambols of a kitten, only to discover that
nothing is peaceful, nothing predictable. As it is narrated in a
letter to William Unwin, the incident that inspired "The Colubriad" exemplifies Cowper's brand of heroic mock-heroic in
two respects—the teller's prompt action within the story, and
his triumph through style over the fearful "paradox" being
dramatized. For the moral that begins the prose version of
this incident (though not its poetic recasting) expresses one of
Cowper's basic obsessions—the inscrutability of the divine
plan, and thus the radical insecurity of his position: "It is a
sort of paradox but it is true.—We are never more in danger
than when we think ourselves most secure, nor in reality more
secure than when we seem perhaps to be most in danger.
Both sides of this apparent contradiction were lately verified
in my experience" (2.68). In prefacing this "apparent contradiction" to his anecdote of dragon-slaying Olney style, and
narrating the story as he does, Cowper both releases his fear
and subdues it.[12] The serpent in the garden is "heroically"
dispatched by the garden's tutelary deity, who demonstrates
the paternal care from which he feels exiled. In schematic
terms, then, Cowper is to kittens as God is *not* to Cowper. On
the surface, however, all is adroit exaggeration and comic
poise:

> *Passing from the greenhouse to the barn I saw three Kittens,*
> *(for we have so many in our retinue) looking with a fixt*
> *attention at something which lay on the threshold of a door*
> *nailed up. I took but little notice of them at first, but a loud*
> *hiss engaged me to attend more closely, when behold! a Viper,*

12. Lady Mary achieves similar ends with different means in her letters to
Lady Mar. See chapter 1, pp. 31–38.

the largest I remember to have seen, rearing itself, darting its
forked tongue, and ejaculating the aforementioned hiss at the
nose of a Kitten almost in contact with his lips. I ran into the
Hall for a hoe with a long handle with which I intended to
assail him, and returning in a few seconds, missed him. He
was gone, and I feared had escaped me. Still however the
Kittens sat watching immoveably upon the same spot. I con-
cluded therefore that sliding between the door and the
threshold he had found his way out of the garden into the
yard. I went round immediately, and there found him in close
conversation with the Old Cat, whose curiosity being excited by
so novel an appearance, inclined her to pat his head repeat-
edly with her forefoot, with her claws however sheathed, and
not in anger, but in the way of philosophical enquiry and
examination. To prevent her falling a victim to so laudable an
exercise of her talents, I interposed in a moment with the hoe,
and performed upon him an act of decapitation, which though
not immediately mortal, proved so in the end.

(2.68–69)

Mutatis mutandis, this prose Colubriad anticipates the subject,
the technique, and the function of his verses "On the Death
of Mrs. Throckmorton's Bullfinch"—"on one level a perfect
performance in the art of sustaining friendly relations," but
"on another, deeper level a poem by one convinced that every
moment was fraught with the most incredible danger—that
the end could come at any time for caged birds and secluded
poets alike."[13]

A mock-heroic style is uniquely equipped to handle such
acts of disclosure/restraint, particularly when terror registers
itself in unabashedly heroic language. Cowper's bulletins
from the spiritual abyss, and his reports on the distress of
others, tend to be couched in versions of Old Testament
prophecy. In a letter about the economic condition of the
Olney lacemakers we can watch him shifting abruptly from
heroic (pain thrust forward) to mock-heroic (pain trans-

---

13. Vincent Newey, *Cowper's Poetry: A Critical Study and Reassessment* (Liverpool: Liverpool University Press, 1982), p. 221.

muted). First he expounds the lacemakers' plight, then pulls back from it:

> *The Measure is like a Scythe, and the poor Lacemakers are the Sickly Crop that trembles before the Edge of it. The Prospect of Peace with America is like the Streak of Dawn in their Horizon, but this Bill is like a Black Cloud behind it, that threatens their Hope of a comfortable Day with utter Extinction. I did not perceive 'till this Moment that I had tack'd two Similes together, a Practise, which, though warranted by the Example of Homer and allowable in an Epic Poem, is rather Luxuriant & Licentious in a Letter; lest I should add a third, I conclude myself with my best Respects to Mrs. Hill . . .*
>
> (1.363)

The letter tames the writer's anxiety, and reassures the recipient, by prying manner loose from matter: serious discussion must cease, Cowper tells Hill, lest further stylistic *faux pas* be the result. By switching contexts (epic/tragedy to letter/comedy) and therefore rules of the rhetorical game, Cowper turns passion into detachment.

Even more important than the rationale of containment is the communicative impulse that prompts Cowper to put his personal stamp upon unpromising material. As contemporary testimony reveals, the mock-heroic voice of the letters represents a stylized version of Cowper's actual conversational persona:

> Nor is it flattery to say, that he possessed the same kind of humour, in a degree not inferior to Mr. Addison himself. With a low voice, and much apparent gravity and composure, he was accustomed repeatedly to surprise his hearers with observations, which not only proved him to be possessed of knowledge and taste, but evinced an extraordinary power of being ludicrous whenever he pleased.[14]

This "extraordinary power of being ludicrous" manifests itself in a wide spectrum of effects, from nascent epistolary

---

14. Anonymous review of Samuel Greatheed's *Sermon on Cowper*, quoted in Ryskamp, p. 100.

grace notes through parodic self-portraits to full-dress narrative. Moreover, setting collaborates with comic persona: "Sir Cowper" fixed in Olney-Weston and contributing reports on village life is a situation fraught with paradox, a daily oxymoron. In short, the gap between rustic situation and gentlemanly observer lends itself to—indeed, insists upon—the comic exaltation of the "low." We are reminded constantly, by juxtapositions tacit as well as explicit, of Fielding's narrator reporting the battle in the parish churchyard: "I hurry you into the Midst of things at once, which if it be not much in the Epistolary Stile, is acknowledg'd however to be very Sublime.—Mr. Morley, Videlicet the grocer, is guilty of such Neglect and Carelessness . . . [that your Mother] begs you will send her Mr. Rawlinson's Address, that she may transfer her Custom to Him" (1.285).

The sly puffery of the trivial is one of Cowper's special achievements. In every meager gazette from his rural backwater lurks another "Nun's Priest's Tale": "We have had a terrible battle in our Orchard; one of our Turkey Hens has killed the other" (3.367); "an army that had quarter'd itself within your walls, exists no longer. I cannot tell you exactly the numbers that have been destroy'd, but victory has daily d[   ]on the side of the Rat[ter whose success was] so brilliant, that 12,[   ]fallen victims to his [   ]he made among their [numb]ers" (3.243). Even before he begins work on his *Iliad,* Cowper dwells whimsically on the distance between Olney and Troy: "As two Men sit Silent after having exhausted all their Topics of Conversation, One says, It is very fine Weather, and the other says, Yes. One Blows his Nose, and the other Rubs his Eyebrow, (by the way this is very much in Homer's Manner). Such seems to be the Case between you and me" (1.369–70). During the long years of translation he will quite often report his own experience in Homeric terms, total saturation in the epic idiom producing several small masterpieces of mock-heroic embellishment. His forty lines per day routine inspires the following simile:

Fine things indeed I have few. He who has Homer to Translate may well be contented to do little else. As when an Ass being harness'd with Ropes to a Sand-Cart, drags with hanging ears his heavy burthen, neither filling the long eccho-ing streets with his harmonious Bray, nor throwing up his Heels behind frolicksome and airy, as Asses less engaged are wont to do—So I, satisfied to find myself indispensibly obliged to render into the best possible English Metre, eight and forty Greek Books of which the two finest Poems in the world con-sist, account it quite sufficient if I may at last atchieve that labour . . .

(3.86)

When he describes the unpacking of a box (3.313–14) or the opening of a beer bottle, the result is another epic miniature:

The day you went, a bottle of Spruce was produced and the cork drawn in the study. A column of the contents immediately spouted to the cieling, nor did it cease to sally in this violent manner till more than two thirds of the liquor were expended. You will imagine that the remaining third was excellent. But it did not prove so. As Mr. Pulteney, while a patriot, speaking in the house of Commons on the subject of public measures, observed that the apparent energy of them was an ill symptom, that they bespoke the delirium of a fever in its last stage, and were not so much efforts as agonies, so it proved in the present instance. All the life, strength and spirit of the good creature were wasted in that last struggle
—placidaque ibi demum morte quievit. [Aeneid 9.445]

(3.316)

Cowper's humorous burlesque of the commonplace extends even to dactylic hexameters on a troublesome cough: "Far be it from me to impose these lines upon you as an extempo-raneous effusion, for, to tell you the truth, I made them on purpose for your edification before I rose this morning" (3.439).

Of Cowper's two sustained exercises in epistolary mock-heroic—his description of the candidate's visit to Orchardside

and his account of a fox hunt on the Throckmorton estate—
the latter is the most successful and the least celebrated. With
the text of the new Oxford edition at our disposal, it is possible for the first time to pay accurate tribute to this masterpiece of sardonic wit, which belongs in the same category as
James Thomson's lines on the hunt in "Autumn" and Fielding's "Hunting Adventure" in *Joseph Andrews* (3.6). It is no
wonder that the letter was censored, for it gives the lie to the
"official" nineteenth-century Cowper, the gentle, Waltonian
recluse whose satire bites no deeper than *sotto voce* mockery of
electoral enthusiasm. Lady Hesketh's note on this letter, the
gloss of an arch-expurgator, underlines the discrepancy between her wishful public image and Cowper's powerful
achievement: "I send this because it contains a Curious account of a Fox-Chace who wou'd believe that my Quiet humane Cousin shd. be in at the Death!" (3.120, n.6).

"Curious" indeed: seldom have epic trappings so pointedly
emphasized the degradation of a sportive contest. By seeming
to accept at face value the huntsmen's high opinion of their
rite ("the slaughtered prey," "a little filth contracted in so
honourable a cause"), the narrator can turn their own preten-
tious language against them without ever needing to resort to
outright condemnation. The satire begins as straightforward
description—but soon apparently neutral, even picturesque
details are invested with satiric force: "Presently we heard a
Terrier belonging to Mrs. Frog, which you may remember by
the name of Fury, yelping with much vehemence, and saw
her running through the thickets within a few yards of us at
her utmost speed as if in pursuit of something which we
doubted not was the Fox" (3.118). The guiding conceit, as in
Thomson and Fielding, is that during the fox hunt men be-
have like animals and animals like men; the composite image
is one of Bacchic "Fury" everywhere:

> *The Gentlemen sat on their horses contemplating the Fox for*
> *which they had toiled so hard, and the hounds assembled at the*
> *foot of the tree with faces not at all less expressive of the most*
> *rational delight, contemplated the same object. The Huntsman*

remounted. He cut off a foot and threw it to the hounds. One of them swallow'd it whole like a Bolus. He then once more alighted, and drawing down the fox by his hinder legs, desired the people who were by this time rather numerous to open a lane for him to the right and left. He was instantly obey'd, when throwing the fox to the distance of some yards, and screaming like a fiend as he is—Tear him in pieces—at least six times repeatedly, he consign'd him over absolutely to the pack, who in a few minutes devour'd him completely.

(3.119)

Cowper dwells intentionally on this savage climax to the entire ritual, during which the Huntsman as head priest throws Reynard-Pentheus to one group of Bacchantes (the hounds) while another group (the hunters) participates vicariously— "with faces not at all less expressive of the most rational delight."

The satiric thrust of Cowper's mock-epic miniature is all the more effective for its restraint: we share the narrator's disgust precisely because it is so tellingly controlled and concisely insinuated. Events promote this reportorial strategy: the fox is run to earth in a privy (a detail restored by King and Ryskamp), and by the time he is dragged out and dismembered, both human and animal protagonists are smeared with excrement:

Being himself by far too staunch to boggle at a little filth contracted in so honourable a cause, he soon produced dead Reynard, and rejoined us in the grove with all his dogs about him. . . . The Fox's tail, or brush as I ought to call it, was given to one of the Hall Foot-boys, who bearing it in his hatband, ran with it to his mistress, and in the height of his transport offer'd it to her fair hand, neither so clean nor so sweet as it had been while the Fox possess'd it. Happily however for Mr. Throg, not being quite so enraptured, she had the presence of mind to decline the offer. The boy therefore for aught I know, remains to this hour in possession both of the tail and the stink that belongs to it.

(3.118–19).

In more senses than one, the "offense is rank, it smells to heaven": in backing away Cowper and the Throckmortons unite physical with moral disgust. After the periphrastic reference to the privy ("videlicet in the Pit of a certain place called Jessamy Hall"), every instance of linguistic elevation heightens our disdain; the more exalted the diction, the baser the proceedings. Cowper seals his condemnation, and ends his description, by quoting from the beginning of *Aeneid* 9 (Iris's message to Turnus):

> *Thus, my Dear, as Virgil says, What none of the Gods could have ventured to promise me, time itself pursuing its accustom'd course has of its own accord presented me with.—I have been In at the death of a Fox—and you now know as much of that matter as I, who am as well inform'd as any Sportsman in England.*

(3.119)

This graceful epilogue constitutes Cowper's final verdict and his final gesture of moral reprobation. He has been "*in* at the death" but not *of* it; the observer's knowledge is his but not the participant's guilt.

The problem of devising access to private thoughts and emotions is one with which every letter-writer must grapple. Cowper's task is especially difficult because of his extreme isolation, spiritual and intellectual as well as geographic. While Lady Mary relies upon the voices of Seneca and Racine, Cowper turns to the emblematic patterns of religious verse and prose. Steeped in Herbert, Bunyan, and the language of the Evangelical revival, he learns from this branch of his literary ancestry ("John Calvin" rather than "John Gilpin") how to convert "intellectual conceptions" into "sensible images."[15] The emblem permits Cowper to objectify, even to allegorize,

---

15. "Emblem, on the other hand, reduces intellectual conceptions to sensible images . . ." See *The Works of Francis Bacon*, ed. James Spedding, Robert Leslie Ellis, and Douglas Denon Heath (New York: Hurd and Houghton, 1864), 9.105 (*Of the Dignity and Advancement of Learning*, v.5). For Herbert's influence on Cowper, see *Adelphi* (King and Ryskamp, 1.9). For a suggestive comparison between *Adelphi* and *Pilgrim's Progress*, see Newey, pp. 30–31.

the least communicable of his feelings. By uniting the visual with the verbal, striking image with pithy interpretation, it holds up to the light even the darkest of his obsessions.

It is no accident that the majority of Cowper's emblems occur in letters to John Newton. Until the estrangement attendant on publication of *The Task,* and even fitfully thereafter, Newton served as Cowper's father confessor—the only correspondent before Samuel Teedon to whom he revealed the full dimensions of his spiritual torment. Furthermore, Newton had collaborated with him on *Olney Hymns,* in which Cowper tried his hand at emblematic renderings of the spiritual life. As Patricia Meyer Spacks has observed, these early "attempts to translate that [psychological] insight into images are rarely and incompletely successful."[16] Spacks's final judgment is not overly harsh: "This is poetry *voulue* with a vengeance . . ."[17] Yet from the standpoint of Cowper's epistolary technique, the clumsy experiments in emblematic religious verse might well be considered a valuable apprenticeship. In his letters Cowper is consistently successful in finding the right objective correlative: we can watch him recasting lifeless or even grotesque images from *Olney Hymns* into effective visual metaphors.

Cowper shares with his predecessor Thomson and his contemporary Johnson the habit of thinking and writing in personified abstractions. His "Dejection," "Melancholy," and "Sympathy" are close kin to the figure of "Observation" who presides over the beginning of *The Vanity of Human Wishes:* "A Dejection of mind which perhaps may be removed by tomorrow, rather disqualifies me for writing, a business I would always perform in good spirits, because Melancholy is catching, especially where there is much Sympathy to assist the contagion" (1.505). This visualizing faculty, reinforced by Cowper's reading and hymn writing, predisposed him to such

16. Patricia Meyer Spacks, *The Poetry of Vision* (Cambridge, Mass.: Harvard University Press, 1967), p. 165.
17. Spacks, p. 171.

symbolic epitomes as the following, an emblem of hope-
lessness that offers a pictorial history of his case:

> *I do not at all doubt the truth of what you say, when you*
> *complain of that crowd of trifling thoughts that pesters you*
> *without ceasing, but then you always have a serious thought*
> *standing at the door of your imagination, like a Justice of*
> *peace with the Riot act in his hand, ready to read it and*
> *disperse the Mob. Here lies the difference between you and me.*
> *My thoughts are clad in a sober livery, for the most part as*
> *grave as that of a Bishop's Servants. They turn too upon*
> *spiritual subjects, but the tallest fellow and the loudest amongst*
> *them all, is he who is continually crying with a loud voice,*
> *Actum est de te, periisti.*
>
> (1.509–10)

Cowper's emblems typically combine biblical echoes with natural phenomena presented and moralized in the manner of a
Renaissance emblem-book:

> *The only consolation left me on this subject is that the voice of*
> *the Almighty can in one moment cure me of this mental infir-*
> *mity. That he can, I know by experience, and there are reasons*
> *for which I ought to believe that he will. But from hope to*
> *despair is a transition that I have made so often, that I can*
> *only consider the hope that may come, and that sometimes I*
> *believe will, as a short prelude of joy to a miserable conclusion*
> *of sorrow that shall never end. Thus are my brightest prospects*
> *clouded, and thus to me is Hope itself become like a wither'd*
> *flower that has lost both its hue and its fragrance.*
>
> (3.425–26)

In this passage Cowper gestures toward a figure of Hope sitting, like Dürer's or Ripa's "Melancholy," with her chin
propped dejectedly in one hand and a withered flower in the
other. In another more complex emblematic description he
conflates two images of spiritual martyrdom, a post propping
up a hedge in wintertime and a soul transfixed by a stake:

> *The weather is an exact emblem of my mind in its present*
> *state. A thick fog invelops every thing, and at the same time it*

freezes intensely. You will tell me that this cold gloom will be succeeded by a cheerful spring, and endeavor to encourage me to hope for a spiritual change resembling it. But it will be lost labor: Nature revives again, but a soul once slain, lives no more. The hedge that has been apparently dead, is not so, it will burst into leaf and blossom at the appointed time; but no such time is appointed for the stake that stands in it. It is as dead as it seems, and will prove itself no dissembler.

(2.200)

The first image enforces a contrast between appearance (both stake and hedge are leafless and therefore *seem* equally life-less) and reality (the hedge will turn green again, the stake never). The second belongs to the metaphysical tradition of pierced, broken, and flaming hearts, a tradition that influenced such Olney hymns as "The Contrite Heart," "Afflictions Sanctified by the Word," "Jehovah-Shalem," and "The Valley of the Shadow of Death."

> What tho' it [God's "chastning rod"] pierc'd my fainting
> heart,
> I bless thine hand that caus'd the smart;
> It taught my tears awhile to flow,
> But sav'd me from eternal woe.
> ("Afflictions Sanctified by the Word," ll. 13–16)

> No drop remains of all the curse,
> For wretches who deserv'd the whole;
> No arrows dipt in wrath to pierce
> The guilty, but returning soul.
> ("Jehovah-Shalem," ll. 9–12)

Cowper's tragedy—the tragedy pictured with such stark simplicity in this emblem—is that he feels his soul pierced but *un*returning.

Seventeenth-century prototypes are even more apparent in another emblem of martyrdom with a crucial difference: "My device was intended to represent, not my own heart, but the heart of a Christian, mourning and yet rejoicing, pierced with thorns yet wreathed about with roses. I have the thorn

Figure 1. Jacobus à Bruck, *Emblemata Moralia,* 1615. (Courtesy of The Newberry Library, Chicago.)

without the rose. My briar is a wintry one, the flowers are wither'd but the thorn remains" (2.127). Two specific analogues from baroque emblem-books will illustrate the kind of "device" Cowper asks Newton to visualize. Jacobus à Bruck's *Emblemata Moralia* includes a wounded heart, fenced around with thorns, from which a flower is growing (fig. 1). The *Sacra Emblemata* of Johann Mannich shows a heart pierced and overgrown with thorns; on one side is a book, on the other bandages. Above and to the left a hand bearing a cross appears from the clouds (fig. 2).[18] The quatrain underneath de-

18. Arthur Henkel and Albrecht Schöne, *Emblemata* (Stuttgart: Metzlersche Verlagsbuchhandlung, 1976), cols. 1030–31.

Figure 2. Johann Mannich, *Sacra Emblemata*, 1624. (Courtesy of The Newberry Library, Chicago.)

scribes the Christian consolation that is withheld from Cowper, who bears the cross but not the crown ("the thorn without the rose"):

> Nec laesum spinis cor lex, unguentave sanant:
> Est solum nostri crux panacea mali.
> Sub cruce quando premor: mihi crux Christi sit asylum.
> In cruce, sit, CHRISTI, gloria, honorque meus![19]

Though it is unlikely that either Bruck or Mannich exerted a

19. "Neither law nor salves heal the heart wounded by thorns. Only the cross is the panacea for our ills. When I am burdened under a cross, may the cross of Christ be a refuge for me. In the cross of Christ be my glory and honor!" (my translation).

direct influence, both typify the tradition that explains and inspires Cowper's private emblem-making.

Although Cowper handles tradition with ease, he is capable of bypassing literary sources to create emblems directly out of country life and landscapes. His acute response to the seasonal cycle intensifies the pathos of this portrait of the artist as blighted fruit tree:

> *Of myself who had once both leaves and fruit, but who have now neither, I say nothing; or only this. That when I am overwhelmed with despair, I repine at my barrenness and think it hard to be thus blighted. But when a glimpse of hope breaks in upon me, I am contented to be the sapless thing I am, knowing that he who has commanded me to wither, can command me to flourish again when he pleases.*
>
> (2.357)

Implicit in this emblem is a connection between sap and divine grace; Cowper is cuing Newton to remember Olney Hymn No. 54, "My Soul Thirsteth for God":

> I want that grace that springs from thee,
> That quickens all things where it flows:
> And makes a wretched thorn, like me,
> Bloom as the myrtle, or the rose.
>
> (ll. 9–12).

Cowper's pastoral surroundings also furnish one of the rare emblems of hopeful expectation to be found in the letters:

> *The Press proceeds like a broad-wheeled wagon, slow and sure. After the correction of the two first sheets, a complete month intervened before I received two more. And before I am favor'd with another pacquet, perhaps another month may be almost expended. So the wild goose in the meadow flaps her wings and flaps them but yet she mounts not. She stands on tip-toe on the banks of Ouse, she meditates an ascent, she stretches her long neck, she flaps her wings again; the successfull repetition of her efforts at last bears her above the ground, she mounts into the heav'nly regions exulting, and*

who then *shall describe her song? To herself at least it makes
ample recompense of her laborious exertions.*

(2.332)

The last and the most powerful of Cowper's emblems registers his overwhelming despair with a single detail from the
Norfolk seascape: "At two miles' distance on the coast is a
solitary pillar of rock, that the crumbling cliff has left at the
high water-mark. I have visited it twice, and have found it an
emblem of myself. Torn from my natural connexions, I stand
alone and expect the storm that shall displace me" (4.450).
The motto is ours to supply—perhaps "sine numine frustra."

Humorous magnifications of Olney minutiae and emblematic renderings of his emotional condition are two ways in
which Cowper manages to objectify, and thus to share, his
private experience. Pictorial description is a third.[20] Readers
of Cowper's poetry have long paid homage to the painterly
handling of landscape in *The Task.* One of the earliest and
most perceptive of these tributes comes from Sainte-Beuve,
who devotes special attention to the prospect scene in Book I:

> ... dans cette description si parfaite qu'on vient de lire, Cow-
> per a su concilier les deux ordres de qualités, la finesse et le
> relief de chaque détail (je dirai même le brillanté sur un ou
> deux points), et la gradation et la suite aérienne de la perspec-
> tive. *On copierait ce paysage avec le pinceau.*[21] (my italics)

More recent investigators have supplemented the findings of
Josephine Miles, whose word count reveals that "eye," "scene,"
and "art" rank among Cowper's favorite nouns, and "see"
among his favorite verbs.[22] Patricia Meyer Spacks, who ex-

20. Throughout the discussion that follows, I have adopted Jean Hagstrum's definition of "pictorialism." See Jean Hagstrum, *The Sister Arts* (Chicago and London: University of Chicago Press, 1958), pp. xxi–xxii.

21. Sainte-Beuve, "William Cowper ou de la Poésie Domestique," in *Caus-
eries du Lundi* (Paris: Garnier Frères, n.d.), 11.177.

22. Josephine Miles, *Renaissance, Eighteenth-Century, and Modern Language
in English Poetry* (Berkeley: University of California Press, 1960), p. 23.

plores the spiritual significance of visual perception in *The Task,* emphasizes Cowper's awareness of spatial organization in the landscapes he describes.[23] Vincent Newey's perceptive analysis of the passage singled out by Sainte-Beuve underpins his conclusion that "in Cowper the human need for *perceptual* order is paramount, and is both reflected in and satisfied by an art-conscious mode of presentation."[24] Yet the very scholars who draw attention to Cowper's visual sensitivity and pictorial finesse have apparently failed to notice the same qualities in those letters they use to explicate his verse. In fact Cowper's letters as well as his poetry exemplify Joseph Warton's belief that "the use, the force, and the excellence of language, certainly consists in raising, *clear, complete,* and *circumstantial* images, and in turning *readers* into *spectators.*"[25]

In his familiar letters Cowper felt a special need to make spectators out of readers. Three explanations for this continuing impulse emerge from a careful study of his epistolary career. First, to pictorialize his environment helped Cowper to order it and to intensify the acts of self-definition and self-illustration typified by the emblematic images we have just been considering. It is true that in many of his descriptions Cowper seems at first glance to be turning away from self to setting, from the inner to the outer life. As he writes to his cousin Mrs. Cowper:

> *Being rather scantily furnished with Subjects that are good for any thing, and Corresponding only with those who have no Relish for such as are good for Nothing, I often find myself reduced to the Necessity, the disagreeable Necessity of Writing about Myself. This does not mend the Matter much, for though in a Description of my own Condition, I discover abundant Materials to Employ my Pen upon, yet as the Task is not very agreeable to me, so I am Sufficiently aware that it is likely to prove Irksome to others. A Painter who should*

23. Spacks, pp. 180–83.
24. Newey, p. 105.
25. Joseph Warton, *An Essay on the Genius and Writings of Pope,* 4th ed. (London: J. Dodsley, 1782), 2.165.

confine himself in the Exercise of his Art to the Drawing of his
own Picture, must be a Wonderfull Coxcomb if he did not
soon grow Sick of his Occupation, and be peculiarly fortunate,
if he did not make others as Sick as Himself.

(1.368–69)

Yet Cowper remains a "Wonderful Coxcomb": his superficially objective renderings in effect continue the autographic process. We do not grow "Sick" of perpetual self-portraiture because of the multiple guises in which it is conducted.

Second, to pictorialize is to facilitate access to the microcosm by illusionism verging on *trompe l'oeil*. Assessing his portrait by L.F. Abbott, Cowper concentrates exclusively on the achievement of a "speaking" likeness, which seems to dissolve the barrier between painted subject and living observer:

To your second enquiry I answer that he has succeeded to
admiration. The likeness is so strong that when my friends
enter the room where my picture is they start, astonish'd to see
me where they know I am not. . . . Every creature that has
seen it has been astonish'd at the strong resemblance; Sam's
boy bow'd to it, and Beau walk'd up to it wagging his tail as
he went, and evidently showing that he acknowledg'd its like
ness to his Master.

(4.156, 160)

In his word-paintings Cowper strives for a similar illusion, by which the subject pictured/described reaches out to viewer/reader and draws him into a shared space. Preeminent among the candidates for such an initiation is Lady Hesketh, former insider become outsider, whom Cowper wishes to bring back into the fold.

Third, to pictorialize is to foster the illusion of stasis, upon which domestic happiness ("meek and constant, hating change") depended (see *The Task* 3.55). For Cowper was obsessed by the passing of time:

There was a time when I could contemplate my present state
and consider myself as a thing of a day with pleasure, when I

number'd the seasons as they pass'd in swift rotation, as a school-boy numbers the days that interpose between the next vacation, when he shall see his parents and enjoy his home again. But to make so just an estimate of life like this is no longer in my power. The consideration of my short continuance here, which was once grateful to me, now fills me with regret. I would live and live always, and am become such another wretch as Mecaenas was, who wish'd for long long life, he cared not at what expence of sufferings.

(3.425)

Unlike the fears of ordinary men, however, his intimations of mortality aroused a special terror: "in the midst of his fear of erratic change and of the inevitability of new and sudden dangers was Cowper's steady awareness of the flow of time, a flow that must, no matter what else it did, bring him to death, and with death to the judgment which he feared because he knew it to be adverse."[26] At the beginning of his poem "On the Receipt of my Mother's Picture out of Norfolk," Cowper paid tribute to "the art that can immortalize, / The art that baffles time's tyrannic claim / To quench it" (ll. 8–10). The capacity to create epistolary miniatures—to *compose* his little world—meant a more solid bulwark, however temporary, against the horrors of dissolution.

Despite his commitment to seeing and making see, Cowper was no Pope or Thomson: in comparison to these major predecessors and many minor poets like John Dyer, he made do with the scantiest of backgrounds in the visual arts. As Jean Hagstrum has emphasized:

A typical poet of the eighteenth century was likely to be an intimate friend of painters, to be surrounded with rather intense artistic activity, to have seen at first hand the masterpieces of Italy, to be himself a collector of prints and sometimes of original oils, and to have read a sufficient amount of art history and criticism to make him familiar with the leading schools and the most important critical clichés.[27]

26. Golden, p. 75.
27. Hagstrum, p. 108.

Only on the last count—general familiarity with art historical schools and critical commonplaces—could Cowper be considered typical. His confession to Mrs. King sums up the poverty of his experience: "I am a great lover of good Paintings, but no Connoisseur, having never had an opportunity to become one. In the last forty years of my life I have hardly seen six pictures that were worth looking at" (3.307). Cowper's various admiring references to Sir Joshua Reynolds do not seem to reflect first-hand knowledge of any specific paintings.[28] Similarly, it cannot be determined whether Cowper ever saw any works by Gainsborough, the contemporary painter who resembles him the most.[29]

We are left with a handful of passages, a sprinkling of metaphors, and a general attitude. Various references in the letters attest to Cowper's familiarity with basic terms and styles (e.g., 1.320, 2.3). He admired the ability of the artist to fashion "A lucid mirror, in which Nature sees / All her reflected features" (*The Task* 1.701–2), and sympathized with the alliance of the sister arts:

> The day before yesterday I saw for the first time Banbury's new Print, the Propagation of a Lie. . . . The Original thought is good, and the exemplification of it in those very expressive features, admirable. A Poem on the same subject, displaying all that is display'd in those attitudes and in those features (for faces they can hardly be called) would be most excellent. The affinity of the two Arts, viz. of Verse and Painting, has been often observed; possibly the happiest illustration of it would be found, if some Poet would ally himself to some such Draftsman as Bunbury, and undertake to write every thing that He should draw.
>
> (3.87–88)

In his own poetry the painter's art quite often supplies a metaphor for creative activity, as in Olney Hymn No. 48 (ll. 21–

28. See Baird and Ryskamp, p. 495.
29. Vincent Newey has suggested that Cowper may have remembered Gainsborough's *The Gypsies*, exhibited and engraved in 1764, when he came to describe them in Book 1 of *The Task*, ll. 557–91. See Newey, p. 337, n. 43.

22), *Hope* (ll. 669–73), and the famous comparison from Book II of *The Task:*

> There is a pleasure in poetic pains
> Which only poets know. . . .
> T'arrest the fleeting images that fill
> The mirror of the mind, and hold them fast,
> And force them sit till he has pencil'd off
> A faithful likeness of the forms he views;
> Then to dispose his copies with such art,
> That each may find its most propitious light,
> And shine by situation, hardly less
> Than by the labour and the skill it cost . . .
>
> (ll. 285–86, 290–97)

It might be argued that an earlier passage displays a condescending, even philistine attitude to the artist and the connoisseur:

> Strange! there should be found,
> Who, self-imprisoned in their proud saloons,
> Renounce the odours of the open field
> For the unscented fictions of the loom;
> Who, satisfied with only pencil'd scenes,
> Prefer to the performance of a God
> Th'inferior wonders of an artist's hands!
>
> (1.413–19)

But what these lines actually stress is the ultimate sterility of any mimetic activity—poetry as well as painting—that preempts or replaces direct experience of God-in-Nature. Any lingering doubts about Cowper's attitude to the visual arts and his capacity for vivid aesthetic response are forcefully dispelled by the letter that describes his reaction to an engraving of Bacon's *Elder Pitt:*

> *I think the figure of Lord Chatham singularly gracefull, and his countenance full of the character that belongs to him. It speaks not only great ability and consummate skill, but a tender and heartfelt interest in the welfare of the charge committed to him. In the figure of the City there is all that*

empressement (pardon a French term, it expresses my Idea better than any English one that occurrs) that the importance of her Errand calls for, and it is noble in its air, though in a posture of supplication. But the figure of Commerce is indeed a perfect beauty, it is a literal truth that I felt the tears flush into my eyes while I looked at her. . . . I have most of the Monuments in the Abbey by heart, but I recollect none that ever gave me so much pleasure. The faces are all expressive and the figures are all gracefull.

(2.174)

Though the technical vocabulary of art criticism may be missing from this passage, sincerity and vitality are not.

It is often forgotten or ignored that Cowper was an amateur artist—coached not by Charles Jervas but by James Andrews, a self-taught painter and engraver who lived in Olney. Cowper took up drawing early in 1780 as a therapeutic diversion:

The Necessity of Amusement makes me sometimes write Verses—it made me a Carpenter, a Bird Cage maker, a Gardener, and has lately taught me to draw, and to draw too with such surprizing Proficiency in the Art, considering my total Ignorance of it two months ago, that when I shew your Mother my Productions, she is all Admiration and Applause.

(1.329)

From the outset he seems to have concentrated on landscapes, and within a year had produced three drawings "which a Lady thought worthy to be framed & glazed" (3.222). Despite rapid progress, however, Cowper soon abandoned this particular diversion. He offered two explanations: that drawing was "an employment hurtful to my eyes" (4.151), and that he was afraid to impair what little reputation he had won for himself: "I then judged it high time to exchange this occupation for another, lest by any subsequent productions of inferior merit, I should forfeit the honour I had so fortunately acquired" (3.222). The "occupation" that replaced drawing appears to have been poetry: *Anti-Thelyphthora,* the work that inaugurated his poetic career, was composed in November 1780, just when

Cowper's year of artistic activity was drawing to a close.[30] The skills he had acquired in one medium he continued to practice in two others—the poetic and the epistolary.

Though up to now the connection has not been perceived, it seems indisputable that Cowper's training as an artist, however brief and rudimentary, influenced his technique as a letter-writer. Striving for the three goals outlined above (to order his microcosm, facilitate access to it, and foster the illusion of stasis), Cowper contrives genre scenes and landscapes whose pictorial syntax finds its closest equivalent in the work of two seventeenth-century Dutch masters, Vermeer and Pieter de Hooch. By "pictorial syntax" I refer specifically to the versatile deployment of four devices: recession through clearly defined spatial compartments, an emphatic foreground/background contrast, concentration on still-life detail, and the creation of a "prepared space" for the viewer.

Though I wish to draw attention to similarities in method and structure, I do not intend to suggest anything so untenable as conscious imitation (though Cowper was aware of the "Flemish pencil").[31] Vermeer and de Hooch can only be considered visual analogues, not sources or even influences. Nevertheless, an *ut pictura epistola* comparison does serve a valuable purpose: it draws attention to the ways in which Cowper's letters aspire to the condition of painting without forfeiting the advantages of verbal mimesis. Their achievement, in short, is to combine the distinctive features of the two sister arts: spatial organization and immediate apprehensibility on the one hand, sequential ordering and gradual absorption on the other. The result is not a primitive anticipation of "spatial form," but a composite art of intimacy.[32]

30. See Baird and Ryskamp, p. 503.

31. See King and Ryskamp, 1.320; 2.3.

32. For the concept of spatial form as originally formulated by Joseph Frank, see the *Sewanee Review* 53 (1945): 221–40, 433–56, 643–53. This essay was reprinted in Frank's *The Widening Gyre* (New Brunswick: Rutgers University Press, 1963). The concept has been modified and extended by W.J.T. Mitchell, "Spatial Form in Literature: Toward a General Theory," in *The Language of Images*, ed. W.J.T. Mitchell (Chicago: University of Chicago Press, 1980), pp. 271–99.

A LANDSCAPE from a DRAWING by MᵣCOWPER the POET.

Figure 3. "A Landscape from a Drawing by Mr. Cowper the Poet." (Reproduced from the *Gentleman's Magazine,* June 1804.)

The only visual record of Cowper's *Kunstjahr* appears in the June 1804 issue of the *Gentleman's Magazine:* an engraving of one of the three landscape drawings he gave to Lady Austen (fig. 3). Because the engraving is so crudely executed it is difficult to assess the quality of the original. In her *Bibliography of William Cowper,* Norma Russell suggests that the landscape was copied "from a drawing-book or print."[33] The vaguely Italianate air—Claude at several removes—certainly rules out Buckinghamshire as the subject. Yet it is equally possible that the drawing represents an imaginary scene. As Cowper told Mrs. King: "Many figures were the fruit of my labours which had at least the merit of being unparallel'd by any production either of Art or Nature" (3.222).

Whatever the source, the drawing does illustrate two of the features we have just noted, features that characterize the expressionistic topography of Cowper's letters: lucid organization, involving an emphatic recessional movement through a

---

33. Norma Russell, *A Bibliography of William Cowper to 1837* (Oxford: Clarendon Press, 1963), p. 138, n. 1.

sequence of distinct spaces; and the juxtaposition of sharply focused foreground activity, usually evocative of happy domesticity, to an unbounded, potentially threatening background. The picture space is organized into three planes, so clearly delimited that they suggest flats on a stage. The eye enters the composition from the left, guided by the swaying trunk of the smaller tree, which bends toward a rustic couple seated on a hummock. The middleground is filled by a clump of overgrown ruins, whose most prominent feature is a blocked-up archway that has been converted into a fountain and watering trough. A dog drinks from the trough while a man gestures in his direction. In the background a promontory crowned with more ruins stretches toward the sea, which is dotted with several boats. A small inlet leads the eye rapidly out into the limitless expanses of water and sky.

Given the significance of oceans and ships in Cowper's private iconography, it is difficult not to interpret the composition in terms of the symbolic antitheses that dominate both letters and poems:

> You from the Flood-controuling Steep
> Saw Stretch'd before your View,
> With conscious Joy, the threat'ning Deep,
> No longer such to You.
>
> Your Sea of Troubles you have pass'd,
> And found the peacefull Shore;
> I Tempest-toss'd and wreck'd at last,
> Come Home to Port no more.
> ("To Mr. Newton on his Return from Ramsgate,"
> stanzas 2, 4)

The shadow that falls over man and dog and reaches toward the happy couple is the shadow that darkens even the calmest of seascapes. The title of this composition might well be *Calabria:* "I know the ground before I tread upon it. It is hollow, it is agitated, it suffers shocks in every direction, it is like the soil of Calabria, all whirlpool and undulation" (2.161).[34]

34. An alternate gloss comes from the letter narrating the events that gave rise to "The Colubriad": see pp. 59–60.

Amateurish as it is, Cowper's drawing does illustrate his ability to guide the viewer into and direct him through the picture space. Similar assistance is offered the reader of the letters, who is invited to participate in a guided tour of the Olney microcosm. In his elegiac description of a favorite copse that has been mercilessly pruned, Cowper actually takes us with him down the path to the pavilion at the center of the Spinney. Like statues lining a garden *allée,* details are "spaced" to mark off the distance traveled and to further the sensation of convergence upon a dramatic eyecatcher—in this case, the violated hermitage:

> *I told you I believe that the Spinney has been cut down, and though it may seem sufficient to have mention'd such an occurrence once, I cannot help recurring to the melancholy theme. Last night at near 9 o'clock we enter'd it for the first time this summer. We had not walked many yards in it, before we perceived that this pleasant retreat is destined never to be a pleasant retreat again. In one more year the whole will be a thicket. That which was once the serpentine walk is now in a state of transformation and is already become as woody as the rest. Poplars and elms without number are springing in the turf, they are now as high as the knee. Before the summer is ended they will be twice as high, and the growth of another season will make them trees. It will then be impossible for any but a sportsman and his dog to penetrate it. The desolation of the whole scene is such that it sunk our spirits. The ponds are dry. The circular one in front of the hermitage is filled with flags and rushes so that if it contains any water not a drop is visible. The weeping willow at the side of it, the only ornamental plant that has escaped the ax, is dead. The ivy and the moss with which the hermitage was lined, are torn away, and the very mats that cover'd the benches, have been stripp'd off, rent in tatters, and trodden under foot. So farewell Spinney. I have promised myself that I will never enter it again. We have both pray'd in it. You for me, and I for you, but it is desecrated from this time forth, and the voice of pray'r will be heard in it no more.*

> (2.362–63)

And when Cowper introduces Lady Hesketh to Orchardside

he walks her the width of the house, orienting her visually at every point:

> *And now I will tell you what you shall find on your first entrance. Imprimis, as soon as you have enter'd the Vestibule, if you cast a look to either side of you, you shall see on your right hand a box of my making. It is the Box in which have been lodged all my hares, and in which lodges Puss at present. But he, poor fellow, is worn out with age, and promises to die before you can see him. On the right hand, stands a cupboard the work of the same Author. It was once a dove-cage, but I transformed it. Opposite to you stands a table which I also made. But a merciless servant having scrubbed it 'till it is become paralytic, it serves no purpose now but of ornament, and all my clean shoes stand under it. On the left hand at the farther end of this superb vestibule you will find the door of the parlour into which I will conduct you and where I will introduce you to Mrs. Unwin (unless we should meet her before) and where we will be as happy as the day is long.*

> (2.476)

The element of activity, of temporal sequence, is kept to a minimum; there is just enough movement subtly to reinforce the impression of proceeding from outer to inner space. The passage constructs a composite image: we peer through a door down the vestibule and into the parlor, where Mrs. Unwin stands waiting. Objects along the central line of recession catch our attention and enliven the act of visual exploration. As in Pieter de Hooch's *The Pantry* (fig. 4), the result of this architectural overlay is to establish the house as a multicelled domestic sanctuary, which offers shelter without threatening confinement. Furthermore, in both de Hooch's painting and Cowper's picture of Orchardside, every nook, cranny, and domestic artifact participates in the affectionate human exchange that focuses the composition: "On the left hand at the farther end of this superb vestibule you will find the door of the parlour into which I will conduct you and where I will introduce you to Mrs. Unwin (unless we should meet her before) and where we will be as happy as the day is long."

This same passage adumbrates two more of Cowper's fa-

Figure 4. Pieter de Hooch, *The Pantry, c.* 1658. (By courtesy of the Rijksmuseum-Stichting, Amsterdam.)

vorite pictorial devices: the lovingly detailed still-life and the preparation of a space for the viewer within the composition itself. Cowper's passionate concentration on individual objects within his microcosm rivals Defoe's, Hopkins's, or Vermeer's. His description of a writing desk, for example, conveys not only the minutest details of physical appearance but also the desk's talismanic status: the rich materials and the adroit craftsmanship are presented as manifestations of their first cause, the discerning Lady Hesketh:

> *Let me sing the Praises of the Desk which my dear Cousin has sent me. In* general, *It is as elegant as possible, In* Par-

ticular, *it is of Cedar, beautifully lacquer'd. When put together, it assumes the form of a handsome small chest, contains all sorts of accommodations, is furnish'd with cut glass for Ink and Sand, and is hinged, handled, and mounted with silver. It is inlaid with Ivory, and also serves the purpose of a Reading-desk. It came stored with Stationary ware of all sorts, and this splendid sheet is a part of it.*

(2.433)

Lawrence Gowing's description of an early still-life by Vermeer perfectly catches the emotional significance of Cowper's icon: "The spherical white jug has been offered up to the light on its round platter: the shining ring of a wine glass has been cradled in careful hands. All are images of satisfaction, of natural volume that is in full, appropriate possession."[35]

This kind of joyful particularity often achieves what the art historian John Rupert Martin has called "the direct involvement of the observer in the spatial-psychological sphere created by the work of art."[36] Direct involvement also occurs when Cowper points to a designated space and indicates that his composition will not be complete until that space is occupied:

> *I long to show you my workshop, and to see you sitting on the opposite side of my table.* We shall be as close pack'd as two wax figures in an old fashioned picture frame. *I am writing in it now. It is the place in which I fabricate all my verse in summer time. . . . The grass under my windows is all over bespangled with dew-drops, and the birds are singing in the apple trees among the blossoms. Never Poet had a more commodious oratory in which to invoke his Muse.*

(2.559, my italics)

In this invitation to Lady Hesketh, Cowper insinuates a picture within a picture. When the gap in the existing scene has been filled up, his portrait of the solitary poet will be replaced

---

35. Lawrence Gowing, *Vermeer* (London: Faber and Faber, 1952), p. 42.
36. John Rupert Martin, *Baroque* (New York: Harper and Row, 1977), p. 168.

by a vibrant conversation piece, framed in the "old fashioned" style.[37]

In several important respects the suite of letters to Lady Hesketh (9 February 1786–12 June 1786) occupies a unique position in Cowper's epistolary oeuvre. It sustains a drama of initiation and anticipation, which builds to a feverish offstage climax. It displays an intensity of affection unmatched by any other group of letters: "the comfort that I have had in our revived correspondence and the joy with which I look forward to an interview with her, are not to be expressed" (2.502). And it succeeds in fully communicating that affection. For contrary to what Cowper tells his uncle, he does manage to express the joy he feels—by picturing the world Lady Hesketh will soon be sharing with him. The letters abound with such proleptic scenes as the one we have just glimpsed; these outline a setting (house, garden, landscape) and position his cousin within it. As their reunion draws closer, Cowper maps the microcosm to-be-shared with increasing energy and precision. The metaphor is his own; what Cowper praises in Lady Hesketh's letters he himself accomplishes in his pictorial guide to Orchardside and environs: "I doubt not that with your Letter in my hand, by way of map, could I be set down on the spot in a moment, I should find myself qualified to take my walks, and my pastime in whatever quarter of your paradise it should please me the most to visit" (3.195). With all the resources of his artistic training Cowper prepares the way for an idyllic *ménage-à-trois*.

37. By situating himself and Lady Hesketh within the summerhouse, Cowper imagines a conversation piece that mixes the two basic categories of setting—"indoors and outdoors, the former more conducive to the portrayal of a middle-class family and exact socio-political definition, the latter to a kind of portrait group that displays an aristocratic family, garden imagery, and symbolism relating art and nature." The outdoor scene represents "not the Garden of Eden but the garden man makes for himself in the fallen world . . ." See the chapter on "The Conversation Piece in Painting and Literature" in Ronald Paulson's *Emblem and Expression: Meaning in English Art of the Eighteenth Century* (Cambridge, Mass.: Harvard University Press, 1975), p. 123.

The four techniques we have been observing separately are brought into play in the tenth letter of the sequence (17 April 1786): recession through spatial compartments, illusionistic detail, symbolic juxtaposition of foreground to background, and the creation of "prepared space." This letter, the tenth of eighteen, introduces Lady Hesketh to the house she will soon be occupying. The complex organization of the picture does not obscure its overall lucidity of design. We view the vicarage from the back, as if we had just come from Cowper's house, through the orchard, and into the vicar's garden. As Cowper explains, Lady Austen had created a gateway which permitted the occupants of both houses to take this agreeable short-cut. As he describes the exterior of the vicarage seen from the gateway, Cowper designates a place for Lady Hesketh, who will soon be sharing this prospect:

> *The Vicarage itself was built by Lord Dartmouth & was not finished 'till some time after we arrived in Olney. Consequently it is new. It is a smart stone building, well sashed, by much too good for the Living, but just what I would wish for you. It has, as you justly conclude from my premises, a garden, but rather calculated for use than ornament or retreat. It is square and well walled, but has neither arbour nor alcove nor other shade except the shadow of the house. But we have 2 gardens my Dear, and 3 Sitting places therein, besides a shady bench, all which are yours. Between your mansion and ours is interposed nothing but an Orchard, into which a door opens out of our garden, and the same door which was made in the garden wall of the Vicarage when Lady Austen lodged there, being opened again (it is now walled up) will afford us the easiest communication imaginable; will save the round about by the town, and make both houses one.*

(2.518–19)

Next Cowper sketches in the background—the world outside, from which the vicarage offers such a pleasant retreat. We look through the house, as it were, to glimpse the landscape stretching in front of it:

> *The house is not in the town, nor more than 40 yards out of it, and has the pleasantest situation that any house can boast in*

Olney. Your Chamber windows look over the river and over the meadows to a village called Emberton and command the whole length of a long bridge described by a certain poet, together with a view of the road at a distance.

(2.519)

Then we peer into the parlor and the kitchen. There is a sense of controlled movement within stasis as Cowper dwells on the arrangement of parlor and kitchen. The eye travels inward from the back garden to examine an assemblage of domestic objects: mahogany chairs and tables in the parlor; tin furniture, china, glasses, and earthenware in the kitchen. At the center of this still-life Cowper invites Lady Hesketh to imagine a modest collection of poetry: "Should you wish for books at Olney, you must bring them with you or you will wish in vain, for I have none but the works of a certain poet Cowper of whom perhaps you have heard, and they are as yet but 2 volumes. They may multiply hereafter, but at present they are no more" (2.520). Thus he puts the finishing touches on a scene which images in every detail his love for its missing centerpiece.

The overall design of the composition will become even clearer if we compare it to Pieter de Hooch's masterpiece, *A Maid with a Child in a Court* (fig. 5). In this painting de Hooch sustains a dynamic interplay between interior and exterior space which helps to draw the viewer into the domestic context inhabited by the three figures. The pictorial organization is complex, but as in Cowper's descriptive set piece, thoroughly "readable": beginning outside and to the right, moving down the corridor to the street, and then returning to the exterior of the building, the eye is urged to explore and to know. Just as in Cowper's composition, it registers both larger units (doorway, pavement, shed, wall) and small details (shutter-bolts, gateposts, broom and bucket, lines and patches of mortar, sprays of tree and vine). It contrasts sheltered enclosure with outside world. Its attention is even drawn to actual texts—in Cowper's letter, his own poems; in de Hooch's painting, his initials and the date included as a cornerstone

Figure 5. Pieter de Hooch, *A Maid with a Child in a Court*, 1658. (Reproduced by courtesy of the Trustees, The National Gallery, London.)

(lower left-hand corner of the doorway) and the half-obscured inscription above the door. As John Rupert Martin indicates, the placement of the figures suggests movement both toward and away from the picture plane:

> The empty foreground which confronts us in De Hooch's *Courtyard* is about to be entered by the maid and child ap-

proaching from the darkened area on the right. Opposed to this advancing movement, however, is the implication of a reverse direction through the narrow passage on the left, the magnetic pull of which is activated by the woman standing at the farther end and looking out into the bright daylight of the open street.[38]

So in Cowper's letter Lady Hesketh is invited to move from the principal vantage point into the house and back toward Orchardside. In painting and letter alike, architecture frames a quiet moment of communion; it also contributes to the illusion of spatial continuum uniting perceiver and perceived.

Cowper's letters to Lady Hesketh after their reunion never regain the capacity to involve the reader totally in his world. Many of them contain memorable sections, [39] but none of them compels our sympathetic attention as completely as those from the February-June 1786 sequence. The principal explanation for this lapse in communicative vitality is that Cowper takes his correspondence (in both senses) somewhat for granted. Lady Hesketh has been initiated; therefore, while the fundamental affection remains, the need to immerse her in and attach her to his microcosm does not.

When Cowper succumbs to his fifth and final depression, his capacity for imaging his experience dwindles along with the capacity to respond to other people's pictures. As he writes to Lady Hesketh:

> *You describe delightful scenes, but you describe them to One, who if he even saw them, could receive no delight from them; who has a faint recollection, and so faint as to be like an almost forgotten dream, that once he was susceptible of pleasure from such causes. The country that you have had in prospect, has been always famed for its beauties; but the wretch who can derive no gratification from a view of nature even under the disadvantage of her most ordinary dress, will have no eyes to admire her in any. In one day, in one moment I should rather have said, she became an universal blank to me,*

38. Martin, pp. 161–62.
39. For instance the description of the kitten, 3.51.

*and, though from a different cause, yet with an effect as
difficult to remove, as blindness itself.*

(4.463)

For all its impact as a biographical document, this letter is a
literary failure, its prose drained of imaginative power. Cowper's inability to "contemplate with rapture" prevents him
from trying to make Lady Hesketh *see* the Miltonic "universal
blank" that erases vision, the spiritual blindness that ex-
punges "nature's works" and cuts him off forever from "the
cheerful ways of men."[40] His letters go black as the power to
capture and project images vanishes. The eye turns inward,
not to the radiance of poetic inspiration but to the autistic
fantasies of despair.

40. "But cloud instead and ever-during dark
Surrounds me, from the cheerful ways of men
Cut off, and for the book of knowledge fair
Presented with a universal blank
Of nature's works to me expunged and rased,
And wisdom at one entrance quite shut out."

(*Paradise Lost* 3.45–50)

Part Two

Love in Several Masques

3

The Allusiveness of Thomas Gray

> His letters were the best I ever saw, & had more novelty and wit.
>
> —*Walpole, "Mr. Thomas Gray"*

> In proportion as a man is witty and humorous, there will always be about him and his a widening maze and wilderness of cues and catchwords, which the uninitiated will, if they are bold enough to try interpretation, construe, ever and anon, egregiously amiss—not seldom into arrant falsity.
>
> —*Lockhart,* Life of Scott

THOMAS GRAY was an inveterate miniaturist. In letters and poems alike he contrived ships in a bottle, which invite painstaking scrutiny lest we miss the wealth of detail packed into the smallest of spaces. When Gray's young friend Norton Nicholls asked him why he had never finished his ambitious "Ethical Essay" on the alliance of education and government, Gray replied in terms that—while ostensibly limited to poetic method—also illuminate his approach to letter-writing: "he explained himself as follows; That he had been used to write only Lyric poetry in which the poems being short, he had accustomed himself, & was able to polish every part; that this having become habit, he could not write otherwise; & that the labour of this method in a long poem would be intolerable . . ."[1]

Gray's foremost aesthetic aim, a rigorous distillation of

1. *Correspondence of Thomas Gray,* 3 vols., ed. Paget Toynbee and Leonard Whibley, rev. H.W. Starr (Oxford: Clarendon Press, [1935] 1971), 3.1291. All subsequent references to this edition will hereafter be noted parenthetically in the text.

thought and feeling, necessarily entails the practice of allusion. For it is only by persistent echoing that such an artist
achieves the desired richness of texture on a reduced scale.
Yet when he makes public appearances Narcissus must at
least pretend to keep Echo far away: in the familiar letter
Gray can give free play to his allusive habits, in poetry the
wholesale appropriation of other men's treasure is cause for
concealment. To friends Gray spoke jauntily of his poetic indebtedness: writing about "The Bard" to Edward Beding-
field, for example, he uses such terms as "borrow'd," "stoln,"
and "pilfer'd," then concludes: "do not wonder therefore, if
some Magazine or Review call me Plagiary: I could shew them
a hundred more instances, wch they never will discover themselves" (2.477). Yet the collected edition of 1768 tells a story
far different from this insouciant confession: there the spar-
seness and the brevity of Gray's notes reflect his determination to avoid the label of "Plagiary." As Roger Lonsdale
observes, "Gray's concern was evidently self-protective rather
than a means of alerting his reader to significant allusions. . . .
The 'imitations' Gray publicly acknowledged in 1768 were
consciously selective and intended to qualify as both accept-
able and even impressive."[2] Thus in his notes to the "Elegy"
Gray confines himself to the tersest recording of debts to Pe-
trarch and Dante; the "Ode on the Death of a Favorite Cat"
and the "Ode to Adversity" are innocent of annotation, and
the reader of the Eton College Ode is directed to two of Dryden's obscurest works. Indeed, to compare the tight-lipped
acknowledgments of *Poems 1768* with Lonsdale's massing of
sources, models, parallels, and echoes is to realize how many
tracks Gray had to cover.[3] In unmistakable contrast to Dry-

2. Roger Lonsdale, "Gray and 'Allusion': The Poet as Debtor," in *Studies in
the Eighteenth Century IV*, ed. R.F. Brissenden and J.C. Eade (Canberra: Australian National University Press, 1979), p. 45.
3. Harold Bloom, himself anxiously influenced by W. Jackson Bate's *The
Burden of the Past and the English Poet*, contends that "in Gray's poetry the
anxiety of style and the anxiety of influence had become indistinguishable . . ." See *The Anxiety of Influence* (New York: Oxford University Press,
1973), pp. 149–50. Yet one need not have recourse to Bloom's paradigm to
register Gray's uneasy attitude toward his own indebtedness.

den and Pope, he could find no better way to accommodate the burden of the past than evasion-by-reticence.[4]

In his influential essay on "The Limits of Allusion in *The Rape of the Lock*," Earl Wasserman contends that the reader of Augustan verse is often meant to trace specific borrowings back to their original context, then to introduce that context into his experience of the poem:

> If this has been an admissible commentary on *The Rape of the Lock*, it would imply that the mode of existence of Pope's poetry—and probably of many other neoclassic poems—ought to be defined broadly enough to include a creative act by the reader. For it suggests that the reader is not only to appreciate the poet's invention in finding appropriate allusions but is actively invited by them to exercise, within poetic reason, his own invention by contemplating the relevances of the entire allusive context and its received interpretation. . . . Such literature as this is constituted not only by its own verbal texture but also by the rich interplay between the author's text and the full contexts it allusively arouses, for these allusive resonances are not peripheral but functional to the meaning of the artistic product.[5]

Yet Wasserman's suggested method of reading does not work for most of Gray's poetry, in which the multiplicity of potential sources and the thorough blending of echoes muffle the precise import of a given borrowing. The difference between Pope's brand of allusiveness and Gray's can be pinpointed by glancing outside the Western literary tradition—to the Japanese poetic technique of *honkadori* or "allusive variation." As Robert Brower and Earl Miner have defined it, *honkadori* "is primarily an echoing of an older poem or poems, not just to borrow material or phrasing, but to raise the atmosphere—something of the situation, the tone, and the meaning—of

---

4. As Roger Lonsdale points out in the article cited above, the creative phase of Gray's poetic career ended with the Pindaric Odes, whose publication coincided with Richard Hurd's "Letter to Mr. Mason on the Marks of Imitation." See Lonsdale, pp. 44–45.

5. *Journal of English and Germanic Philology* 65 (1966): 443–44.

the original."[6] The almost subliminal effects created by diffuse borrowing should not be confused with the contrapuntal patterns of allusive variation: "If a poet merely uses an old phrase that does not add to the dimension of the new poem, or if the phrasing has half a dozen precedents, the poet has borrowed from the tradition; he has not created an allusive variation. Moreover, the allusion must be specific and meaningful."[7] Only on rare occasions, such as the echo of *Purgatorio* 8 in the opening line of the "Elegy," are Gray's allusions "specific and meaningful." Attempts to argue otherwise must somehow come to terms with the embarrassment of choice and the distorting resonance of the echo chamber.

The conscious deployment of allusive variation, on the other hand, proves to be the single most distinctive feature of Gray's familiar letters. It is his prose and not his poetry that "creates meanings, comprehends judgments, and animates experiences, by bringing into play other works of literature and their very words."[8] Christopher Ricks's eloquent description of allusiveness in Dryden and Pope also serves to identify Gray's basic epistolary strategy—one almost entirely missing, as we have just noted, from his poetic oeuvre. The reader of Gray's letters is called upon to play an active role by recognizing sources and comparing original setting to epistolary adaptation. The significance of a particular letter will often depend upon a complex web of oblique references—to literature primarily, but also to other "texts," such as the circumscribed world of Pembroke College, Cambridge. Gray could assume in all of his regular correspondents an intimate acquaintance with these texts and therefore the means to unravel his "web" (the poet's own word). "I am a sort of spider," he writes to West, "and have little else to do but spin it over again, or creep to some other place and spin there" (l.194).

---

6. Robert H. Brower and Earl Miner, *Japanese Court Poetry* (Stanford: Stanford University Press, 1961), p. 14.

7. Brower and Miner, p. 287.

8. Christopher Ricks, "Allusion: The Poet as Heir," in *Studies in the Eighteenth Century III*, ed. R.F. Brissenden and J.C. Eade (Canberra: Australian National University Press, 1976), p. 209.

Allusive patterning allows this reticent miniaturist to speak out eloquently, compactly, and intensely. It constructs the version of himself he chose to transmit in private, an epistolary voice which can be identified by at least five qualities: invariable pithiness of expression; decorous communication of intense emotion; ribald sense of humor; acuity of description, narration, and critical judgment; and a tendency to philosophical disengagement combined with an affirmation of intellectual and social community. This chapter will consider each of these qualities in turn, as they illustrate Gray's allusiveness of mind and pen.

I

Gray's penchant for allusion of almost every kind is tied closely to the Tacitean model upon which he based his prose. This stylistic exemplar both promotes and necessitates a sustained allusiveness. In early 1742 Richard West, who had made the mistake of judging the *Annals* "a little tedious," is roundly lectured by Gray for *lèse-majesté*. Gray proceeds to analyze Tacitus's achievement in terms that relate the historian's methodology to his distinctive style: "A man, who could join the *brilliant* of wit and concise sententiousness peculiar to that age, with the truth and gravity of better times, and the deep reflection and good sense of the best moderns, cannot choose but have something to strike you. . . . I remember a sentence in his Agricola that (concise as it is) I always admired for saying much in a little compass" (1.188–89).

"Saying much in a little compass" says much in a little compass about Gray's own practice. While West was reading and translating Tacitus, Gray was writing a tragedy, *Agrippina*, based on the *Annals* and Racine's *Britannicus*. During this same period Gray also tried his hand at translating Thucydides, a kindred stylist. In another letter to West he reflects on the inadequacies of English as a vehicle for duplicating the essence of the original:

> *I think you have translated Tacitus very justly, that is freely, & accommodated his thoughts to the Turn & Genius of our*

> *Language, which at the same time I commend your Judge-*
> *ment, is no commendation of the English tongue, which is too*
> *diffuse, & daily grows more & more enervate, & one shall*
> *never be more sensible of this, than in turning an Author like*
> *Tacitus. I have been trying it in some parts of Thucydides*
> *(who has a little resemblance of him in his Conciseness) &*
> *endeavour'd to do it closely, but found it produced mere*
> *Nonsense.*
>
> (1.196)

Yet his acute understanding of the difficulties involved did
not deter him from perfecting a workable English equivalent
to the Tacitean idiom—a style that will avoid "dry Con-
ciseness" (1.241) while catching the intensity, compression,
and variety of the Latin. One measure of Gray's success is that
we find ourselves compelled to read his letters exactly as we
do Tacitus: slowly, patiently, attentively, with tolerance for
contorted syntax and alertness to every nuance of diction.
Each paragraph, and often each sentence, must be taken
apart and reassembled before it will yield up its full meaning.
Implication is all: rarely are ironies less than subtle, judgments less than oblique. With the resources of this style at his
disposal, Gray can provide in every letter he writes what
Geoffrey Tillotson has called "a closely knitted monologue of
personal comment on persons and things . . ."[9]

The monologues begin when Gray first comes up to Cambridge, where in a state of desperate loneliness he sends cries
of help to Horace Walpole. These early love letters, for they
are nothing less than that, coyly encode their emotion: in
Roger Martin's words, "Il invente mille postures pour le di-
vertir, mille fictions pour préciser le tableau de son existence,
pour lui faire partager sa vie."[10] Walpole is nudged toward a
variety of literary sources, which require identification before
message and tone can be deciphered. Gray most often cues

9. Geoffrey Tillotson, "On Gray's Letters," in *Essays in Criticism and Research* (Cambridge: Cambridge University Press, 1942), p. 118.
10. Roger Martin, *Essai sur Thomas Gray* (London: Oxford University
Press, 1934), p. 73.

his reader by means of mimicry: "who am I now," he asks, and "why do you suppose I have adopted this particular voice?" Like Swift in *A Tale of a Tub,* he impersonates at top speed, darting in and out of a succession of identities. These playful, almost burlesque "turns" show Gray at his most elusively allusive.

The game begins in the earliest surviving letter, whose substratum consists of Gray's passionate desire for Walpole's company, his distress at the lack of genuine reciprocity, and his determination to keep their friendship continuously vital. Yet Gray shies away from either a direct statement of longing or anything that might be construed as recrimination. For all its bantering tone, the beginning of the letter does make clear the basic source of discontent; however, just as Gray begins to approach the sensitive topic of Walpole's silence, he launches into a mock tirade:

> *I believe by your not making me happy in a longer letter than that I have just received, you had a design to prevent my tireing you with a tedious one; but in revenge for your neglect I'm resolved to send you one five times as long: S^r, do you think, that I'll be fob'd off with eleven lines and a half? after waiting this week in continual expectation, & proposing to myself all the pleasure, that you, if you would, might give me: Gadsbud! I am provoked into a fermentation! when I see you next, I'll firk you, I'll rattle you with a Certiorari: let me tell you; I am at present as full of wrath & choler, as—as—you are of wit & goodnature; though I begin to doubt your title to the last of them, since you have balked me in this manner . . .*
>
> (1.1–2)

The two models for this shrill harangue are both theatrical: Mistress Quickly in 2 *Henry IV* and Sir Paul and Lady Plyant in *The Double Dealer.* In the first scene to which Gray alludes, Mistress Quickly attempts to have Falstaff arrested for his debts and for breach of promise: he has exploited her by making love and even promising marriage in order to maintain his credit. Mistress Quickly in desperation finally looses the bailiffs: "A hundred mark is a long one for a poor lone woman to bear, and I have borne, and borne, and borne, and have been fubb'd off, and fubb'd off, and fubb'd off, from this day to that day, that it is a shame to be thought on."[11] However, Falstaff has little difficulty in persuading her, by dint of empty promises and repeated blandishments, to "draw thy action."

Act II of *The Double Dealer* includes a similar explosion of pique:

> *Sir Paul.* Gads bud! I am provoked into a Fermentation, as my Lady *Froth* says; was ever the like read of in Story?
> *Lady Plyant.* Sir *Paul* have patience, let me alone to rattle him up.
> *Sir Paul.* Pray your Ladyship give me leave to be Angry—I'll rattle him up I Warrant you, I'll firk him with a *Certiorari.*
> *Lady Plyant.* You firk him, I'll firk him my self; pray Sir *Paul* hold you Contented.[12]

Sir Paul, who claims he cannot be tamed when once roused to anger, is promptly squashed by Lady Plyant; his wife claims to be chaste, but succumbs easily to Careless's seductive blandishments. The two scenes are linked by their humorous malapropisms, by their hollow threats of legal action, and by characters whose splenetic outbursts denote not anger so much as the need to be pacified. By tapping into these scenes Gray signals to Walpole that his anger, like Sir Paul and Lady Plyant's toward Mellefont, is largely counterfeit, but that, like Mistress Quickly, he expects to be soothed with loving attentiveness.

Throughout the early letters to Walpole, Gray adopts a variety of female roles: Widow Blackacre, Patient Griselda, Lady Wishfort, even Ovid's Europa. His favorite voice, however, remains Mistress Quickly's, the irate and befuddled widow. He quotes twice more from 2 *Henry IV*, both times in a context of disguised reproach:

11. All Shakespearean quotations are taken from *The Riverside Shakespeare,* ed. G. Blakemore Evans et al. (Boston: Houghton Mifflin, 1974).

12. *The Complete Plays of William Congreve,* ed. Herbert Davis (Chicago and London: University of Chicago Press, 1967), p. 143.

> *Thou has been for this month, like an auctioneer's mallet,*
> *just a-coming! just a-coming! and pray what has next Thurs-*
> *day in it, more than last Wednesday, to make me expect you*
> *with any tolerable Certainty? when these two eyes behold thee,*
> *I question, whether I shall believe them: three long months is a*
> *long while, for a poor lone woman to bear; and I have born,*
> *& born, and been fub'd off, and fub'd off from this day to that*
> *day by you, thou Honey-suckle Villain (as Mrs Quickly says)*
> *oh! thou art an infinitive thing upon my score of impatience.*
> *remember you are a day in my debt for every hour you have*
> *made me wait, & I shall come upon you for the payment, &*
> *perhaps with interest . . .*
>
> (1.25)

Here Gray conflates two speeches: "I am undone by his
going, I warrant you, he's an infinitive thing upon my score.
Good Master Fang, hold him sure. Good Master Snare, let
him not scape. . . . Ah, thou honeysuckle villain! wilt thou kill
God's officers and the King's?" (2.1). Gray is drawn to this
scene by its comically rendered themes of exploitation and
abandonment. At the same time, he deliberately inserts "of
impatience" to soften the allusion and to relate it more con-
vincingly to his state of mind. Walpole, Gray wittily suggests,
is indeed "Honey-suckle" (viz. "homicidal"), for his hopes are
dying, killed by neglect. Gray's application of the Quickly
speeches to his own plight is both an astute act of dramatic
criticism (for it recognizes that the widow is actually seeking to
be "reimbursed" with love) and a tactful registration of griev-
ance.

The shrill chatter of another theatrical widow is put to
work in much the same way when Gray writes, "To mie Nuss
att London." He asks his "Honner'd Nurse" to bring down
from London a good dose of "spirit of ridicule," for the ailing
writer has been unable to fill her prescription for this precious medicine in Cambridge:

> *now I would not put you to this trouble, if I could provide*
> *myself of the Ingredients here; but truly, when I went to the*
> *Poticaries for a drachm of Spirit of Ridicule; the saucy Jack-*

anapes of a Prentice-Boy fleered at me, I warrant ye, as who
should say, you don't know your Errand: so by my troth, away
ambles me I (like a fool as I came) home again, & when I
came to look of your Receipt; to be sure, there was Sp^t of
RIDICULE in great Letters, as plain as the nose in one's
face: & so, back hurries I in a making-Water-while, as one
may say . . .

(1.6)

Here Gray both quotes and imitates the extravagant abuse of
Wycherley's Widow Blackacre. In the scene alluded to, the
widow threatens to bring "my Action of Detinue or Trover"
to recover her missing documents. Gray, who has been enduring a widowed existence at Peterhouse, presents his letter
as an equivalent action of trover, in order to recover the
friend he once possessed.[13]

The same conceit grows even more extravagant in a letter
written two months later:

well! be it, as it will, you have got my Soul with you already; I
should think, 'twould be better, for you to bring it hither to the
rest of me, than make my body take a journey to it; besides it
would be cheaper to me, for that can come down in the coach
with you; but my limbs must pay for their passage up. I hate
living by halves, for now I lead such a kind of I don't know
how—as it were—: in short, what the devil d'ye mean by
keeping me from myself so long?

(1.21)

In this letter another deprived widow makes herself heard,
Congreve's pathetic Lady Wishfort: "but pray, don't importune, don't press, dear Sr Celadon; oh Jesus! I believe, if you
should importune, I shall—be very coming . . ." (1.21). In Act
III of *The Way of the World,* Lady Wishfort tries to feign reluc-
tance at the thought of a fervent suitor:

13. *Trover:* "the name of an action, which a man hath against one, who,
having found any of his Goods, refuseth to deliver them upon demand." See
The Plays of William Wycherley, ed. Arthur Friedman (Oxford: Clarendon
Press, 1979), p. 447, n. 1.

But art thou sure Sir *Rowland* will not fail to come? Or will a
not fail when he does come? Will he be Importunate *Foible*,
and push? For if he shou'd not be Importunate—I shall never
break Decorums—I shall die with Confusion, if I am forc'd to
advance—Oh no, I can never advance—I shall swoon if he
shou'd expect advances.

Unfortunately Gray finds himself in Lady Wishfort's condition, caught between the desire to preserve his dignity and
the need to feel wanted: ". . . And that you may not fail me, I
believe I shall see you at London beforehand; Almanzor per-
suades me, and I have a months mind to it myself; tho' I think
it a foolish undertaking enough would you advise me to
come, or not? for I stand wavering" (1.20–21). The dilemma
is humiliating but inescapable. It underlies the letter signed
"yours to command, Patient Grissel," which makes even clearer Gray's almost masochistic need for blandishments at any
price: "it seems to be at this time of year, that the humour
usually takes you to tell us stories about your coming, but
however I would rather be deceived, than hear nothing at all
of it; so say something of it pray; every body in Cambridge
knows better than I" (1.60).

Gray's gnawing insecurity, his fear that social and geographical distance will impair their friendship, directs his
choice of two classical allusions: to Horace's *Odes* 3.9 and to
Ovid's tale of Europa and the bull from *Metamorphoses* 2. In
both instances fragmentary quotation is intended to evoke the
original context and thereby to create a penumbra of anxiety,
all the while preserving a light-hearted surface elegance. The
first of these allusions opens a letter:

My Dearest Horace
  Donec gratus eram tibi
*I was happier than Dr Heighington, or his Wife Lydia; how-
ever I find being from you agrees as ill with me, as if I never
had felt your absence before . . .*

(1.27)

The ode in question takes the form of a dialogue between two estranged lovers. The man begins:

> Donec gratus eram tibi
> nec quisquam potior bracchia candidae
> cervici iuvenis dabat,
> Persarum vigui rege beatior.[14]

The dialogue ends with the promise of reconciliation:

> quamquam sidere pulchrior
> ille est, tu levior cortice et improbo
> iracundior Hadria
> tecum vivere amem, tecum obeam libens![15]

In Gray's letter the overt endearment ("Donec gratus eram tibi") is darkened by the possibility of a breach, the anxiety that this Horace will prove "levior cortice." The same shadow falls directly across Gray's letter of congratulation on Walpole's appointment to the Inspectorship of Imports and Exports:

> *My Dear*
> *I should say Mr Inspector general of the Exports & Imports,*
> *but that appellation would make but an odd figure in con-*
> *junction with the two familiar monosyllables above written,*
> *for, Non bene conveniunt, nec in unâ sede morantur Majestas*
> *& amor, which is being interpreted, Love does not live at the*
> *Custom-house: however by what style, title, or denomination*
> *soever you please to be dignified or distinguish'd hereafter,*
> *you'll never get rid of these two words . . .*
>
> (1.71–72)

Gray plucks his tag from the beginning of Ovid's version of the rape of Europa:

---

14. "While I was dear to thee and no more favoured youth flung his arms about thy dazzling neck, I lived in greater bliss than Persia's king." Unless noted otherwise, all quotations and translations from Greek and Latin are taken from the respective volumes of the Loeb Classical Library.

15. "Though he is fairer than the stars, and thou less stable than the tossing cork and stormier than the wanton Adriatic, with thee I fain would live, with thee I'd gladly die."

non bene conveniunt nec in una sede morantur
maiestas et amor; sceptri gravitate relicta
ille pater rectorque deum, cui dextra trisulcis
ignibus armata est, qui nutu concutit orbem,
induitur faciem tauri . . .[16]

Once again the original context enhances and complicates the significance of the quotation. Gray is inviting Walpole to act like Jupiter: to set aside his newly acquired *maiestas* and to affirm his love by sweeping down from London to Cambridge.

Gray's premonition that social and financial inequality will drive a wedge between them was in fact borne out by events on the Grand Tour. Though we can never know the exact circumstances of their quarrel, Walpole's confession to William Mason many years later strongly suggests that his hauteur was at fault:

> *I was too young, too fond of my own diversions, nay, I do not doubt, too much intoxicated by indulgence, vanity, and the insolence of my situation, as a prime minister's son, not to have been inattentive and insensible to the feelings of one I thought below me. . . . I treated him insolently: he loved me and I did not think he did.[17]*

On the evidence of Gray's letters from Cambridge, it is difficult to understand how Walpole ever reached so groundless a conclusion.

The passionate affection that explains and enlivens Gray's letters to Walpole recurs at the end of his life when he befriends, and then loses, the young Swiss aristocrat Charles Victor de Bonstetten. In the handful of letters to and about Bonstetten, Gray comes as close as he ever does to telling the

16. "Majesty and love do not go well together, nor tarry long in the same dwelling-place. And so the father and ruler of the gods, who wields in his right hand the three-forked lightning, whose nod shakes the world, laid aside his royal majesty along with his sceptre, and took upon him the form of a bull" (2.846–50).

17. *Horace Walpole's Correspondence*, 42 vols., ed. W.S. Lewis et al. (New Haven: Yale University Press, 1937–83), 28.68 (To Mason, 2 March 1773).

full extent of his love. While the youthful letters express passion in terms of verbal gamesmanship, these melancholy signals of distress scarcely contain their anguish. Unlike Lady Mary, however, Gray does not press into service a new language to do justice to his feelings; rather he turns again to allusive variation and the safety of indirection.

The first letter to Bonstetten begins with a lament that time has passed with interminable slowness since his departure: "Never did I feel, my dear Bonstetten, to what a tedious length the few short moments of our life may be extended by impatience and expectation, till you had left me: nor ever knew before with so strong a conviction how much this frail body sympathizes with the inquietude of the mind" (3.1117). Gray compares his plight to a figure from Oriental folklore: "I am grown old in the compass of less than three weeks, like the Sultan in the Turkish Tales, that did but plunge his head into a vessel of water and take it out again (as the standers-by affirm'd) at the command of a Dervish, and found he had pass'd many years in captivity and begot a large family of children" (3.1117–18). Addison had popularized this story in *Spectator* No. 94, an essay that advocates one of Gray's most cherished convictions:

> I have before shewn how the unemployed Parts of Life appear long and tedious, and shall here endeavour to shew how those Parts of Life which are exercised in Study, Reading, and the Pursuits of Knowledge are long but not tedious; and by that Means discover a Method of lengthening our Lives, and at the same Time of turning all the Parts of them to our Advantage.[18]

Addison goes on to discuss the relativity of time by quoting first Locke and then Malebranche; he then retells two stories from the *Turkish Tales*. The second of these is the fable to which Gray alludes. Addison concludes the essay by reinforc-

18. *The Spectator*, ed. Donald F. Bond (Oxford: Clarendon Press, 1965), 1.398.

ing his original proposition and embellishing it with an elaborate simile:

> The Hours of a wise Man are lengthened by his Ideas, as those of a Fool are by his Passions: The Time of the one is long, because he does not know what to do with it; so is that of the other, because he distinguishes every Moment of it with some useful or amusing Thought; or in other Words, because the one is always wishing it away, and the other always enjoying it.

> How different is the View of past Life, in the Man who is grown old in Knowledge and Wisdom, from that of him who is grown old in Ignorance and Folly? The latter is like the Owner of a barren Country, that fills his Eye with the Prospect of naked Hills and Plains which produce nothing either profitable or ornamental; the other beholds a beautiful and spacious Landskip divided into delightful Gardens, green Meadows, fruitful Fields, and can scarce cast his Eye on a single Spot of his Possessions, that is not covered with some beautiful Plant or Flower.[19]

In his letter Gray alludes not only to the story itself but also to the larger Addisonian context. The result is to imply that longing for Bonstetten has not only disrupted his quiet scholarly routine and upset a precarious mental equilibrium, but that it has caused him to doubt the truth of the very conviction he had previously shared with Addison—a belief in the supreme value of "Study, Reading, and the Pursuits of Knowledge." Gray had followed Addison's advice: looking about his rooms at Pembroke, filled with bulbs, herbs, and various botanical specimens, he could quite literally "scarce cast his Eye on a single Spot of his Possessions, that is not covered with some beautiful Plant or Flower." As he had written to Norton Nicholls: "my gardens are in the window, like those of a Lodger up three pair of stairs in Petticoat-lane or Camomile-street, & they go to bed regularly under the same

19. *The Spectator* 1.401–2.

roof that I do" (3.1065). These specimens represent only one aspect of the multifarious scholarly activity with which, in Addison's phrase, he had been "filling up those empty spaces of Life which are so tedious and burthensome to idle People." Yet the advent and the departure of Bonstetten have made all this activity seem purposeless, empty make-work.

The first and last paragraphs of Gray's letter disclose, as Jean Hagstrum has noted, "a man on the rack, even his frail body sympathizing with the unquiet of his mind . . ."[20] In startling contrast the central paragraph preaches self-control by importing a long quotation from the sixth book of Plato's *Republic*. The ostensible audience for this stoical sermon is Bonstetten, the more urgent candidate Gray himself. The larger juxtaposition of Platonic askesis (paragraph two) to emotional display (paragraphs one and three) is matched by the placing of the Turkish allusion within its Addisonian frame. In this way what might have been a single illustrative comparison comes to participate in the overall struggle between self-discipline and unbearable pain.

The letter to Nicholls announcing Bonstetten's departure for the Continent conveys the same depth of distress by means of a brief citation from *King John:*

> here am I again to pass my solitary evenings, wch hung much lighter on my hands, before I knew him. this is your fault! pray let the next you send me, be halt & blind, dull, unapprehensive & wrong-headed. for this (as Lady Constance says) Was never such a gracious Creature born! & yet—but no matter! burn my letter that I wrote you, for I am very much out of humour with myself & will not believe a word of it. you will think, I have caught madness from him (for he is certainly mad) & perhaps you will be right. oh! what things are Fathers & Mothers! I thought they were to be found only in England, but you see.
>
> (3.1115)

---

20. Jean Hagstrum, "Gray's Sensibility," in *Fearful Joy: Papers from the Thomas Gray Bicentenary Conference at Carleton University*, ed. James Downey and Ben Jones (Montreal, London: McGill-Queen's University Press, 1974), p. 9.

Though he only quotes one line, Gray manages to convey the full weight and substance of Constance's lament for her son:

> I am not mad, I would to heaven I were!
> For then 'tis like I should forget myself.
> O, if I could, what grief should I forget! . . . .
> For since the birth of Cain, the first male child,
> To him that did but yesterday suspire,
> There was not such a gracious creature born . . . .
> Grief fills the room up of my absent child,
> Lies in his bed, walks up and down with me,
> Puts on his pretty looks, repeats his words,
> Remembers me of all his gracious parts,
> Stuffs out his vacant garments with his form;
> Then, have I reason to be fond of grief?
>
> (3.4.48–50, 79–81, 93–98)

Shakespeare's imagery imprints itself so thoroughly on Gray's mind that when he writes to Bonstetten two weeks later, he echoes Constance yet again: "My life now is but a perpetual conversation with your shadow.—The known sound of your voice still rings in my ears.—There, on the corner of the fender you are standing, or tinkling on the Pianoforte, or stretch'd at length on the sofa" (3.1127). In the letter to Nicholls, Gray catches as if by osmosis the tone of her exclamatory speech— language pushed as far as it can go under the pressure of extreme anguish. He will not, like Constance, rave extravagantly or tear his hair; but he will adjust his habitual manner to conform to his heightened emotional state, and imply a sense of loss by conjuring up her frantic wail. Allusive variation permits Gray to suggest that he feels both a parent's love for Bonstetten, and, like Constance's attachment to Arthur, more than a parent's love: "therefore never, never / Must I behold my pretty Arthur more" (3.4.88–89).

II

Our brief look at the literary matrix of Gray's most revealing letters has tended to slight the comic genius that permeates his epistolary oeuvre. Ever since William Mason wielded his pruning shears, biographers and critics have over-stressed Gray's serious side. In his Alexander Lectures on literary biography, Leon Edel takes the orthodox position when he describes Gray as a "passive, quiet individual, bookish, learned, given to reverie and self-consolation, a good Christian, a melancholy man, who holds that all is vanity . . ."[21] Yet the picture that emerges from the total corpus of surviving letters corresponds only in part to this image of scholarly introversion. In fact Gray's inventive sense of humor sparked a wide variety of comic effects, from the slyest irony to the most ribald pun. The majority of the letters confirms Walpole's judgment: "Gray never wrote anything easily but things of humour: humour was his natural and original turn."[22] Those "things of humour" that depend upon allusion for their comic impact fall into four main categories: "offensive" satirical thrusts, "defensive" jokes unfurled against disappointment or disillusion, arch self-ridicule, and genial mockery of friends.

Given sufficient provocation, Gray was a good hater and a waspish commentator. The author of "The Candidate" and "On Lord Holland's Seat Near Margate" yields to no one in the etching of unforgettable satirical portraits. Gray's account of the death of Dr. Thomas Chapman, Master of Magdalene College, Cambridge, rivals this pair of inspired poetic squibs in its biting precision and adept insinuation of literary analogues:

> *Our friend Dr. Chapman (one of its [Cambridge's] nuisances) is not expected here again in a hurry. He is gone to his grave with five fine mackerel (large and full of roe) in his belly. He eat them all at one dinner; but his fate was a turbot on Trinity Sunday, of which he left little for the company besides bones. He had not been hearty all the week; but after this sixth fish he never held up his head more, and a violent looseness carried him off.—They say he made a very good end.*
>
> (2.693)

21. Leon Edel, *Literary Biography* (London: Rupert Hart-Davis, 1957), p. 54.

22. *Horace Walpole's Correspondence* 1.367.

This grotesque medical bulletin might seem callous were it not for the distancing effect of two literary allusions, to Pope and to Shakespeare. Together with Gray's clipped narrative style, these bring to the fore the black humor latent in the event itself. The deliberate reminiscence, "his fate was a turbot," jogs our memory of Pope's *Epistle to Cobham:*

> A salmon's belly, Helluo, was thy fate;
> The doctor call'd, declares all help too late:
> 'Mercy! cries Helluo, mercy on my soul!
> Is there no hope?—Alas!—then bring the jowl.'[23]

These two couplets form part of a rapid series of types ("Old Politicians," the lecherous "rev'rend sire," the "frugal Crone," "Narcissa," "The Courtier smooth," "Old Euclio"), all of which illustrate Pope's thesis that the ruling passions govern human behavior up to the very end. We die as we have lived: "Consistent in our follies and our sins, / Here honest Nature ends as she begins" (ll. 226–27). Gray's echo of Pope turns Dr. Chapman into a type of the glutton (*helluo* in Latin), whose bizarre death we are licensed to relish with amused detachment. Why should one feel compassion, the text implies, for something less than a human being? Lady Mary, who also learned her technique from Pope, manages a similar satiric reduction: "He [Lord Carlton] was taken ill in my Company at a Consort at the D[uchess] of Marlbrô's, and dy'd 2 days after, holding the fair Dutchesse by the hand, and being fed at the same time with a fine fat chicken, thus dying, as he liv'd, indulging his Pleasures" (2.48).

Helluo is one analogue, Polonius the other. The mad Ophelia has no violets to distribute, for "they wither'd all when my father died. They say 'a made a good end" (*Hamlet* 4.5). The reminiscence sets the parallels vibrating: Dr. Chapman has met as freakish a death as Polonius; he was also

23. Alexander Pope, *Poetical Works,* ed. Herbert Davis (London: Oxford University Press, 1966), p. 290 (ll. 238–41). All subsequent quotations are taken from this edition.

judged, in Gray's circle at least, "a foolish prating knave." We have no more cause to be grieved by the death of Dr. Chapman, Gray's report insinuates, than to mourn the demise of the loquacious Lord Chamberlain.

The power of humor to caricature the behavior of others also serves to arm Gray against disappointment and self-doubt. When he learns of his failure to win the Regius Professorship of Modern History, for example, he can distance himself with a joke: "I received my answer very soon, wch was what you may easily imagine, but join'd with great profession of *his desire to serve me* on any future occasion, & many more fine words, that I pass over, not out of modesty, but for another reason. so you see I have made my fortune, like S^r Fr: Wronghead" (2.787–88). Gray wittily berates himself for ever having believed the assurances of the powerful; at the same time he implies that Bute is no better than the lord who gulls Sir Francis Wronghead, the naive country squire in Vanbrugh and Cibber's *The Provoked Husband:*

> *Sir Francis.* "Sir Francis," says he, "I shall be glad to serve you any way that lies in my power." So he gave me a squeeze by the hond, as much as to say, "Give yourself no trouble, I'll do your business." With that he turned him abawt to somebody with a colored ribbon across here, that looked, in my thowghts, as if he came for a place too.
> *Manly:* Ha! So, upon these hopes you are to make your fortune!
> *Sir Francis:* Why, do you think there's ony doubt of it, sir?[24]

Gray's comic poise, which depends on a detached view of personal misfortunes and idiosyncracies, expresses itself most fully in his whimsical prose equivalents to the "Ode on the Death of a Favourite Cat." Gray originally introduced this poem to Walpole with parodic allusions to Acts 19:15 and *Aeneid* 4.433:

> *As one ought to be particularly careful to avoid blunders in a compliment of condolence, it would be a sensible satisfaction to*

24. Sir John Vanbrugh and Colley Cibber, *The Provoked Husband*, ed. Peter Dixon (Lincoln: University of Nebraska Press, 1973), p. 105.

me (before I testify my sorrow, and the sincere part I take in
your misfortune) to know for certain, who it is I lament. Zara
I know & Selima I know. . . . Till this affair is a little better
determined, you will excuse me if I do not begin to cry: "Tem-
pus inane peto, requiem, spatiumque doloris."

(1.271)

As this early letter demonstrates, both the Bible and Virgil
contain abundant materials for comic self-inflation. On the
verge of a summer trip to Old Park, for example, Gray imagines himself an English Aeneas, surveying the construction of
a latter-day Carthage: "I have no other apprehension, if I
should come into the North, than that of somehow incom-
moding you & your family; & yet I believe my strong inclination to see you & your Carthage will prevail over so reason-
able an apprehension" (2.779). The reference is to Virgil's
description of the Phoenician building program:

> miratur molem Aeneas, magalia quondam,
> miratur portas strepitumque et strata viarum.
> instant ardentes Tyrii, pars ducere muros
> molirique arcem et manibus subvolvere saxa,
> pars optare locum tecto et concludere sulco. . . .
> qualis apes aestate nova per florea rura
> exercet sub sole labor, cum gentis adultos
> educunt fetus, aut cum liquentia mella
> stipant et dulci distendunt nectare cellas,
> aut onera accipiunt venientum, aut agmine facto
> ignavum fucos pecus a praesepibus arcent;
> fervet opus redolentque thymo fragrantia mella.[25]

Gray recurs to the same epic simile in a letter to James Brown,
written from Old Park that same summer: "The house rings

25. "Aeneas marvels at the massive buildings, mere huts once; marvels at
the gates, the din and paved high-roads. Eagerly the Tyrians press on, some
to build walls, to rear the citadel, and roll up stones by hand; some to choose
the site for a dwelling and enclose it with a furrow. . . . Even as bees in early
summer, amid flowery fields, ply their task in sunshine, when they lead forth
the full-grown young of their race, or pack the fluid honey and strain their
cells to bursting with sweet nectar, or receive the burdens of incomers, or in
martial array drive from their folds the drones, a lazy herd; all aglow is the
work and the fragrant honey is sweet with thyme" (1.421–25, 430–36).

all day with carpenters and upholsterers, and without doors we swarm with labourers and builders" (2.781).

Gray's second source for mock-epic drollery, the Bible, furnishes several ludicrously inappropriate exemplars. In one of his letters to Thomas Wharton he alludes to the beginning of Exodus, thereby suggesting that the original convenant of friendship with the Wharton children needs to be renewed and extended. Otherwise he risks misunderstanding and even expulsion: "I have no idea of the family at present, & expect to see a multitude of little new faces, that know not Joseph" (2.872). Not only is Gray like Joseph, he also has a claim to be compared with Jonah: "I this day passed thro' the jaws of a great Leviathan, that lay in my way, into the belly of Dr Templeman, Super-Intendent of ye reading-room, who congratulated himself on the sight of so much good company" (2.629). As is true in the case of the Virgilian allusion, the humor derives from a set of farfetched parallels. In Gray's comic vision the storm-tossed Mediterranean has been replaced by the backwaters of Bloomsbury, the dreadful whale by the Keeper of the British Museum Reading Room, and terrified Jonah by a studious poet-antiquarian. This is total immersion of a delightfully different sort.

Gray's allusive games-playing extends to his circle of intimate friends, who are not spared the occasional deftly aimed barb. William Mason is a prime target. He is summoned to Wharton's estate in the language of the Song of Songs: "have done with your tricks, & come to Old-Park, for the peaches & grapes send forth a good smell, & the voice of the Robin is heard in our land" (3.977). Although Gray had half-seriously echoed the Song of Songs in one of his earliest letters to Walpole (1.14–16), the biblical diction here is used solely for the sake of comic incongruity. Gray was given to mockery of Mason's physical appearance: the nickname "Scroddles" suggests what other letters make amply clear. When a rumor of impending marriage reached Cambridge, for example, Gray asked the putative bridegroom: "I rejoice. but has she common sense, is she a Gentlewoman? has she money? has she a nose? I know, she sings a little, & twiddles on the harpsichord, hammers at sentiment, & puts herself in an attitude, admires a cast in the eye, & can say Elfrida by heart: but these are only the virtues of a Maid" (2.821–22). Mason was indeed short, plump, and ill-featured, with a large nose and a slight squint. Gray's casting of him as the Bride—"my love, my fair one," sweet of voice and comely of countenance—is therefore doubly inappropriate.

Even Mason's physical infirmities are fair game: "as to mine Host of the Minster his eyes are very bad (in imitation of Horace) & he is besides tied down here to residence" (2.878). Gray alludes to *Satire* 1.5, Horace's account of a journey to Brundisium. On the first leg of the trip Horace traveled with the rhetorician Heliodorus. At Anxur, where they were due to meet Maecenas, Horace put salve on his sore eyes: "hic oculis ego nigra meis collyria lippus / illinere."[26] The allusion not only makes light of Mason's complaint; it also pays a sly compliment to Gray's superior learning, for Heliodorus is described as "Graecorum longe doctissimus."[27]

On his way to Durham, Gray twits Wharton about the "barbarous" people and climate of "the remote parts of the North": "for if we are overturn'd, & *tous fracassés,* or if the Mob at Leeds cut us off, as friends to Turnpikes; or if the Waters be out, & drown us; or (as Herodotus says) if we can go no farther *for feathers,* in all these cases, & many more, we may chance to fail you" (2.876, 1.378–79). Gray is reminding Wharton of a passage from Book IV of Herodotus's *Histories,* which mentions the country to the north of the Scythians, where "none (they say) can see or travel further, by reason of showers of feathers; for earth and sky are overspread by these, and it is this which hinders sight" (4.7). Herodotus explains "feathers" as snow: "Northward of that country snow falls continually, though less in summer than in winter, as is to be expected" (4.31). Part of Gray's joke resides in the fact that his visit to Old Park is taking

26. "Here I put black ointment on my sore eyes" (ll. 30–31).
27. "far most learned of all Greeks" (l. 3).

place in mid-July, part in the tacit comparison between County Durham and a land so far beyond the civilized pale that no reliable information about it exists. Gray may also have in mind, and expect Wharton to recognize, the theory of Swift's "Modern Wit" in *A Tale of a Tub*—that among "our *Scythian* Ancestors . . . the Number of *Pens* was so infinite, that the *Grecian* Eloquence had no other way of expressing it, than by saying, *That in the Regions, far to the* North, *it was hardly possible for a Man to travel, the very Air was so replete with* Feathers."[28] One of the added dangers of the North Country, Gray seems to be saying in jocular fashion, is a glut of "Moderns" to retard the progress of an unreconstructed "Ancient."

III

Like the figured bass in musical notation, allusive variation shrinks a complex harmonic design into a handful of signs. It cues the reader to constitute for himself a variety of melodic lines; it also hints at the most appropriate dynamic markings. As we have observed, Gray often relies upon allusion to suggest his passionate feelings or direct his humorous impulses. The same device also sharpens critical judgments, enlivens storytelling, and expands descriptive passages.

Gray employs a two-tiered allusion to emphasize and to complicate his judgment of Mark Akenside's *Pleasures of the Imagination.* Soon after the poem appeared he wrote to Wharton: "it is often obscure, & even unintelligible, & too much infected with the Hutchinson-Jargon. in short it's great fault is that it was publish'd at least 9 years too early" (1.224). Gray would advise Akenside, Wharton's "young Friend," to follow Horace's counsel to Young Piso:

> si quid tamen olim
> scripseris, in Maeci descendat iudicis auris
> et patris et nostras, nonumque prematur in annum,

28. Jonathan Swift, *A Tale of a Tub,* ed. Herbert Davis (Oxford: Basil Blackwell, 1939), p. 94.

membranis intus positis: delere licebit
quod non edideris; nescit vox missa reverti.[29]

Gray's brisk sentence judges Akenside's work according to
one of the essential canons of classical poetics, and finds it
wanting: the poem will improve only if Akenside is prepared
to let time winnow the good from the merely modish, in this
instance Francis Hutcheson's fashionable terminology. Gray
can comment as incisively as he does—"in short"—because of
Wharton's knowledge of the Horatian tradition and their
shared belief that the precepts of the *Ars Poetica* still hold true
for contemporary poetry.

The second tier of the Horatian allusion works at cross
purposes to the first. Gray's reference to the *Ars Poetica*,
viewed in the context of the entire paragraph, actually places
ironic limitations on the value of his critical activity. The specific reminder of Horace develops on further consideration
into an echo of the most famous of Pope's imitations of
Horace, the *Epistle to Dr. Arbuthnot*, which Gray had read and
admired:[30]

> Seiz'd and ty'd down to judge, how wretched I!
> Who can't be silent, and who will not lye:
> To laugh, were want of goodness and of grace,
> And to be grave, exceeds all Pow'r of face.
> I sit with sad civility, I read
> With honest anguish, and an aching head;
> And drop at last, but in unwilling ears,
> This saving counsel, 'Keep your piece nine years.'
>
> (ll. 33–40)

Like Pope in *Arbuthnot*, Gray deplores the ignorance, insi-

---

29. "Yet if ever you do write anything, let it enter the ears of some critical
Maecius, and your father's, and my own; then put your parchment in the
closet and keep it back till the ninth year. What you have not published you
can destroy; the word once sent forth can never come back" (ll. 386–90).

30. See Gray's letter to Walpole, 14 January 1735 (1.18).

pidity, and even venality of what passed for informed critical judgment:

> *You desire to know, it seems, what Character the Poem of your young Friend bears here. I wonder to hear you ask the Opinion of a Nation, where those who pretend to judge, don't judge at all; & the rest (the wiser Part) wait to catch the Judgement of the World immediately above them, that is, Dick's Coffee-House, & the Rainbow: so that the readier Way would be to ask Mrs This & M^{rs} T'other, that keeps the Bar there.*

$$(1.223–24)$$

At one level he associates himself with Pope, as critic if not as poet. Both are members of an embattled minority, the uncorrupted few who see clearly, judge cogently, and write independently. On the other hand, Gray is far from being plagued with requests for his opinion and assistance; no one flies to Cambridge as they besieged Twickenham. And in making a snap judgment on the basis of a cursory examination he is perhaps guilty of the same fault as the Dick Minims at the Inns of Court: "and so methinks in a few Words, a la Mode du Temple, I have very pertly dispatch'd what perhaps may for several Years have employed a very ingenious Man worth 50 of myself" (1.224).

The same ambivalent attitude is conveyed by a second, more explicit allusion to *Arbuthnot*. When Gray solicits Walpole's opinion of *Elfrida*, his cover letter mixes flattery with ironic self-deprecation and disguised reproach: "You will take me for a mere poet, and a fetcher and carrier of singsong, if I tell you that I intend to send you the beginning of a drama, not mine, thank God, as you'll believe, when you hear it is finished, but wrote by a person whom I have a very good opinion of" (1.343). Gray's apparently casual adaptation of Pope draws into his letter an entire passage from the original:

> I sought no homage from the Race that write;
> I kept, like Asian Monarchs, from their sight:
> Poems I heeded (now be-rym'd so long)

No more than thou, great GEORGE! a birth-day song.
I ne'er with wits or witlings pass'd my days,
To spread about the itch of verse and praise;
Nor like a puppy daggled thro' the town,
To fetch and carry sing-song up and down . . .

(ll. 219–26)

The attitude exemplified here is prophetic of Gray's refusal
to accept the laureateship six years later: he will not under
any circumstances write birthday songs or "spread about the
itch of verse and praise." As before, the brief reference to
Arbuthnot brackets Gray with Pope; it also comments with
tongue-in-cheek on the difference between them.

At the same time Gray glances sardonically at Walpole himself, a true "fetcher and carrier of singsong." Indeed he had
just written to his overzealous friend to insist that, since Walpole was responsible for spreading about copies of the "Elegy," he must arrange for prompt and authoritative publication: "As you have brought me into a little Sort of Distress,
you must assist me, I believe, to get out of it, as well as I can"
(1.341). Gray had discussed the subject more frankly with
Wharton: "the Stanza's, wch I now enclose to you, have had
the Misfortune by M^r W$^{:s}$ Fault to be made still more publick,
for wch they certainly were never meant, but it is too late to
complain" (1.335). In his letters to Walpole the closest Gray
comes to direct complaint is the two-pronged allusion to *Arbuthnot*. Not only does the phrase quoted describe Walpole's
activities, but the original context supports another, sharper
criticism. The verse paragraph from which Gray extracts his
epithet introduces the character of Bufo:

Fed with soft Dedication all day long,
Horace and he went hand and hand in song.
His Library (where busts of Poets dead
And a true Pindar stood without a head)
Receiv'd of wits an undistinguish'd race,
Who first his judgment ask'd, and then a place:
Much they extoll'd his pictures, much his seat . . .

(ll. 233–39)

From an uncharitable standpoint, Walpole the literary patron, antiquarian, placeman, and creator of Strawberry Hill and its Press might well be considered a latter-day counterpart to Bufo. Even the names confirm this pairing: "Horace and he went hand and hand in song."

Gray's description of the "improvements" at Oatlands Park refines the technique of allusive pointing down to the subtlest of reminiscences. In a letter to Wharton, who shared his taste for picturesque landscape, Gray contrasts the natural beauties of Hampton with the artificial geometry of Lord Lincoln's estate. At Hampton, "every little gleam of sunshine, every accident of light, opens some new beauty in the view, & I never saw in so small a spot so much variety, & so many natural advantages, nor ever hardly wish'd more for your company to partake of them" (2.578). At Oatlands, on the other hand, Lord Lincoln:

> is hurting his view by two plantations in front of his terrace, that regularly answer one another, & are of an oval form with rustic buildings in the middle of them, a farm, dairies, &c:. they stand on the opposite side of the water, & (as they prosper) will join their shade to that of the hills in the horizon, exclude all the intermediate scene of enclosures, meadows, & cattle feeding, & reduce that great distance to nothing. this seems to be the advice of some new Gardiner, or Director of my Lord's Taste; his Successor perhaps may cut all down again.
>
> (2.578)

Both in substance and diction this critique aligns itself with Pope's description of Timon's Villa in the *Epistle to Burlington:*

> No pleasing Intricacies intervene,
> No artful wildness to perplex the scene;
> Grove nods at grove, each Alley has a brother,
> And half the platform just reflects the other.
>
> (ll. 115–18)

Gray had visited both Oatlands and Hampton, as he tells Wharton, with the Dowager Viscountess Cobham, whose gardens at Stowe serve as Pope's exemplar of true taste in landscape architecture. It is therefore appropriate, and intentional, that the moral of Gray's story corresponds to Pope's: Lord Lincoln did not "Consult the Genius of the Place in all" (l. 57); he has ignored or slighted "spontaneous beauties" (l. 67); and, like Pope's "Prodigal," he has spent his money lavishly "to purchase what he ne'er can taste," and what will soon be undone by another (l. 4). Gray invites Wharton to recognize that his faultfinding, far from being idiosyncratic, is ratified and supplemented by a close alliance with the principal poetic theoretician of the picturesque.

There is nothing in the least subtle about Gray's expression of contempt for Frederick the Great's poetry. His scorn for half-baked deism tricked out in contemptible verse sends him directly to Juvenal for the most appropriate reinforcement: "The Town are reading the K: of Prussia's Poetry (Le Philosophe sans Souci) & I have done, like the Town. they do not seem so sick of it, as I am. it is all the scum of Voltaire and Ld Bolingbroke, the *Crambe recocta* of our worst Free-thinkers, toss'd up in German-French rhyme" (2.670). Gray has adapted a metaphor from *Satire 7*, Juvenal's attack on the Bufos of Imperial Rome:

> Declamare doces? o ferrea pectora Vetti,
> cum perimit saevos classis numerosa tyrannos.
> nam quaecumque sedens modo legerat, haec eadem stans
> perferet atque eadem cantabit versibus isdem;
> occidit miseros crambe repetita magistros.[31]

Gray changes "repetita" to "recocta": Frederick's cabbage, instead of being served up *ad nauseam*, consists of the warmed-over dregs of "our worst Free-thinkers."

31. In Rolfe Humphries's lively translation:
Or do you teach declamation? What iron nerve must be needed
While your class, by the score, knocks off tyrannical monarchs
Each schoolboy, in turn, gets up and, standing, delivers
What he's just read sitting down, in the most monotonous singsong.
This is the kind of rehash that kills unfortunate masters.
(ll. 150–54).
See *The Satires of Juvenal*, trans. Rolfe Humphries (Bloomington: Indiana University Press, 1958), p. 97.

Juvenal's *Satire* praises the Emperor Hadrian, himself a skilled poet and critic, for patronizing distinguished men of letters: "hoc agite, o iuvenes. circumspicit et stimulat vos / materiamque sibi ducis indulgentia quaerit."[32] Frederick by contrast not only encourages the worst elements in contemporary literature (Gray could not abide Voltaire), but further lowers standards with his own execrable poetry.[33] The rewritten and redirected phrase from *Satire* 7 associates Gray's disapproval with Juvenal's weighty condemnation. It also urges Wharton to savor the ironic reversal that has occurred: the emperor, in Juvenal's day a genuine poet and enlightened patron, has now sunk into the ranks of the scribblers.

When Gray writes up his Lake Country journal for Wharton or deliberately composes a georgic setpiece, his prose registers the activity of an all-seeing eye:

> the grass was cover'd with a hoar-frost, wch soon melted, & exhaled in a thin blewish smoke . . . to the left the jaws of Borodale, *with that turbulent Chaos of mountain behind mountain roll'd in confusion; beneath you, & stretching far away to the right, the shining purity of the* Lake, *just ruffled by the breeze enough to shew it is alive, reflecting rocks, woods, fields, & inverted tops of mountains, with the white buildings of* Keswick, Crosthwait*church, &* Skiddaw *for a background at distance.*
>
> (3.1079–80)

In most of his letters, however, Gray limits himself to a few concise details of weather and landscape. Only as a joke will he indulge in pictorial flourishes: "in the east the sea breaks in upon you, & mixes its white transient sails & glittering blew expanse with the deeper & brighter greens of the woods & corn. this last sentence is so fine I am quite ashamed. but no

---

32. "Your prince, your patron, is watching, urging you to produce material worth his indulgence" (ll. 20–21).

33. Gray's first twentieth-century editor, Duncan Tovey, heartily endorses his opinion. Tovey adds in his note on this passage: "But Frederick's trash is often worse than 'warmed-up cabbage.'" See *The Letters of Thomas Gray*, ed. D.C. Tovey (London: G. Bell and Sons, 1909–12), 2.137, n. 1.

matter! you must translate it into prose" (3.927). His usual
practice is much closer to this terse report: "It rains, 'tis Sunday, this is the country" (1.49). Gray's instinct for compression
in all aspects of the letter—narrative, judicial, and descriptive—teaches him to rely on allusion for the array of tones and
details he chooses not to supply directly.

Two examples from a wealth of possibilities will demonstrate how Gray manages to hint a complete tableau. When a
trio of Florentine aristocrats visits Cambridge, their entou-
rage reminds him of Scarron: "Nicolini with a whole Coach-
full of the Chattichees has been at Cambridge in an Equipage
like that of Destiny & his Comrades in the Roman Comique.
they said they had been in the Meridional Parts of Great-Brit-
ain, & were now visiting the Oriental" (1.287). *Le Roman Comique* opens with the description of a troupe of traveling actors, whose leader has taken the stage name of "Le Destin":

> . . . il était entre cinq et six quand une charrette entra dans les
> halles du Mans. Cette charrette était attelée de quatre boeufs
> fort maigres, conduits par une jument poulinière dont le poul-
> ain allait et venait à l'entour de la charrette comme un petit fou
> qu'il était. La charrette était pleine de coffres, de malles et de
> gros paquets de toiles peintes qui faisaient comme une
> pyramide . . .[34]

By importing this Longhi-like genre scene into his letter,
Gray manages to imply that the Italians, despite their ped-
igree, appeared both raffish and risible. The passage from
Scarron not only supplies a visual flourish, it establishes a
point of view and an atmosphere.

The same holds true for Gray's description of Netley Abbey, which intensifies the atmospheric gloom of Gothic ruins
with the nocturnal imagery of Shakespeare's *King John:*

> *the sun was* all too glaring & too full of gauds *for such a
> scene, wch ought to be visited only in the dusk of the evening.
> . . . the Abbey was never very large. the shell of its church is*

34. Paul Scarron, *Le Roman Comique*, ed. Emile Magne (Paris: Garnier
Frères, 1973), p. 3.

almost entire, but the pillars of the iles are gone, & the roof has tumbled in, yet some little of it is left in the transept, where the ivy has forced its way thro', & hangs flaunting down among the fretted ornaments & escutcheons of the Benefactors.

(2.843)

Gray quotes from John's speech of dark suggestion to Hubert de Burgh as they plot the murder of Arthur:

> The sun is in the heaven, and the proud day
> Attended with the pleasures of the world,
> Is all too wanton and too full of gawds
> To give me audience. If the midnight bell
> Did with his iron tongue and brazen mouth
> Sound on into the drowsy race of night;
> If this same were a churchyard where we stand,
> And thou possessed with a thousand wrongs;
> Or if that surly spirit, melancholy,
> Had bak'd thy blood and made it heavy, thick. . . .
> Then, in despite of brooded watchful day,
> I would into thy bosom pour my thoughts.

(3.3.34–43, 52–53)

Although Gray was unable to visit the ruined abbey at the witching hour, he can insinuate the atmosphere of dark deeds that fits the place. The Shakespearean allusion is all the more appropriate given the fact that Netley Abbey was founded by John's son Henry, whose succession to the throne was eased by Arthur's death.

IV

Elusion, allusion, illusion: three connected strands, three abiding concerns. Even in the most private of messages to the most intimate of friends, Gray takes refuge in obliquity. On every occasion the urge to correspond is matched by the need to keep private. We have watched him achieve both objectives by allusive gesturing toward a larger context. It is time to take note of the symbolic dimension of this technique. Gray the Christian Platonist recognizes the world of shadows for what it is: living in the actual he preserves his loyalty to the real. At times he will dramatize his awareness of the double-layered cosmos by sudden allusive withdrawal to the philosophical plane. Such appeals from shifting actuality to eternal truth must be considered Gray's elusive version of a credo.

Gray vindicates the study and practice of philosophy in a short homily "à la Grecque," most of which is derived from the fifth book of Cicero's *Tusculan Disputations:*

> *I am very sorry to hear you treat philosophy and her followers like a parcel of monks and hermits, and think myself obliged to vindicate a profession I honour, bien que je n'en tienne pas boutique (as mad. Sévigné says). The first man that ever bore the name, if you remember, used to say, that life was like the Olympic games (the greatest public assembly of his age and country), where some came to show their strength and agility of body, as the champions; others, as the musicians, orators, poets, and historians, to show their excellence in those arts; the traders, to get money; and the better sort, to enjoy the spectacle, and judge of all these. They did not then run away from society for fear of its temptations: they passed their days in the midst of it: conversation was their business: they cultivated the arts of persuasion, on purpose to show men it was their interest, as well as their duty, not to be foolish, and false, and unjust; and that too in many instances with success: which is not very strange; for they showed by their life that their lessons were not impracticable; and that pleasures were no temptations, but to such as wanted a clear perception of the pains annexed to them. But I have done preaching à la Grecque.*
>
> (1.262–63)

In his "Reminiscences of Gray," Norton Nicholls stresses the poet's conviction that virtue must be man's primary goal:

> Ability, talents, genius, the highest acquisitions of science, & knowledge were in his opinion of little account compared with *virtue* which he often used to quote to me from Plato is nothing but "the exercise of right reason."—I remember in the early

part of my acquaintance with him saying that some person was
"a clever man"—he cut me short & said "Tell me if he is good
for any thing?"

(3.1288)

To Nicholls, Gray quoted Plato, to Walpole, Pythagoras, who
defined and exalted the philosopher's virtuous way of life:

> Pythagoram autem respondisse similem sibi videri vitam homi-
> num et mercatum eum, qui haberetur maximo ludorum appa-
> ratu totius Graeciae celebritate: nam ut illic alii corporibus
> exercitatis gloriam et nobilitatem coronae peterent, alii emendi
> aut vendendi quaestu et lucro ducerentur, esset autem quod-
> dam genus eorum idque vel maxime ingenuum, qui nec plau-
> sum nec lucrum quaererent, sed visendi causa venirent studi-
> oseque perspicerent quid ageretur et quo modo, item nos
> quasi in mercatus quandam celebritatem ex urbe aliqua sic in
> hanc vitam ex alia vita et natura profectos alios gloriae servire,
> alios pecuniae; raros esse quosdam, qui ceteris omnibus pro
> nihilo habitis rerum naturam studiose intuerentur; hos se ap-
> pellare sapientiae studiosos, id est enim philosophos, et ut illic
> liberalissimum esset spectare nihil sibi acquirentem, sic in vita
> longe omnibus studiis contemplationem rerum cognitionem-
> que praestare.[35]

In this letter Gray comes close to offering an apology for his

35. "Pythagoras, the story continues, replied that the life of man seemed
to him to resemble the festival which was celebrated with most magnificent
games before a concourse collected from the whole of Greece; for at this
festival some men whose bodies had been trained sought to win the glorious
distinction of a crown, others were attracted by the prospect of making gain
by buying or selling, whilst there was on the other hand a certain class, and
that quite the best type of free-born men, who looked neither for applause
nor gain, but came for the sake of the spectacle and closely watched what was
done and how it was done. So also we, as though we had come from some city
to a kind of crowded festival, leaving in like fashion another life and nature
of being, entered upon this life, and some were slaves of ambition, some of
money; there were a special few who, counting all else as nothing, closely
scanned the nature of things; these men gave themselves the name of lovers
of wisdom (for that is the meaning of the word philosopher); and just as at
the games the men of truest breeding looked on without any self-seeking, so
in life the contemplation and discovery of nature far surpassed all other pursuits" (5.3).

exclusive dedication to scholarship: "sic in vita longe omnibus studiis contemplationem rerum cognitionemque praestare." He will not set up shop as a professional philosopher, but he will pattern his life after the ideals that Pythagoras and Cicero have celebrated. To these he adds the goal of active involvement—something he was never able in practice to achieve. Yet in his stoical retirement he can match Madame de Sévigné's claim: "Il se trouvera à la fin que moi, qui ne lève point boutique de philosophie, je l'exercerai plus qu'eux tous. Ma Providence me sert admirablement dans ces occasions."[36] The last sentence of a gossip-laden chronicle to Brown points abruptly toward an immutable scheme of values that shrinks the daily routines of scholarship into relative insignificance: "do not pout, but pray let me hear from you, & above all do, come & see me, for I assure you, I am not uncomfortably situated for a Lodger, & what are we, but Lodgers?" (2.633). With a simple rhetorical question Gray jolts his reader out of the sphere of the particular and the habitual, where antiquarians squabble, maneuver, and live beyond their means. We are asked instead to share the vantage point on human life offered by Cicero in his *De Senectute:*

Quid habet enim vita commodi? Quid non potius laboris?
Sed habeat sane: habet certe tamen aut satietatem aut modum.
Non libet enim mihi deplorare vitam, quod multi et ei docti
saepe fecerunt, neque me vixisse paenitet, quoniam ita vixi, ut
non frustra me natum existimem, *et ex vita ita discedo tamquam
ex hospitio, non tamquam e domo;* commorandi enim natura divorsorium nobis, non habitandi dedit.[37]

(my italics)

36. Madame de Sévigné, *Correspondance,* ed. Roger Duchêne (Paris: Gallimard, 1972–78), 3.704.
37. "For what advantage has life—or, rather, what trouble does it not have? But even grant that it has great advantage, yet undoubtedly it has either satiety or an end. I do not mean to complain of life as many men, and they learned ones, have often done; nor do I regret that I have lived, since I have so lived that I think I was not born in vain, and I quit life as if it were an inn, not a home. For Nature has given us an hostelry in which to sojourn, not to abide" (23.84).

Without disrupting the light-hearted tone of the letter, which describes a ludicrous dispute among the Keepers of the British Museum, Gray distances himself from the antics he reports. The Ciceronian echo introduces a sophisticated duality of perspective: serious long shot overlays comic close-up. The total effect is reminiscent of Pope's superimposition of worlds in *The Rape of the Lock:* living in boudoir and salon, we are nudged by reminders of what lies outside.

> Snuff, or the fan, supply each pause of chat,
> With singing, laughing, ogling, and all that.
> Mean while, declining from the noon of day,
> The sun obliquely shoots his burning ray;
> The hungry Judges soon the sentence sign,
> And wretches hang that jury-men may dine;
> The merchant from th'Exchange returns in peace,
> And the long labours of the Toilet cease.
>
> (3.17–24)

The result in both Gray and Pope is a provocative tension between sympathy and judgment, involvement and detachment.

A similar reminder of the essential verities colors Gray's reaction to the news that Pitt had accepted a pension and a title for his wife: "oh that foolishest of Great Men, that sold his inestimable diamond for a paltry peerage & pension: the very night it happen'd was I swearing, that it was a damn'd lie, & never could be: but it was for want of reading Thomas a Kempis, who knew Mankind so much better, than I" (2.771). As he vents his sense of betrayal, Gray reproves himself for ever having believed in Pitt's integrity and steadfastness of purpose, for ever having thought that the Great Commoner, alone among England's leaders, was untainted by the weaknesses of lesser men. However, events have proved him wrong, and reminded him forcibly of a chapter from the *De Imitatione Christi:* "Quod omnibus non est credendum, et de facili lapsu verborum."[38] The first two sentences of this chap-

---

38. "That all men are not to be trusted, and that the pronouncements of men are misleading" (my translation). See *Le Manuscrit Autographe de Thomas a Kempis et "L'Imitation de Jésus-Christ"*, ed. L.M.J. Delaissé (Paris-Bruxelles: Aux Éditions "Érasme" S.A., 1956), chap. 45 (p. 367).

ter aptly describe Gray's reaction: "Da michi auxilium domine de tribulatione: quia vana salus hominis. Quam sepe ibi non inveni fidem ubi me habere putavi."[39] Still recovering from the exposure of Pitt's feet of clay, Gray remembers the question Thomas à Kempis asks and the answer he provides: "Sed quare mihi misero non melius providi? Cur etiam tam facile aliis credidi? Sed homines sumus, nec aliud quam fragiles homines sumus, etiamsi angeli a multis estimamur et dicimur Cui credam domine? Cui, nisi tibi? Veritas es, que non fallis, nec falli potes."[40]

The allusion to Thomas à Kempis is entirely consistent with Gray's habit throughout his letters: a passing reference, deceptive in its simplicity, directs the reader to examine a thought, phrase, or image *in situ*, and to juxtapose original context to new surroundings. At the same time it carries a special weight of meaning. As R.W. Ketton-Cremer has noticed: "towards the close of his life there are many indications in his letters of a strengthening of faith, a more complete acceptance of the teachings of his Church."[41] Yet Gray's piety, like his wit, affection, and learning, shuns the ordinary channels of communication. Faith and acceptance are there—to be deduced.

Gray's allegiance to the community of believers is expressed in and through his commitment to the academic societies of Peterhouse and Pembroke College, Cambridge. Most of his correspondents were members or former members of these two institutions. Gray assumes that even those who have left the fold will wish to be kept up-to-date. As he tells Wharton: "I am half ashamed to write University News

39. "Give me aid, Lord, in my tribulation; for human assistance is useless. How often have I not found faithfulness where I thought to find it" (my translation).

40. "But why did not I, wretched one, provide better for myself? Why moreover did I trust men so readily? But we are men, nor anything other than men, even if we are thought by many to be angels, and called such. In whom shall I trust, Lord? In whom, if not you? You are the truth, who neither deceives nor can be deceived" (my translation).

41. R.W. Ketton-Cremer, *Thomas Gray: A Biography* (Cambridge: Cambridge University Press, 1955), p. 193.

to you, but as perhaps you retain some little Leven of Pembroke Hall, your nursing Mother, I am in hopes you will not be more than half-ashamed to read it" (1.318). Here an allusion to a shared text (Isaiah 49:23) introduces a spate of allusions to another, the collegiate society. In fact many of Gray's letters remind one of elliptical columns from an alumni magazine, whose inside jokes, commentary, and nomenclature exclude the uninitiated. For example, Gray's invitation to spend Christmas at Pembroke erects a one-way mirror, reflective yet opaque:

> *Of all loves come to Cambridge out of hand, for here is Mr Dillival & a charming set of Glasses, that sing like nightingales, & we have concerts every other night, & shall stay here this month or two, & a vast deal of good company, & a Whale in pickle just come from Ipswich. & the* Man *won't die, & Mr Wood is gone to Chatsworth, & there is no body but you, & Tom, & the curl'd Dog, and don't talk of the charge, for we will make a subscription: besides we know, you always come, when you have a mind.*

> (2.766)

As we shall observe in Johnson's letters to Mrs. Thrale, allusions of this kind define a community of interest not so much by virtue of the information conveyed as the shorthand used to convey it. You and I, such letters proclaim, are cognoscenti, with shared access to a world apart. Therefore amplification is unnecessary. I write to you out of this world; prior knowledge and friendly intuition permit you to flesh out my bulletin, to interpret it accurately, and even to live imaginatively within it. By acquainting ourselves with Gray's allusive mode, we are empowered to do likewise.

4

Horace Walpole: The Letter-Writer as Chameleon

I have done nothing but slip out of my domino into bed, and out of bed into my domino.
—*Walpole to West, 27 February 1740*

. . . I will not correct my historic errors: I am not apt to recant my tenets, nor will give up the only king that I have defended; especially as I shall never enter the *sanctum sanctorum,* where one's religion like a chameleon takes the hue of the place the instant one enters it. One quality of the chameleon I have, and rejoice in having; the orbit of my eye allows me to look backward—other creeping things only see before them, and think but of advancing: I keep my eye on what I have always been, and choose to be uniform.
—*Walpole to Lady Ossory, 30 January 1783*

"**D**AMN the man, how various he is!"[1] Instead of his archrival Sir Joshua Reynolds, Gainsborough might have been describing Walpole the letter-writer, who exceeds even Gray in the variety and versatility of his impersonations. Usually accurate in self-appraisal, Walpole discerns a chameleon's gift for looking backward, yet fails to comment on the most striking of all his epistolary talents, the ability to "take the hue" of his immediate audience. So deft and so complete are his transformations, in fact, that Walpole can be said to remake his identity from correspondence to corre-

1. Quoted by Robert Wark in his edition of Sir Joshua Reynolds's *Discourses on Art* (San Marino: Huntington Library, 1959), p. xxxii.

spondence.[2] Although he scorned "the saucy Caliban,"[3] he practices what Johnson preached: "a letter is addressed to a single mind of which the prejudices and partialities are known, and must therefore please, if not by favouring them, by forbearing to oppose them."[4] Both by "favouring" and by "forbearing to oppose," Walpole strives for a unique fit between writer and receiver. As he boasts to Lady Ossory: "the less I am understood by anybody but the person I write to, so much the better" (32.385).

Both Gray and Walpole dart in and out of a succession of identities; both take delight in playing witty games with their correspondents, and in contriving to insinuate what might have been openly declared. Yet even at his most elusively allusive, Gray preserves a quiddity independent of the role of the moment. Walpole's versatility, on the other hand, comes to seem an unsettling and pervasive flaw. Macaulay diagnosed the problem: "His features were covered by mask within mask. When the outer disguise of obvious affectation was removed, you were still as far as ever from seeing the real man. He played innumerable parts, and over-acted them all."[5] Why did Gray, who also "played innumerable parts," overact none of them? One answer is that his parade of identities always takes place *within* a given letter: never does one role dominate an entire correspondence. Walpole's disguises, on the other hand, are so complete, so varied, and so long-lasting,

2. Nothing could be further from the truth than William N. Free's contention that Walpole's "[epistolary] character does not change from one correspondence to another, although different sides of it might receive emphasis at different times." See "Walpole's Letters: The Art of Being Graceful," in *The Familiar Letter in the Eighteenth Century*, ed. Howard Anderson, Philip B. Daghlian, and Irvin Ehrenpreis (Lawrence: University of Kansas Press, 1966), p. 166.

3. *Horace Walpole's Correspondence*, 42 vols., ed. W.S. Lewis et al. (New Haven: Yale University Press, 1937–83), 29.106. References to this edition will hereafter be noted parenthetically in the text.

4. Samuel Johnson, *Lives of the English Poets*, ed. G.B. Hill (Oxford: Clarendon Press, 1905), 3.207.

5. T.B. Macaulay, "Horace Walpole," in *Critical and Historical Essays* (London: Longman, Green, Longman, and Roberts, 1860), 2.99.

that we come to wonder what (if anything) lies beneath the domino. Was there in fact a "real man" left when carnival time came to an end? Though this question can never be settled, it haunts the investigation that follows.

In Wayne C. Booth's vocabulary of rhetorical criticism, the writer of fiction creates a version of himself, "the implied author," while insinuating an identity for his audience, "the implied reader."[6] The master of the familiar letter is engaged in a similar enterprise—an act of creative adaptation whose success ultimately depends on a harmonious union of the two identities in question ("implied sender" and "implied recipient," if you will). In fact, epistolary intimacy might be defined as a process of making and matching, a series of reciprocal adjustments between the writer's self-presentation and the kind of correspondent he fashions for himself.[7] Every successful letter-writer correlates manner to audience: the "implied author" of Lady Mary's letters to Lady Mar is not the same as the presence that registers itself in writing to Lady Bute; nor is the "Cowper" we meet in the correspondence with William Unwin identical to the "Cowper" of the letters to John Newton. Yet in no other letter-writer of the eighteenth century do we encounter so flexible a repertoire of voices as in the complete span of Walpole's work. For almost every correspondent he finds a distinctive angle of approach: *quot homines tot personae.*[8] In practice there proves to be no better way of measuring these angles than by collating different ver-

6. See Wayne C. Booth, *The Rhetoric of Fiction* (Chicago and London: University of Chicago Press, 1961), especially p. 138. Also *The Reader in the Text: Essays on Audience and Interpretation,* ed. Susan R. Suleiman and Inge Crosman (Princeton: Princeton University Press, 1980), pp. 7–9.

7. I have borrowed the phrase "making and matching" from E.H. Gombrich's *Art and Illusion* (Princeton: Princeton University Press, 1960), where it describes the way in which an artist tests his conceptual schemata by close observation of "external" Nature, and revises them accordingly. A similar process could be said to govern the creation of "implied author" and "implied reader" during the course of a familiar correspondence.

8. This is why, as W.S. Lewis has noticed, we are so often able "when reading his side of a correspondence . . . to form such a clear picture of the person to whom he is writing" (28.xxiii).

sions of the same event, whether it be an attack of gout or the trial of a peer, the latest refinement in landscape architecture or the death of Lord Waldegrave. Starting with five sets of paired letters, we will progress to Walpole's array of reports on three major events: the coronation of George III, his trip to Paris in 1765, and the Gordon Riots of 1780.

To present a given subject to a specialized audience is to handle it one way, to a lay audience quite another. This principle governs Walpole's treatment of all his favorite topics, gout and landscape gardening among them. Both were enthusiasms, but of much different kinds; both provided indispensable fodder for letters, but letters designed for correspondents who inhabited separate worlds. In the context of letters to Lady Ossory—the former Duchess of Grafton, now living in social exile on her second husband's Bedfordshire estates—attacks of gout are not to be taken seriously. Walpole stands outside his affliction, contemplating the disease and its effects with humorous detachment. In one letter he pictures himself, swaddled in his bootikins, as the mummy of an Egyptian crane:

> *When a fit of the gout has just turned the corner, one flatters oneself that nothing bad can happen, and one talks with an impudent air of immortality—how you would smile if you saw the figure my immortality makes at this moment! I fancy I look very like the mummy of some sacred crane which Egyptian piety bundled up in cered cloths, and called preserving. The very bones of the claw I write with, are wrapped in a flannel glove.*
>
> (32.43)

In another letter Walpole sketches two improbable comparisons, the first to an heroic St. Lawrence in the style of Titian, the second to a childish William Pitt, staggering from his bed of pain to harangue the House of Commons:

> *Had you come hither, Madam, at your return from Winterslow, you would have found me about as much at ease as St Laurence was upon his gridiron; and though I have been in no danger as he was, I think I may say I have been* saved,

but so as by fire, *for I do not believe roasting is much worse than what I have suffered—one can be broiled too but once; but I have gone through the whole fit twice, it returning the moment I thought myself cured. I still dandled in the arms of two servants, and not yet arrived at my go-cart—In short, I am fit for nothing but to be carried into the House of Lords to prophesy.*

(32.43–44)

Paradoxically, he wins more sympathy for himself by striking these pictorial "attitudes"—the party game in which Emma, Lady Hamilton was to create such a sensation. Instead of admiring a famous picture or statue made glorious flesh, we laugh with and take pity on the sufferer who can make a joke of his plight. Walpole "upon the gridiron" evokes the same initial response as Lismahago climbing down the ladder in his nightshirt: "O, what a subject!—O, what *caricatura!*—O, for a Rosa, a Rembrandt, a Schalken!— . . . O, what *costume!* St. Andrew! St. Lazarus! St. Barrabas!' "[9] The crucial difference is that Walpole has placed himself in this risible posture. He earns our sympathy by caricaturing his pains rather than cataloguing them.

To William Cole, a fussy Anglican clergyman and a fellow-sufferer, Walpole can describe his symptoms from inside. Knowledge is taken for granted, remedies traded, fits and twinges compared and discussed. Clinical summaries require no apology or disguise:

I have been extremely ill indeed with the gout all over, in head, stomach, both feet, both wrists and both shoulders. I kept my bed a fortnight in the most sultry part of this summer, and for nine weeks could not say I was recovered. . . . My relapses have been endless; I cannot yet walk a step; and a great cold has added an ague in my cheek for which I am just going to begin the bark. The prospect for the rest of my days is gloomy.

(1.95, 301)

9. Tobias Smollett, *The Expedition of Humphry Clinker*, ed. James L. Thorson (New York and London: W.W. Norton and Co., 1983), p. 277 (J. Melford's letter of 3 Oct.).

We the gout-free react to these complaints as Lady Ossory would have: we find them tedious and self-indulgent, we judge the writer querulous and more than a little hypochondriacal. However, *Cole* did not, as Walpole realized. On this subject, to this correspondent, he chose to break his own rule that "the evils of life are not good subjects for letters" (1.301)—but only evils served up straight, one should add.

The same distinction between specialized and non-specialized audiences prevails in a pair of letters (to Lady Ossory and Lord Strafford) that describes a dolmen transplanted by Henry Seymour Conway from Jersey to Park Place, Berkshire. Unlike the emphatic contrast we have just observed, however, the variations in tone and detail are less obvious, just as the difference between the recipients, negligible at first glance, requires close scrutiny to assess. The information conveyed in both letters is the same, with emphasis placed on the siting of the megalithic circle. To Lady Ossory, Walpole treats the dolmen as a charming plaything, a garden folly like any other but with the fringe benefit of authenticity:

> . . . *I have been to Park Place on a pilgrimage to little Master Stonehenge, alias, the Druids' Temple from Jersey, which is now erected on the back of an eminent hill, with two wings of fir groves at small distances, and is seen from the garden over a long ridge of firs that shoot up from the side of the beautiful descending valley. Every morsel of stone that formed the circle originally is placed to an inch in its primitive position; and though the whole is diminutive, yet being seen on the horizon, it looks very high-priestly, and in that broken country may easily be taken for respectable ruins of an ancient castle, or Caractacus's own summer residence.*
>
> (34.14–15)

Walpole gently mocks his own interest in this "morsel of stone"—"little Master Stonehenge," "Caractacus's own summer residence." When writing to Strafford, by contrast, he takes the subject and his reaction to it more seriously, as befits a correspondent who has "improved" his own grounds and commissioned a Gothic temple from the "Committee of Taste" at Strawberry Hill:[10]

I have been at Park Place, and assure your Lordship that the Druidic temple vastly more than answers my expectation. Small it is, no doubt, when you are within the enclosure, and but a chapel of ease to Stonehenge; but Mr. Conway has placed it with so much judgment, that it has a lofty effect, and infinitely more than it could have had, if he had yielded to Mrs Damer's and my opinion, who earnestly begged to have it placed within the enclosure of the home grounds.

(35.396)

There is a hint of *The Castle of Otranto* in the picturesque vista Walpole fashions for Lord Strafford:

It now stands on the ridge of the high hill without, backed by the horizon, and with a grove on each side at a little distance; and being exalted beyond and above the range of firs that climb up the sides of the hill from the valley, wears all the appearance of an ancient castle, whose towers are only shattered, not destroyed; and devout as I am to old castles, and small taste as I have for the ruins of ages absolutely barbarous, it is impossible not to be pleased with so very rare an antiquity so absolutely perfect, and it is difficult to prevent visionary ideas from improving a prospect.

(35.396)

Without ceasing to be a toy ("chapel of ease to Stonehenge"), the dolmen by the end of this passage has acquired dignity as a potent stimulus to "visionary ideas." Walpole stresses the evocative power of the sight because of his firsthand knowledge of Strafford's own garden architecture at Wentworth Castle: "Without doors all is pleasing: there is a beautiful (artificial) river with a fine semicircular wood overlooking it, and the temple of Tivoli placed happily on a rising towards the end. There are obelisks, columns, and other buildings, and above all, a handsome castle, in the true style, on a rude

10. See W.S. Lewis, *Horace Walpole* (New York: Pantheon Books, 1961), p. 115.

mountain . . ." (35.267). The more we know of the shared experiences and tastes that knit together letter-writer and correspondent, the more we stand to appreciate Walpole's infal-
lible sense of congruity.

Three additional pairs of letters illustrate the adjustments
Walpole is continually making when he writes about the same
subject to both outsiders and insiders. The outsiders are of
two kinds: either those to whom a courteous response is due
but who will never become real friends, or intimates such as
Sir Horace Mann who have lost touch with current events and
personalities. The insiders are best typified by George Montagu and Lady Ossory, who know the upper reaches of English society from close personal experience.

The first of these three pairs concerns Walpole's acknowl-
edgment of congratulations on his accession to the earldom of
Orford. His note to Lady Ossory (10 December 1791) is delicately balanced between resignation and pride. On the one
hand, the earldom is merest vanity, an affliction rather than a
blessing. On the other, it is a part of his heritage, his identity
even, that cannot be abjured. Walpole glosses over the painful
aspects of the affair—the empty title, the heavily encumbered
estates: "It is a story much too full of circumstances, and too
disagreeable to me to be couched in a letter—Some time or
other I may perhaps be at leisure and composed enough to
relate in general" (34.134). In doing so he adheres to the
same rule he had violated by complaining of gout to William
Cole ("the evils of life are not good subjects for letters"). But
propriety is not the only consideration: for Walpole to brush
aside Lady Ossory's compliments would be to falsify his own
ambivalent reactions and to fracture the twin codes of eti-
quette and friendship. On this of all subjects it behooves him
to act with perfect breeding. Rising above the multiple vexa-
tions inflicted on him by the earldom, he therefore returns
compliment for compliment, gracefully pairing Lady Ossory
with his predecessor the third Earl: "I had reason to think
that he ["my poor nephew"] had disgraced by totally omitting
me—but unhappy as his intellects often were, and beset as he
was by miscreants, he has restored me to my birthright, and I

shall call myself obliged to him, and be grateful to his memory as I am to your Ladyship, and shall be as I have so long been your devoted servant, by whatever name I may be forced to call myself" (34.134). For all its *nolo episcopari* undercurrents, this is the letter of one aristocrat to another: Walpole knows that Lady Ossory will understand the importance of "my birthright," and the concept of *noblesse oblige* that accompanies it. A mess of pottage the earldom may be, but at least it has not been sold to another.

To the Scottish antiquarian John Pinkerton, Walpole sends a much different letter, one of the few in his entire oeuvre that might be said to buttress Macaulay's claim: "We are never sure that we see him as he was. We are never sure that what appears to be art is not merely habit which has become second nature."[11] Especially when one compares this letter to others written at the same time (to Hannah More and Mary Berry as well as to Lady Ossory), it becomes painfully obvious that Walpole is making elaborate excuses in advance for his failure to read promptly the manuscript of Pinkerton's *History of Scotland.* Furthermore, he is telling Pinkerton what Pinkerton wants to hear: the new title is meaningless, and causes him nothing but trouble. When Walpole writes to Lady Ossory he brings out the best in himself and his correspondent; when he writes to Pinkerton, he caters to a lowest common denominator in both.

Without any evidence external to this letter, we could characterize Pinkerton quite accurately as an ambitious, exigent flatterer on-the-make, "whose hatred of nobility appears in many pars of his biographical Sketch [of Walpole]. . . and though he pretends to praise H. Walpole, he often bitterly satirizes him."[12] From the very beginning Walpole's claims ring false: "As I am sure of the sincerity of your congratula-

---

11. Macaulay, 2.118.
12. Robert Nares's note in Edmond Malone's copy of Pinkerton's *Walpoliana*, quoted by James M. Osborn. See "Horace Walpole and Edmond Malone" in *Horace Walpole: Writer, Politician, and Connoisseur*, ed. Warren Hunting Smith (New Haven and London: Yale University Press, 1967), p. 322, n. 44.

tions, I feel much obliged by them . . ." (16.313). This disingenuous assertion is but the first of many. Throughout the
letter Walpole poses as the distraught, fastidious valetudinarian, whose unwanted elevation to the peerage leaves
only a taste of ashes in the mouth. His catalogue of woes piles
exaggeration upon exaggeration: the earldom "destroys my
tranquillity"; the estate is "loaded with debt"; he does not
"understand the management" of Houghton; the lawyers
have plagued him with "endless conversations"; he has been
left "weak and dispirited," with only a "rag of life" hanging
about him. Each one of these claims is inflated, imaginary, or
equivocal. Style alone gives the game away: the master of the
colorful idiom, the elegantly turned phrase, the precise for-
mulation, wraps himself on this occasion in a blanket of wool-
ly syntax and evasive generality. Pinkerton has pushed
Walpole to take on the role of munificent patron, who will be
paid in flattery for services rendered; Walpole duly obliges,
but the strain warps his prose and distorts his matter.

Rarely can we say, as in these two letters, that Walpole is
patently insincere in one and undeniably honest in the other.
More often than not, shifts in emphasis and alterations in
content can be explained by considering how much the correspondent is likely to know already of the matter at hand.
When Walpole describes the trial and execution of Earl Ferrers to George Montagu, or the simultaneous death of Lord
Waldegrave and resignation of Bute, he handles these events
as social phenomena, the equivalent of reports "under the
article of White's Chocolate House" from *The Tatler*. To Sir
Horace Mann, the expatriate envoy who had left England for
good c. 1737, they must be elaborated as installments of an
ongoing chronicle—the epistolary "History of My Own
Time" that the Mann letters were ultimately intended to be.[13]
As Walpole explained to Lady Ossory, who replaced Montagu
in the role of social correspondent:

13. See Walpole's "Advertisement" to the Mann correspondence, 17.1–2;
also R.W. Ketton-Cremer, *Horace Walpole*, 3rd ed. (Ithaca: Cornell University
Press, 1966), pp. 97–98.

Pray don't think I am tired of your stories. Nothing is so
pleasant as the occurrences of society in a letter. I am always
regretting in my correspondence with Madame du Deffand
and Sir Horace Mann, that I must not make use of them, as
the one has never lived in England, and the other not these
fifty years, and so any private stories would want notes as
much as Petronius. Sir Horace and I have no acquaintance in
common but the kings and queens of Europe.

(32.320)

Walpole sends his friends in-the-know a variety of partial, elliptical reports—private stories that need no notes because
the correspondent is totally *au fait*. Mann, interested but ignorant, requires a trot to elucidate the text. Therefore Walpole's
letters to him necessarily combine briefing with storytelling.

From 16–18 April 1760 Lawrence, Earl Ferrers was tried
before the House of Lords for the murder of his steward.
Ferrers was found guilty, and executed on 5 May. Reporting
on the trial to Mann, Walpole concentrates on the discrepancy between the villainy of the defendant and the solemnity
of the proceedings: "The behaviour, character, and appearance of the criminal by no means corresponded to the dignity
of the show" (21.388). He comments only in passing on the
judges, and not at all on the audience. The letter to Montagu,
on the other hand, dwells on the appearance and behavior of
the peers and peeresses: "There are so many young peers,
that the show was fine even in that respect; the Duke of Rich-
mond was the finest figure. The Duke of Marlborough with
the best countenance in the world, looked clumsy in his robes.
He had new ones, having given away his father's to the valet
de chambre" (9.280–81). Walpole is much more intrigued by
the trial as a social event than as a judicial proceeding. He
picks out of the crowd figures Montagu will recognize, and
flicks each one with the lash of ridicule:

But never was a criminal more literally tried by his peers, *for*
the three persons who interested themselves most in the exam-
ination, were at least as mad as he, Lord Ravensworth, Lord
Talbot and Lord Fortescue—indeed the first was almost fran-

tic. *The seats of the peeresses were not near full; and most of
the beauties absent; the Duchess of Hamilton and my niece
Waldegrave, you know, lie in—but to the amazement of everybody, Lady Coventry was there—and what surprised me much
more, looked as well as ever. I sat next but one to her, and
should not have asked if she had been ill—yet they are positive
she has few weeks to live. She and Lord Bolingbroke seemed to
have very different thoughts, and were acting over all the old
comedy of eyes.*

(9.279–80)

Because he knows next to nothing of the victims, such "quizz-
ing" would only baffle Mann.

Walpole's focus shifts firmly to the protagonist in the pam-
phlet-length account of the execution he compiles for Mann's
benefit. Nowhere else in this correspondence do we feel more
strongly the influence of Prince Posterity. Only twice does
Walpole turn from his circumstantial narration to address the
recipient; both of these taps on the shoulder take the form of
rhetorical questions. The first is little more than a device to
begin the letter with a flourish: "What will your Italians say to
a peer of England, an earl of one of the best families, tried,
for murdering his servant, with the utmost dignity and solemnity, and then hanged at the common place of execution for
highwaymen, and afterwards anatomized?" (21.394–95). The
second proves the most token of concessions to his immediate
reader: "How will you decipher all these strange circumstances to Florentines?" (21.400). With these two negligible
exceptions, Mann *per se* drops out completely—or rather, is
subsumed into Walpole's hypothetical reader of the future.
All private jokes and allusions are stripped away, all *dramatis
personae* identified, all peculiarities of dress and behavior un-
obtrusively explained, all necessary background information
inserted into the story without slowing its momentum. Mann
reacted to this approach exactly as he was meant to: "The
whole process, and particularly the catastrophe, is an interesting historical narrative" (21.410).

"Occurrences of society" rather than "historical narrative"

justify and enliven the letter to Montagu. The story of the execution is told, not for its own sake, but as the occasion for two mocking jabs, the first at the blindly imitative behavior of the mob, the second at the excesses of the Methodists:

> *The mob was decent, admired him, and almost pitied him—so they would Lord George, whose execution they are so angry at missing. I suppose every highwayman will now preserve the blue handkerchief they have about their necks when they are married, that they may die like a lord. With all the frenzy in his blood, he was not mad enough to be struck with his aunt Huntingdon's sermons—the Methodists have nothing to brag of in his conversion, though Whitfield prayed for him and preached about him—even Tyburn has been above their reach. I have not heard that Lady Fanny dabbled with his soul—but I believe she is prudent enough to confine her missionary zeal to subjects where the body may be her perquisite.*

(9.283–84)

Mann receives a polychrome pageant worthy of Froissart, Montagu an ironic little *conte* in the manner of Voltaire. The moral of the story comes at the beginning: "Madness, that in other countries is a disorder, is here a systematic character. It does not hinder people from forming a plan of conduct, and from even dying agreeably to it" (9.283).

Montagu's insider status exerts a different kind of influence on the letter (8 April 1763) in which Walpole announces two deaths: the literal demise of Lord Waldegrave and the political suicide of Lord Bute. Two days later he writes to Mann about the same events. The structure of both letters is similar: the first half describes a domestic, the second a national drama. In the earlier letter, however, we encounter Walpole's version of "writing to the moment": "Amidst all my own grief, and all the distress which I have this moment left, I cannot forget you, who have so long been my steady and invariable friend. I cannot leave it to newspapers and correspondents to tell you my loss. Lord Waldegrave died today" (10.58). Caught up in a private tragedy, Walpole packs his description of Waldegrave's deathbed with dramatic touches:

snatches of dialogue between the dying man and his physicians; the arrival of the express from London; the tears of his
valet. Confident of Montagu's interest and emotional involvement—a confidence borne out by Montagu's letter of con-
dolence—he sends a stage-by-stage report, accompanied by
choral lament and expostulation: "It was indeed too late! too
late for everything. . . . Vain to recollect, how particularly
kind he, who was kind to everybody, was to me!" (10.59). By
comparison the second half of the letter, the political gazette,
's both compressed and detached. Walpole is too much the
historian, and the epistolary artist, to slight the momentous
news of Bute's resignation, or to unbalance a letter that has
set out to juxtapose two "unexpected revolutions." Yet the
intensity that permeates the first half has slackened: the actor
quits centerstage and takes a seat in the auditorium.

The theme of mortal illness, actual and metaphorical, unites
the two halves of the letter to Mann: "At a time when the
political world is in strange and unexpected disorder, you
would wonder that I should be here. . . . The same day that put
an end to Lord Waldegrave's life gave a period too to the
administration of Lord Bute, his supplanter" (22.126, 128).
Walpole's goal is to fashion an historical diptych; accordingly,
Mann is furnished with a capsule summary of the progress of
Waldegrave's disease: "He was taken ill on the Wednesday, the
distemper showed itself on the Friday, a very bad sort, and
carried him off that day sennight" (22.127). Walpole explains
why Waldegrave had never been inoculated, launches into a
brief eulogy, accuses the physicians of incompetence, then
concentrates on the plight of his widowed niece, who "has
nothing left but a moderate jointure of a thousand pounds a
year, three little girls, a pregnancy, her beauty, and the testi-
monial of the best of men" (22.127). The distraught young
woman of the Montagu letter, whose shock and grief touch us
directly, has been turned into the heroine of a sentimental
romance: "Since the death of Lady Coventry she is allowed the
handsomest woman in England: as she is so young, she may
find as great a match and a younger lover—but she never can

find another Lord Waldegrave!" (22.128). Walpole's reactions take on a ritualized quality: they invite Mann to respond as if to the plot of another *Nouvelle Héloïse.*

In the second half of the letter (the right-hand leaf of the diptych) Walpole analyzes political developments and dissects motives, for unlike Montagu, Mann cannot be expected to pick up the nuances of the new administration. To his memorandum Walpole appends a final paragraph, which comments philosophically on the sudden changes, then circles back to the subject with which the letter began. Its two chief concerns, related only metaphorically at the outset, are neatly tied together:

> *The poor man who is gone could have been of the utmost consequence at this moment to accomplish some establishment; he had been offered and had refused the greatest things—no bad ingredient in reconciling others. In that or any other qualification I know few equal to him! Adieu!*
>
> (22.131)

Though there is no gainsaying the sincerity of Walpole's grief for his friend, his anxiety for Lady Waldegrave, and his concern for the chaotic political situation, the report to Mann deliberately holds all such matters at arm's length. Whether emotion had actually subsided into tranquillity is impossible to judge. One fact is obvious, however: Walpole's doctrine of epistolary decorum dictates that it should *appear* to have done so.

THE CORONATION OF GEORGE III

The first of Walpole's reports on the coronation, his letter to George Montagu (24 September 1761), mixes the sublime and the ridiculous, belittlement and admiration, the nobility of Lord Errol (who "looked like one of the giants in Guildhall, new-gilt") and the vanity of the Duchess of Bedford (who "looked like an orange-peach, half red and half yellow"). Yet Walpole lingers with most relish on various examples of affectation; he comes to celebrate and stays to mock. Montagu is

treated to an account of the ceremony in Westminister Abbey
that begins and ends with the antics of a fool:

> *My Lady Harrington, covered with all the diamonds she
> could borrow, hire, or tease, and with the air of Roxana, was
> the finest figure at a distance; she complained to George
> Selwyn, that she was to walk with Lady Portsmouth, who
> would have a wig, and a stick—"Pho," said he, "you will
> only look as if you was taken up by the constable"—she told
> this everywhere, thinking the reflection was on my Lady
> Portsmouth. . . . Lord Talbot piqued himself on backing his
> horse down the Hall, and not turning its rump towards the
> King, but he had taken such pains to dress it to that duty,
> that it entered backwards; and at his retreat the spectators
> clapped, a terrible indecorum, but suitable to such Bar-
> tholomew Fair doings. He put me in mind of some King's
> fool, that would not give his right hand to the King of
> Spain, because he wiped his backside with it.*
>
> (9.387–89)

Walpole makes little attempt to recreate setting, atmosphere,
or ritual: individual actors rather than the glittering panorama catch his eye, as he turns the coronation into the pup-
pet show he had declared it to be at the beginning of the letter
(9.386). So selective is his emphasis, so stylized his satirical
renderings of appearance and gesture, that we temporarily
forget what might have been made of the same occasion—a
letter such as those devoted to the trial and execution of the
Rebel Lords, for example, which combine sharp close-ups
with a generous assortment of long shots. Two factors steer
Walpole away from documentation and incline him to "Bar-
tholomew Fair doings": Montagu his "social" correspondent,
a fellow connoisseur of aristocratic oddities, and the lingering
influence of Lady Mary Wortley Montagu.

In 1751 Walpole had read Lady Mary's letters to Lady Mar
and praised them extravagantly: "They are charming! have
more spirit and vivacity than you can conceive. . . . in most of
them, the wit and style are superior to any letters I ever read
but Madame Sévigné's" (20.281–82). In 1786 he annotated

eighteen of them for Lady Ossory, including the letter on the Coronation of George II (34.260). The more one studies Walpole's coronation letter to Montagu, the more persuasive the link with Lady Mary's becomes (see above, pp. 11–12). Certainly Walpole did not set out to imitate her closely: he could not have done so, even if he had wanted to, for the manuscripts had long ago been returned to their owner, and there is no evidence that copies were taken. Instead of an exact model, Lady Mary furnishes a precedent and a procedure: on this grandest of all possible occasions, her letter authorizes him to be as partial (in both senses) and as irreverent as he likes.

Writing, like Walpole, to a privileged insider with a taste for caricature, Lady Mary sets in motion a small company of human marionettes. In both coronation letters the particular occasion functions largely as a catalyst for an exhibition of folly, made delectable by the power of wit. The participants are reduced to types, even to objects—the Duchess of Bedford to a mottled peach, the Countess of Portland to a mummy. Historical pageantry, dimly glimpsed in the background, frames a procession of grotesques.

Lady Mary's influence continues to make itself felt in Walpole's letters to Henry Seymour Conway and his wife Lady Ailesbury. Since Walpole knows that these two will compare letters, he takes special pains to vary contents and tone: the sober professional soldier receives a brisk enumeration of salient points, his sympathetic wife a joking romp through the day's events. The highlights of both letters, however, consist of specimens of vanity, pomposity, and farcical misbehavior. To Conway, Walpole writes of Lady Townshend, a relic from the previous coronation: "My Lady Townshend said she should be very glad to see a coronation, as she never had seen one. 'Why,' said I, 'Madam, you walked at the last?' 'Yes, child,' said she, 'but I saw nothing of it: I only looked to see who looked at me'" (38.123). He also recounts a Feydeau-like mishap involving the Duke of Newcastle, who was surprised by the Queen upon the royal chamberpot: "Of all the incidents of the day, the most diverting was, what happened to the Queen. She had a retiring-chamber, with *all* conveniences, prepared behind the altar. She went thither—in the *most convenient,* what found she but—the Duke of Newcastle!" (38.122). Walpole leaves this anecdote out of his letter to Lady Ailesbury, but offers in compensation a gallery of satirical sketches in Lady Mary's mode. The subject of the first sketch is the Countess Cowper, who objected to her place in the procession next to Lady Macclesfield, a woman of humble birth and dubious morals: "yet I was not so *perilously* angry as my Lady Cowper, who refused to set a foot with my Lady Macclesfield, and when she was at last obliged to associate with her, set out on a round trot, as if she designed to prove the antiquity of her family, by marching as lustily as a maid of honour of Queen Gwiniver" (38.126). To the same category belong "Lady Portsmouth, who had put a wig on, and old Exeter, who had scratched hers off; Lady Stamford, the Dowager Effingham, and a Lady Say and Sele with her tresses coal black and her hair coal white" (38.127). From her observations at the Coronation of George II, Lady Mary had concluded: "In General I could not perceive but the old were as well pleas'd as the Young, and I (who dread growing Wise more than any thing in the World) was overjoy'd to observe one can never outlive one's Vanity" (2.86). The same combination of mocking irony and rueful philosophy marks Walpole's summing up: "Well! it was all delightful, but not half so charming as its being over—the gabble one heard about it for six weeks before, and the fatigue of the day, could not well be compensated by a mere puppet-show, for puppet-show it was, though it cost a million" (38.127).

In his letter to Sir Horace Mann, Walpole selects only those anecdotes that have intrinsic appeal, such as the Duke of Newcastle incident or those that contrast with the England Mann had known thirty years before. A social inventory of the kind he had just sent to Montagu and Lady Ailesbury would be pointless: as Walpole himself observes, "I tell you nothing of who looked well; you know them no more than if I told you of the next coronation" (21.535). The first third of the letter hatches in the background he had not bothered to delineate before: "hammering of scaffolds, shouting of people, relieving guards, and jangling of bells, was the concert I heard from twelve to six . . ." (21.534). A long coda compares the astronomical prices paid at this coronation with those of 1727: Walpole knows that Mann will be interested in the exact index of inflation and extravagance, whereas his other correspondents require no such economic data.

As it happens, the letter to Mann is the least vital of the four—not so much because of the differences among correspondents as Walpole's commitment on this occasion to registering certain kinds of detail. He takes most pleasure in fishing for oddities, and only a fraction of his catch is suitable for the foreigner Mann has in effect become. Furthermore, the whole subject has begun to grow stale by the time Mann's turn comes round. Ideally Walpole would have exerted himself to supply the kind of panoramic view that Gray shares with James Brown—a long letter with a firm narrative line, scrupulous attention to details of setting and dress, and a comprehensive roster of protagonists:

> *I set out at half an hour past four in the morning for the Coronation, & (in the midst of perils & dangers) arrived very safe at my Ld Chamberlain's Box in Westminister Hall. it was on the left hand of the throne over that appropriated to the Foreign Ministers. opposite to us was the Box of the Earl Marshal, & other Great Officers, & below it that of the Princess, & younger Part of the Royal Family. next them was the royal sideboard. then below the steps of the Haut-pas were the tables of the Nobility on each side quite to the door, behind them boxes for the sideboards, over these the galleries for the Peers Tickets, & still higher the boxes of the Auditor, the board of Green-Cloth, &c: all these throng'd with people head above head, all dress'd, & the Women with their Jewels on.*

(2.752–53)

This exact, atmospheric *veduta*, which might almost be a set of notations for a festival panorama, recalls Walpole's own letter to Mann on the execution of Earl Ferrers. Because he comes last and knows least, however, Mann hears more of prices than of peers.

THE TRIP TO PARIS, 1765

Walpole set out for France on 9 September 1765, determined to recover from "the greatest disillusionment of his life,"[14] the ingratitude of Henry Seymour Conway. To his other friends he had given poor health and a surfeit of politics as the motives for his jaunt to Paris; to Montagu he hints at the true reason, and describes the cure he has chosen to undertake:

> *I advise you to do as I do: when I meet with ingratitude, I take a short leave both of it and its host. Formerly I used to look out for indemnification somewhere else; but having lived long enough to learn that the reparation generally proved a second evil of the same sort, I am content now to skin over such wounds with amusements, which at least leave no scars.*
>
> (10.174)

Though Walpole claims that "nothing strikes me; everything I do is indifferent to me" (10.175), the rest of the letter, and the other letters he writes throughout the Parisian sojourn, emphatically contradict this claim.

In tune with his assertion to Montagu—"the trifles that amuse my mind, are the only points I value now" (10.171)— Walpole lists the ways in which he has already contrived "to trifle away the day as I like" (10.175). These include shopping, the theatre, the opera, and late suppers. He also sounds the *o tempora, o mores* theme that is elaborated in subsequent letters from Paris: the city is dirtier than he remembered, "the French stage is fallen off" (10.175), conversation is fatally infected by pedantic literary topics and by rampant attacks on religion and government. Walpole affects to write as one retired veteran to another: in Paris he is managing to disengage himself from serious concerns as completely as Montagu in rural Northamptonshire. "In short, I have done

14. Ketton-Cremer, p. 204.

with the world, and only live in it, rather than in a desert, like you" (10.177).

For John Chute the man of exquisite social refinement, the acute observer of foreign customs, Walpole gathers together an assortment of curious minutiae under the general heading, "the total difference of manners between them and us, from the greatest object to the least" (35.112). Chute brings out Walpole's talent for observing and reporting the representative particular—just that feature of dress, deportment, or setting that epitomizes a scene. Because Chute shares his passion for trifles, from flimsy occasional poetry to neo-Gothic chimneypieces, Walpole can descend without apology to the most humble details:

> *The very footmen are powdered from the break of day, and yet wait behind their master, as I saw the Duc of Praslin's do, with a red pocket handkerchief about their necks. Versailles like everything else is a mixture of parade and poverty; and in every instance exhibits something most dissonant from our manners. In the colonnades, upon the staircases, nay in the antechambers of the royal family, there are people selling all sorts of wares. While we were waiting in the Dauphin's sumptuous bedchamber, till his dressing-room door should be opened, two fellows were sweeping it, and dancing about in sabots to rub the floor.*
>
> (35.112)

With pinpoint accuracy Walpole captures the incongruity of such Breughelesque intrusions into would-be tableaux by Le Brun. He emphasizes the gap between public facade and private frailty, the "mixture of parade and poverty" that is comic in its startling juxtapositions but tragic in its implications.

This relish for incongruities continues to inform Walpole's description of the French royal family. His group portrait takes the "parade and poverty" theme one step further by imaging the inner bankruptcy of the Bourbons:

> *You are let into the King's bedchamber just as he has put on his shirt; he dresses and talks good-humouredly to a few,*

glares at strangers, goes to Mass, to dinner and a-hunting. The good old Queen, who is like Lady Primrose in the face, and Queen Caroline in the immensity of her cap, is at her dressing-table, attended by two or three old ladies, who are languishing to be in Abraham's bosom, as the only man's bosom to whom they can hope for admittance. Thence you go to the Dauphin, for all is done in an hour. He scarce stays a minute; indeed poor creature, he is a ghost and cannot possibly last three months. The Dauphiness is in her bed- chamber, but dressed and standing: looks cross, is not civil, and has the true Wesphalian grace and accents. The four Mesdames, who are clumsy plump old wenches, with a bad likeness to their father, stand in a bedchamber in a row, with black cloaks and knotting bags, looking good-humoured, not knowing what to say, and wriggling as if they wanted to make water. This ceremony too is very short: then you are carried to the Dauphin's three boys, who you may be sure only bow and stare. The Duke of Berry looks weak and weak-eyed: the Count de Provence is a fine boy; the Count d'Artois, well enough. The whole concludes with seeing the Dauphin's little girl dine, who is as round and fat as a pudding.

(35.112–13)

Like Goya in *The Family of Charles IV,* Walpole depicts "the corner baker and his wife after they won the lottery"[15]—an ill-favored, undignified collection of human oddities, man- ifestly unsuited to their ceremonial role ("clumsy plump old wenches . . . not knowing what to say, and wriggling as if they wanted to make water"). Fred Licht's account of Goya's paint- ing fits the empty posturing of Walpole's royal troupe:

Goya's portrait of the royal family strips the group portrait of all such ulterior significance. The family has not come to- gether in order to vouchsafe their subjects a vision of their august presence. Instead, they have congregated in the artist's studio in order fatuously to admire their own image. Not all their finery (which seems usurped, as Gautier implied) can

15. Théophile Gautier's description, quoted in Fred Licht's *Goya: The Ori- gins of the Modern Temper in Art* (New York: Harper and Row, 1979), p. 68.

give us the sense of royalty. Their stance has no authority; they are not spiritually larger than life. . . . They do not dominate the space in which they move, as do the unforgettably self-assured personages of Van Dyck or Boucher. They stand about rather sheepishly . . .[16]

Here, as in the coronation letter of George Montagu, Walpole "hits off" satirical likenesses with a few deft strokes, convincing us by sheer dexterity of his accuracy and authority. It is fitting that Chute the virtuoso, once a seeker after paintings and virtu for Houghton and now a collector in his own right, should receive this *catalogue raisonné* of ignoble specimens.

On 19 November Walpole responds to Gray's letter of c. 12 November, which had inquired solicitously after Walpole's health, and, "at the hazard of being called an old woman," had recommended various prophylactics and remedies against the gout (14.140–41). Gray writes as "a fellow-sufferer with you, about your own age"; after describing his "prescriptions," he begs for information and reassurance: "You will do me pleasure (if you are able) in telling me yourself how you do, for I have nobody but your servants to inform me" (14.141).

Walpole matches his response very closely to Gray's letter, drawing on a lifetime's knowledge of his correspondent's tastes and prejudices. Roughly the first third of the letter is devoted to a short treatise on his gout—more detailed than even the bulletins to Cole. Though he knows that an apology for this sort of medical report is not necessary, given the tenor of Gray's letter from "a fellow-sufferer," he includes it anyway, contriving thereby to ridicule his obsession in the process of indulging it: "You are very kind to inquire so particularly after my gout: I wish I may not be too circumstantial in my answer; but you have tapped a dangerous topic; I can talk gout by the hour" (14.142). As the rest of the paragraph bears out, Walpole keeps in mind the various shades of meaning that "particularly" could support: "one by one, severally, singly, individually"; "for a specific purpose"; "minutely, cir-

16. Licht, pp. 79–80.

cumstantially, in detail"; "in a special degree"; "personally, familiarly, intimately." To this particular friend on this particular subject, Walpole luxuriates in the particulars of his case. And Gray was gratified: "I am very much obliged to you for the detail you enter into on the subject of your own health; in this you cannot be too circumstantial for me . . ." (14.146).

Walpole manages the transition from health to travels by endorsing Gray's scornful opinion of "French nostrums or people of quality's receipts" (14.141);

> *I laughed at your idea of quality receipts, it came so apropos: there is not a man or woman here that is not a perfect old nurse, and who does not talk gruel and anatomy with equal fluency and ignorance. One instance shall serve; Madame de Bouzols, Marshal Berwick's daughter, assured me there was nothing so good for the gout as to preserve the parings of my nails in a bottle close stopped. When I try any illustrious nostrum, I shall give the preference to this.*
>
> (14.143)

The absurdity of aristocratic prescriptions is equaled by the indelicacy of aristocratic conversation:

> *The Dauphin is at the point of death; every morning the physicians frame an account of him, and happy is he or she who can produce a copy of this lie, called a* bulletin. *The night before last, one of these was produced at supper where I was; it was read, and said, he had had* une évacuation fétide—*I beg your pardon, though you are not at supper. . . . They talk of a* chienne chaude, *or the dangerous time of a woman's age, as they would talk of a knotting bag.*
>
> (14.143–44)

Having echoed and reinforced Gray's prejudices on two counts—the gout and the grotesque ignorance of the French nobility—Walpole then touches on the plague of *philosophes*, just as if he had been responding to the letter in which Gray contemptuously labels Frederick the Great's poetry "the *Crambe recocta* of our worst Free-thinkers" (see above, pp. 123–24). To Montagu, Walpole had vented a milder complaint: "Freethinking is for one's self, surely not for society; besides one has settled one's way of thinking, or knows it cannot be settled; and for others, I do not see why there is not as much bigotry in attempting conversions from any religion as to it" (10.176). To Gray, Walpole writes with a vehemence that foreshadows his tirades against the French Revolution.[17] What did he "really" feel: polite distaste or angry aversion? It is impossible to tell, so completely has the letter-writer taken on the color of his correspondent.

Thus on every subject Walpole dovetails his report with the interests and antipathies of his friend. The letter to Gray is one of those that provides irrefutable support for W.S. Lewis's claim: "Were we to read 'new' letters to Cole or Montagu or Mason that had no obvious clue to the identity of the recipients, we should have little difficulty in assigning the letters correctly" (28.xxiii). The "implied author" gives back the image of the "implied reader"; the chameleon merges with his background.

Though he owed primary allegiance to Madame de Sévigné, "Notre Dame de Livry," Walpole could on occasion model his letters after the epistolary soufflés of Vincent Voiture. In his twenties he dismisses Voiture's style as "affected stuff" (30.75), but in his forties, stricken with "a passion" for Lady Mary Coke and the Duchess of Grafton, he turns himself into another *mercure galant*, who speaks the extravagant language of the Hotel de Rambouillet. In his *Memoirs of George III* Walpole describes the Duchess as "a woman of a commanding figure, though no regular beauty, graceful, full of dignity and of art too, passionate for admiration" (34.240). His letters mirror that grace, dignity, and art, while gratifying the passion for admiration. Like Voiture, Walpole puts into practice "le don d'être à la fois spirituel et naturel, un style également raffiné et cursif, la facilité et l'art unis pour faire valoir les moindres sujets par la façon de les traiter."[18] This gift

17. See Robert A. Smith, "Walpole's Reflections on the Revolution in France," in *Horace Walpole: Writer, Politician, and Connoisseur*, pp. 91–114.
18. Pierre Moreau, "Voiture," in *Dictionnaire des Lettres Françaises: XVIIe Siècle* (Paris: Librairie Arthème Fayard, 1954), p. 1016.

might be compared to the ormolu mounts with which the
French encrusted their delicate Chinese porcelain: a gilded
tracery of compliment embellishes, surrounds, and coalesces
with the fabric of the letter, itself the most insubstantial of
commodities. Like the bowls and jars displayed in this fashion,
Walpole's letters in the style of Voiture belong to a minor
category of rococo decorative arts. Yet they display a special
kind of painstaking craftsmanship, trivial as the result may
seem.

The characteristic tone of Walpole's correspondence with
the Duchess is established in the first sentence of the earliest
surviving letter:

> *If anything could make me amends, Madam, for not seeing
> the finest figure in the world walk at the Coronation, it would
> be the letter and the* découpure *that I have received from
> your Grace: I will carry the latter to that ceremony, to prevent
> the handsomest peeresses from gaining any advantage in my
> eyes by an absence that I fear they are all wicked enough to
> enjoy.*

> (32.1)

Walpole contrives a delicate strain of hyperbole that avoids
the pitfalls of sterile frivolity on the one hand and offensive
gallantry on the other. His admiration is exaggerated but
sincere, his courtship at once a light-hearted joke and a genuine expression of devotion. The elaborate compliments are
turned with a refined gallantry that both flatters (because it is
fundamentally accurate) and amuses (because it is fundamentally asexual):

> *With all your favours your Grace has mixed a little un-
> kindness—when I was to answer your letter, you must know I
> should wish to write of nothing but you—you enjoin me to talk
> of the Queen. . . . To begin then, Madam, she is of the best
> proportioned height in the world; her person is so exactly
> formed, that it would please though motionless, and yet she has
> an air of as much dignity as is compatible with the most
> amiable softness; her eyes have more fire, her teeth are whiter,
> her hair is better disposed, her neck—oh! Lord bless me, I*

forgot—it was the Queen I was to describe—She is nothing of all this; she is as unlike the description I have been giving as—as—as—as every woman in the world is but one.

(32.2–3)

Walpole maintains the charm and the humor of these "high-flown but innocuous gallantries" by appealing to the testimony of others and by portraying himself as a ridiculous January to the Duchess's dazzling May:[19]

What do I, or can I say to you, that all the world would not say to you, if you had the same indulgence for them that you have for me? . . . . what is to preserve the equilibrium of mine, when I receive such flattering letters from your Grace?— what?—why, alas! the reflection on the cause that makes you think such letters of no consequence; that I am a poor old withered skeleton, and that you may write to me as safely as to your great-grandfather.

(32.12)

Like any other suitors, great-grandfathers are allowed to present bouquets, even to send *billets-doux;* like eunuchs in the harem, however, they can do no harm.

From Paris Walpole writes to the Duchess in the character of a "wrinkled Adonis" (32.13), one of the identities he had assumed before crossing the Channel:

If your Grace thinks that I am turned coxcomb in my grey years, look you, Madam, you know nothing of the matter or of me. If you have been told that the French are blind, you have been as ill-informed. The nymphs I live with, it is true, are ancient; but nothing in their behaviour has given me a hint that they admire an antique swain—They have known better things. Six weeks more of gout have not added to my natural roses and lilies; and though my poor legs have been swelled to a degree of Hibernian respectableness, they are dwindled back to their former invisibility. Now does your Grace any longer believe that I have been charming and have charmed?

(32.21)

19. Ketton-Cremer, p. 239.

The topics he had treated directly and at length in the letters to Montagu, Chute, and Gray are here compressed, hinted at, or glossed over: "I talk French very indifferently, hold dissertations worse, don't understand eating, nor descant on its consequences, laugh at their philosophers, and never play at whisk. Judge if I am admired, when all these points are capital!" (32.21–22). In each paragraph a rapid catalogue of diversions and temptations climaxes in a compliment to the Duchess or a declaration of unswerving attachment; the "historic" content of the letter—Paris, November 1765—does little more than undergird the multiple gesture of gallantry.

The letter ends with the most elaborate of compliments, which reintroduces the letter-writer in his role of aging Adonis. Walpole imagines a mythological tableau, an exalted version of himself riding in a chariot with the Duchess as Venus (a comparison with which she was familiar from his "Epigram on the Duchess of Grafton going abroad. . . . just after the transit of Venus"). This tableau is immediately subverted, however: lover of Venus he may be, but he also remains a thin-shanked valetudinarian.

> *My stay, I doubt, will be longer; I dare not venture on inns and sea in winter, nor even in a car drawn by doves. Paris must be my Paphos till warmer weather. Nobody of my make but Grammont's Germain (my predecessor* aux jambes menues) *could fly from conquest to conquest, and from Paris to London, when it freezes. We make a sad figure with pinched cheeks and blue noses. I will return by violet-tide, and if your Grace is really jealous, as I trust, of Madame de Monaco, I will sacrifice her to you the first moonlight night after my arrival—provided there is no dew.*
>
> (32.25)

The final proviso—human frailty qualifying heroic ardor—epitomizes the nature of their epistolary relationship at this early stage. Instead of coarsening into self-parody, Walpole's improbable adaptation of the classical progress-piece balances the tender and the grotesque. We are left with a teasing little capriccio on a stately theme: not Reynolds's *Lady Sarah Bun-*

bury Sacrificing to the Graces but *The Honourable Horatio Walpole Sacrificing to Her Grace of Grafton.*

The first spate of reports from Paris, September – December 1765, draws to a relaxed and genial close in a letter to George Selwyn. Writing to a celebrated man of wit, Walpole abstains from a deliberate parade of cleverness; writing to an habitué of Parisian society, he tones down displays of local color; writing to a devout Francophile, he softens or suppresses negative opinions. Because Selwyn had equipped him with letters of introduction to various social luminaries, Walpole concentrates on tracing his developing relationships with these (now mutual) friends, chief among them Madame du Deffand. A refugee from English politics, he refuses to dwell on French parliamentary affairs, preferring instead to share his literary pilgrimages with a fellow votary of Madame de Sévigné:

> *The Hôtel de Carnavalet sends its blessings to you. I never pass it without saying an* Ave Maria de Rabutin Chantal, gratiae plena! *The Abbé de Malherbe has given orders that I should see Livry whenever I please. Pray tell me which convent was that of* Nos Soeurs de Sainte Marie, *where our friend used to go on the evening that Madame de Grignan set out for Provence?*
>
> (30.206–7)

The letter furthers the impression of solidarity by dismissing with composure those very subjects that had fired Walpole's indignation two months earlier:

> *I forgot to tell you that I sometimes go to Baron d'Olbach's, but I have left off his dinners, as there was no bearing the authors, and philosophers, and savants, of which he has a pigeon-house full. . . . In short, nonsense for nonsense, I like the Jesuits better than the philosophers. . . . Madame de Deffand says I have* le fou moquer, *and I have not hurt myself a little by laughing at whisk and Richardson, though I have steered clear of the chapter of Mr Hume; the only Trinity now in fashion here.*
>
> (30.208–9)

To a far greater extent than in the letters we have just been considering, this "idle" patchwork of news and gossip (30.207), stitched together by means of the artless "à propos," conforms to Walpole's pronouncement that "letters ought to be nothing but extempore conversations upon paper" (33.318). Like all Walpole's letters it is a performance, but a performance thoroughly content to remain—and to be judged—impromptu.

THE GORDON RIOTS

The Gordon Riots of 1780 began on Friday, 2 June, when a large anti-Catholic mob, led by the fanatical Lord George Gordon, presented a petition to the House of Commons for repeal of the Toleration Act of 1778. The mob laid siege to both Houses of Parliament until late that evening, then proceeded to plunder and set fire to the chapels of the Sardinian and Bavarian embassies. During the weekend several Catholic schools, houses, and chapels in the vicinity of Moorfields were put to the torch. On Tuesday, 6 June the rioters ransacked and burned the houses of Justice Hyde, Sir John Fielding, and Lord Mansfield; attacked Newgate, freed the prisoners, and set the building aflame; and "liberated" the inmates of Bridewell and the New Prison. On 7 June, "Black Wednesday," attacks on private property, Protestant as well as Catholic, proliferated, and the army was finally called out to restore order. During the afternoon and evening mob action reached a pitch of violence and wanton destruction: Holborn Distilleries were plundered and fired, as well as the King's Bench and Fleet Prisons. Late that night, the Bank of England was repeatedly (though unsuccessfully) attacked. By Thursday, 8 June ten thousand troops were patrolling the streets of London. On Friday order had finally been reestablished, and Lord George Gordon committed to the Tower. It has been estimated that during the week of violence over 450 rioters were either killed or wounded; damages ran into the hundreds of thousands.[20]

20. This paragraph is based on the information collected by J. Paul de Castro in *The Gordon Riots* (London: Oxford University Press, 1926).

Walpole wrote to six people about the riots. These letters fall into two categories: the dispatches sent to Lady Ossory, William Mason, and Sir Horace Mann (in which Walpole writes "to the moment"), and retrospective epitomes drawn up for William Cole, Lord Harcourt, and Lord Strafford. The dispatches can be grouped in three distinct phases, which correspond to Walpole's movements during the week of troubles. In schematic form:

PHASE 1
{
To Lady Ossory, Saturday 3 June (London)
To Mason, Sunday 4 June (Strawberry Hill)
To Mann, Monday 5 June (Strawberry Hill)
To Lady Ossory, Tuesday 6 June (Strawberry Hill)
}

PHASE 2
{
To Lady Ossory, Wednesday 7 June (London)
To Lady Ossory, Thursday 8 June (London)
To Lady Ossory, Friday 9 June (London)
To Mason, Friday 9 June (Strawberry Hill)
}

PHASE 3
{
To Lady Ossory, Saturday 10 June (Strawberry Hill)
To Mann, Wednesday 14 June (Strawberry Hill)
}

A rapid summary of Walpole's activities will provide a context for this outline. On Friday morning, 2 June, he arrived in London from Strawberry Hill. During the day he saw nothing out of the ordinary save for "a few blue cockades here and there" (33.174), worn as badges of the Protestant Association. That evening at eight he called on his niece the Duchess of Gloucester; about nine the Duke arrived from the House of Lords, and described the tumult there. Then Walpole supped with General Conway, who told him what had passed in the House of Commons. The Phase 1 reports to Lady Ossory, Mason, and Mann (3 June – 6 June) are based on these two eyewitness accounts, and on news from his cousin Thomas Walpole, who rescued the wife of the Sardinian ambassador.

On Saturday, 3 June, Walpole returned to Strawberry Hill, where he remained until Wednesday, 7 June, hearing only rumors (33.181, 183). Wednesday evening marks the beginning of Phase 2: Walpole traveled about the city "to learn and see and hear" (33.185–86)—first to Gloucester House, where he watched the flames from the King's Bench Prison; then to Lord Hertford's; then to General Conway's, where he had supper and watched "either the Fleet prison or the distiller's" on fire (33.187). After supper he returned to the Hertfords' house, then traveled back to "my garrison in Berkeley Square" (33.186), from which he wrote to Lady Ossory in the small hours of the morning. On Thursday he paid another visit to Gloucester House, and received further intelligence from his printer Kirgate, his niece Mrs. Keppel, Lady Albemarle, and Conway. Early Friday afternoon Walpole left for Strawberry Hill, writing to Mason that same evening and to Lady Ossory and Lord Harcourt on Saturday. The following Monday he wrote to Strafford, and on Thursday to Cole.

Of the three sets of letters that emerge directly out of the flux of events, the one to Lady Ossory most nearly resembles a series of dispatches from the front. In fact Walpole describes himself as a war correspondent at the beginning of the first letter about the riots: "I know that a governor or a gazetteer ought not to desert their posts, if a town is besieged, or a town is full of news—and therefore, Madam, I resume my office . . ." (33.174). But Walpole's interpretation of this office ensures that the gazettes to Bedfordshire—jaunty and well-bred, always graphic but never painful—remain suitable for consumption at the teatable. Exploiting a style of sudden pauses, choppy rhythms, and abrupt splicing of details, he makes himself into a messenger who is determined to inform without alarming, to purvey news without tears.

The tone of the first letter (3 June) is half-shocked, half-amused. Walpole's description of the disheveled peers, though it professes outrage, contains a playfully subversive element of knockabout farce:

> *The Duke had reached the House with the utmost difficulty,*
> *and found it sunk from the temple of dignity to an asylum of*
> *lamentable objects. There were the Lords Hilsborough, Storm-*
> *ont, Townshend, without their bags, and with their hair*
> *dishevelled about their ears, and Lord Willoughby without his*
> *periwig, and Lord Mansfield, whose glasses had been broken,*
> *quivering on a woolsack like an aspen. Lord Ashburnham had*
> *been torn out of his chariot, the Bishop of Lincoln ill-treated,*
> *the Duke of Northumberland had lost his watch in the holy*
> *hurly-burly, and Mr Mackinsy his snuff-box and spectacles.*
> *Alarm came that the mob had thrown down Lord Boston and*
> *were trampling him to death—which they almost did. They*
> *had diswigged Lord Bathurst on his answering them stoutly,*
> *and told him he was the Pope and an old woman—thus*
> *splitting Pope Joan into two.*
>
> (33.175–76)

Such phrases as "holy hurly-burly," and comparisons as
"quivering on the woolsack like an aspen," suggest that, in the
hands of a Samuel Foote, this scene might easily have been
transformed into an amusing afterpiece. The undercurrent
of flippancy continues into the second letter; back at Strawberry Hill, Walpole is disposed to make light of the whole
matter: "I know no more of Saint George Gordon, but that I
would change his last name into Cordon, and baptize him
with a halter" (33.180–81).

Even the letters from Phase 2, written after Walpole returned to London on "Black Wednesday," react to the catastrophe with boyish high spirits: "I am heartily glad I am come
to town, though never was a less delicious place; but there was
no bearing to remain philosophically in the country, and hear
the thousand rumours of every hour, and not know whether
one's friends and relations were not destroyed" (33.183–84).
As they are presented to Lady Ossory, the riots provide an
opportunity for chivalric fun and games:

> *It will probably be a black night—I am decking myself with*
> *blue ribbands like a May-day garland—horsemen are riding*

by with muskets. I am sorry I did not bring the armour of
Francis I to town, as I am to guard a Duchess Dowager and
an heiress—will it not be romantically generous if I yield the
latter to my nephew?

(33.186)

Walpole deliberately underplays the disaster by speeding
through the unmitigated horrors and dwelling whenever possible on ludicrous or picturesque sidelights, such as the incident of Lord George and the King: "If anything can surprise
your Ladyship, it will be what I am going to tell you. Lord
George Gordon went to Buckingham House this morning
and asked an audience of the King—Can you be more surprised still?—He was refused" (33.185).

Even at the most serious stage of the riots Walpole's point
of view remains fundamentally spectatorial. "Horrible" the
events may be (33.187), but in this correspondence they are
made to resemble the horrors of Gothic fiction, which cause
an almost agreeable *frisson*. Walpole surveys the scene from a
distance, while positioning Lady Ossory behind him, as it
were, so that she is always at several removes from the action:

I was at Gloucester House between nine and ten. The servants
announced a great fire; the Duchess, her daughters and I
went to the top of the house, and beheld, not only one but two
vast fires, which we took for the King's Bench and Lambeth;
but the latter was the new prison, and the former at least was
burning at midnight. . . . Thence I went to General Conway's,
and in a moment a servant came in and said there was a great
fire just by. We went to the street door and thought it was St
Martin's Lane in flames, but it is either the Fleet prison or the
distiller's.

(33.187)

In contrast to Pepys's account of the Great Fire, for example,
the narrator never quits his lofty vantage point: we seem to be
watching a *son et lumière* spectacle rather than the Gordon
Riots themselves. The closest Walpole brings himself and his
reader to direct engagement is the encounter with various

witnesses, who arrive like messengers in classical tragedy to describe the terrible events that have been occurring offstage:

> *Henry and William Conways [sic] arrived and had seen the populace break open the toll-houses on Blackfryars Bridge and carry off bushels of halfpence which fell about the streets, and then they set fire to the toll-houses. General Conway's porter has seen five distinct conflagrations.*
>
> *Lady Hertford's cook came in, white as this paper.* He is a German Protestant; *he said his house had been attacked, his furniture burnt, that he had saved one child and left another with his wife whom he could not get out; and that not above ten or twelve persons had assaulted his house. . . . I sent my own footman to the spot in Woodstock Street; he brought word there had been eight or ten apprentices who made the riot, that two life-guard-men had arrived and secured four of the enemies.*

(33.188–89)

Yet at the end of the same letter that collects this testimony Walpole dismisses the subject with a witticism, just as if he had been attending a performance of a Shakespearean tragedy: "as it is now three in the morning, I shall wish you good night and try to get a little sleep myself, if Lord George Macbeth has not murdered it all—I own I shall not soon forget the sight I saw from the top of Gloucester House!" (33.190).

When in Phase 3 Walpole steps forward to convey his own feelings of sorrow, the style plunges abruptly into an ersatz tragic idiom. Newly minted language turns stale; vivid perceptions are replaced by shopworn sentiments. The more Walpole exclaims, the more his emotions seem mechanically fomented:

> *Last night when sitting silently alone, horror rose as I cooled—and grief succeeded, and then all kinds of gloomy presages. For some time people have said, where will all this end? I as often replied, where will it begin?—It is now begun, with a dreadful overture; and I tremble to think what the chorus may be! The sword reigns at present—and saved the*

*capital! What is to depose the sword?—is it not to be feared
on the other hand, that other swords may be lifted up?—What
probability that everything will subside quietly into the natural
channel?—nay, how narrow will that channel be, whenever
the prospect is cleared by peace! What a dismal fragment of an
empire!—yet would that moment were come, when we are to
take a survey of our ruins!—That moment I probably shall
not see.*

(33.194–95)

The glut of empty questions draws our attention to a rhetorical posturing that seems manufactured for propriety's
sake. Fortunately Walpole discards the inauthentic rant at the
end of his last dispatch:

*. . . mercy on us! we seem to be plunging into the horrors of
France in the reigns of Charles VI and VII!—yet, as extremes
meet, there is at this moment amazing insensibility—within
these four days I have received five applications for tickets to
see my house! one from a set of company who fled from town
to avoid the tumults and fires. I suppose Aeneas lost Creüsa by
her stopping at Sadler's Wells.*

(33.196)

We are back in the cosy world of Strawberry Hill, where epic
figures shrink to human dimensions, and foibles rather than
atrocities are the order of the day. The nightmare has turned
out to be rather picturesque after all.

The letters to William Mason contrast sharply with those to
Lady Ossory: devoid of lively details and bantering asides,
they encumber a minimum of narration with a maximum of
lugubrious commentary. Walpole justifies this imbalance by
pointing out that Mason already knows what has happened:
"All yesterday I had not a minute's time to write you a line, so
you will have seen all the particulars in the common papers"
(29.51). Yet in no other major correspondence does the fact
that he has been scooped stop Walpole from reporting the
news in his own special way. When he writes to Mason, on the
other hand, his primary purpose is to sound what W.S. Lewis

has called "the dolorous note of doom" (28.xxx). A sour, cynical, and disgruntled correspondent gets what he gives— in this instance, long harangues against Gordon and the dire consequences of religious fanaticism:

> *Nothing ever surpassed the abominable behavior of the ruffian apostle that preached up this storm. I always, you know well, disliked and condemned the repeal of the popish statutes, and am steadfast in that opinion, but I abhor such Protestantism as breathes the soul of popery, and commences a reformation by attempting a massacre. The frantic incendiary ran backwards and forwards naming names for slaughter to the mob: fortunately his disciples were not expert at assassination, and nobody was murdered for the gospel's sake. . . . Violence, unsupported by general national union, will, like Lord [George] Gordon's frenzy, but precipitate destruction, and in its progress be imbued with every act of injustice. That lunatic, whom I should less severely condemn if I saw nothing in him but lunacy, is horridly black in my eyes, for you know it is my most conscientious opinion that no man has a right to expose any life but his own on any disputable tenet in religion or government, still less on suspicions or jealousies: but I wander, from indignation against him, and will finish lest I dissert, instead of amusing you with news.*

> (29.52, 54–55; my italics)

To use Walpole's own word, Mason the rabid political partisan receives his just "disserts."

On Tuesday, 6 June, when he had no reason to suspect that Friday's troubles were not subsiding, Walpole told Lady Ossory that he would be going to town the following day (33.183). To Mason he puts a heroic construction on his return: "I could not bear to sit here in shameful selfish philosophy, and hear the million of reports, and know almost all I loved in danger, without sharing it" (29.55). The disingenuous extravagance of this claim sets the mood for Walpole's second letter (Friday, 9 June), which makes liberal use of words like "slaughter," "desperadoes," and "villains." If in the Ossory letters Walpole labors to preserve a humorous touch, here he strains for the histrionic. Events are seen through a thick rhetorical varnish, which reduces everything to the same "browner horror":

> *My printer whom I had sent out for intelligence came not*
> *home till past nine the next morning, I feared he was killed,*
> *but then I heard of such a scene. He had beheld three sides of*
> *the Fleet market in flames, Barnard's Inn at one end, the*
> *prison on one side and the distiller's on the other, besides*
> *Fetter and Shoe Lanes, with such horrors of distraction,*
> *distress etc., as are not to be described; besides accounts of*
> *slaughter near the Bank.*
>
> (29.56)

These horrors "are not to be described" not because they are indescribable: the letters to Lady Ossory and Horace Mann prove the contrary. Rather, Walpole is composing a jeremiad-philippic, in which specific details merely constitute the vehicle for extended denunciation. He has switched genres: story-telling has given way to pamphleteering.

We can watch Walpole blurring the vivid images of riotous disorder in accordance with his shift in purpose. One brief comparison will illustrate this Masonic seachange. For Lady Ossory, Walpole sketches a scene that anticipates *A Tale of Two Cities:* "Some hundreds are actually dead about the streets with the spirits they plundered at the distiller's; the low women knelt and sucked them as they ran from the staved casks" (33.193). In the version sent to Mann, the precise verbs of action ("plundered," "knelt," and "sucked") disappear: "At the great popish distiller's they swallowed spirits of all kinds, and Kirgate saw men and women lying dead in the streets under barrows as he came home yesterday" (29.59). The women have become statistics rather than subjects worthy of Rowlandson or Daumier.

Like the hero of one of Mason's own forgettable dramas, Walpole struts and frets in a haze of stock tragic diction:

> *I have so much exerted my no strength, and had so little*
> *sleep these two nights, that I came hither today for some rest. It*

will be but grim repose. . . . *My bosom I think, does not
want humanity, yet I cannot feel pity for Lord Mansfield. I
did feel joy for the four convicts who were released from Newgate within twenty-four hours of their execution, but ought not
a man to be taught sensibility, who drove us cross the
Rubicon? I would not hurt a hair of his head: but if I sigh for
the afflicted innocent, can I blend him with them? . . . If I live
to see you again,—but ifs are the subterfuges of those that
cannot support present unhappiness; whoever can descry connection between* this *instant and anything that is to come is
the* maximus *of all Apollos. Adieu.*

(29.59–61)

The haze has lifted in the letters to Sir Horace Mann, which
in substance as well as tone fall between the letters to Lady
Ossory on the one hand and those to William Mason on the
other. In his description of the "siege of Parliament" Walpole
offers a plentiful supply of particulars, but orders them in a
neutral fashion—neither as material for farce nor as fuel for
sermonizing:

*In the meantime, the peers going to their own chamber, and
as yet not concerned in the petition, were assaulted—many of
their glasses were broken, and many of their persons torn out
of the carriages. Lord Boston was thrown down and almost
trampled to death; and the two secretaries of state, the Master
of the Ordnance and Lord Willoughby were stripped of their
bags or wigs, and the three first came into the House with their
hair all dishevelled. The chariots of Sir George Saville and
Charles Turner, two leading advocates for the late toleration,
though in opposition, were demolished; and the Duke of Rich-
mond and Burke were denounced to the mob as proper objects
for sacrifice.*

(25.53–55)

His attitude to Lord George is shrewd and levelheaded, the
operative term "indignant" rather that "outraged":

*You will be indignant that such a mad dog as Lord George
should not be knocked on the head. Col. Murray did tell him
in the House that if any lives were lost, his Lordship's should*

join the number—nor yet is he so lunatic as to deserve pity.
Besides being very debauched, he has more knavery than mis-
sion. What will be decided on him I do not know—every man
that heard him can convict him of the worst kind of sedition—
but it is dangerous to create a rascal a martyr.

(25.55)

Always mindful of Mann's status as expatriate outsider, Walpole augments the summary accounts sent to Lady Ossory. In
his letter to Ampthill of 3 June he had skimmed over the
plundering of the Bavarian embassy: "Old Haslang's chapel
has undergone the same fate, all except the ordeal. They
found stores of mass-books and run tea" (33.178). The same
subject in the letter to Mann (5 June) warrants two sentences
as well, but these explain as they narrate:

Old Haslang's chapel was broken open and plundered; and as
he is a prince of smugglers, as well as Bavarian minister,
great quantities of run tea and contraband goods were found
in his house. This one cannot lament, and still less, as the old
wretch has for these forty years usurped a hired house, and
though the proprietor for many years has offered to remit his
arrears of rent, he will neither quit the house nor pay for it.

(25.54–55)

As in his description of the coronation, Walpole tells Mann
everything he needs to know without ostentatious glossing.

Walpole's sardonic attitude to Lord George and the week's
madness has not altered in his second letter: "The Pope needs
not be alarmed: the rioters thought much more of plundering those of their own communion, than his Holiness's flock.
To demolish law and prisons was their next great object; and
to release prisoners, the only gospel-work they performed"
(25.61). Walpole augments his previous report with several
discrete fragments of information, but declines to piece together anything approaching a complete history:

It is all unaccountable, and I can yet send you no consistent
narrative. Much appears to have been sudden fury, and in
many places the act of few. In other lights it looks like plan

*and deep premediation—whether it will ever be unravelled I
know not: or whether, like the history of darker ages, falsehood
will become history, and then distant periods conjecture that we
have transmitted very blundered relations—but when I know
so little of what has passed before my own eyes, I shall not
guess how posterity will form their opinions.*

(25.63–64)

Walpole's refusal to strike attitudes or indulge in snap judgments does credit to his maturity as an epistolary historian: he
will not risk letting the moods or ideologies of the moment
warp the understanding of those future readers whom Mann
represents. The difference between the Walpole of the letters
to Mason and the Walpole of the letters to Mann is the difference between Junius and Gibbon, a cartoon by Gillray and
a portrait by Sir Thomas Lawrence.

Just as he was about to receive Walpole's diatribe on the
Gordon Riots, William Mason wrote to Lord Harcourt, complaining of "very long political and literary letters from a certain friend of ours who is at times so spitfire and at times so
frighted . . ." (29.39, n. 1). Cruel as this gibe certainly is, it also
contains an element of truth: Walpole's second "spitfire" harangue to Mason precedes by a day his "frighted" report to
Lord Harcourt. In a letter of elaborate, almost obsequious
courtesy—a courtesy which Harcourt duly made fun of to
Mason[21]—he writes as one member of the aristocracy to another, giving thanks that "your Lordship and all my friends
escaped massacre" and rejoicing that "the frantic
wretches . . . seem to be awed" (35.503, 505). This letter exposes in its most blatant and therefore least attractive form the
hauteur of the man who, in Macaulay's phrase, "never for a
moment forgot that he was an Honourable,"[22] the man who
could write about the riots: "Two fortunate circumstances are

21. "I called on him the other morning and though I was not quite his
dearest, or his *best* Lord, as formerly, I was well enough received, and as I had
nothing to reproach myself with regard to him *I* was not the least embar-
rassed . . ." (29.353).
22. Macaulay, 2.99.

amazing, that a large portion of the town was not burnt, and that not a single person of any name is killed" (25.62). Yet despite Walpole's assumption of a shared outlook, his brittle commentary and feeble witticisms betray a fundamental lack of ease; what should be included and how it should be told are unresolved issues. The letter-writer describes his own effort as a rapid drawing: "How poor a sketch have I given your Lordship of what Guicciardin would have formed a folio!" (35.505). But to the reader of the preceding letters to Lady Ossory and Sir Horace Mann, it resembles nothing so much as a shaky studio copy after a masterly original.

To Lord Harcourt, Walpole sends a L'Allegro sketch, to Lord Strafford an Il Penseroso postmortem, half editorial and half moral essay. Secure in his longstanding friendship with Strafford, Walpole has relaxed: no longer does he quip nervously, as to Harcourt, or lash out hysterically, as to Mason. Though it summarizes Walpole's activities during the riots, the letter is focused on three larger issues: religion, politics, and the consequences of excessive ambition. It begins on a poised, reflective note:

> *If the late events had been within the common proportion of news, I would have tried to entertain your Lordship with an account of them; but they were far beyond that size, and could only create horror and indignation. Religion has often been the cloak of injustice, outrage and villainy: in our late tumults, it scarce kept on its mask a moment; its persecution was downright robbery; and it was so drunk, that it killed its banditti faster than they could plunder.*
>
> (35.354)

The first half of the second paragraph, which telescopes the events of the past week, introduces a Whiggish meditation on the lessons to be learned from this tragedy:

> *It will still be not quite an unhappy country, if we reflect that the old constitution, exactly as it was in the last reign, was the most desirable of any in the universe. It made us then the first people in Europe . . . but can we take a better path than that*

*which King William pointed out to us? I mean the system he
left us at the Revolution. I am averse to all changes of it—it
fitted us just as it was.*

(35.355)

Finally, Walpole asks a question that, alone of all his numerous rhetorical queries on the subject of the riots, seems to
emerge from a genuine concern for what he deeply values:
"Oh! when shall we have peace and tranquillity?" (35.355).
The question ushers in a peroration that might be taken for
part of an *Idler* essay, so powerfully do style and subject bring
Johnson to mind:

> *I have long doubted which of our passions is the strongest—
> perhaps every one of them is equally strong in some person or
> other—but I have no doubt but ambition is the most detestable,
> and the most inexcusable; for its mischiefs are by far the most
> extensive, and its enjoyments by no means proportioned to its
> anxieties. The latter, I believe, is the case of most passions—
> but then all but ambition cost little pain to any but the pos-
> sessor. An ambitious man must be divested of all feeling but
> for himself. The torment of others is his high road to hap-
> piness. Were the transmigration of souls true, and
> accompanied by consciousness, how delighted would Alexander
> or Croesus be to find themselves on four legs, and divested of a
> wish to conquer new worlds, or to heap up all the wealth of
> this!*

(35.355–56)

The compassion, the discernment, the Olympian perspective,
the gnomic truths set forth in balanced clauses: these traits
witness to a maturity we do not customarily associate with
Walpole, and mark an improbable rapprochement between
two less than kindred spirits.

The transformations of voice and viewpoint come to an end
with Walpole's letter to William Cole (15 June 1780). Beginning with the dispatches to Lady Ossory, we have encountered
a richly varied parade of identities: the vivacious gazetteer, the
choleric politician, the equable historian, the aristocratic but-
terfly, and the meditative moralist. In this final piece of testi-

mony Walpole assumes the mask of a placid, molelike
antiquarian, who yearns chiefly for the uninterrupted pursuit
of his researches into the heraldic arms of the Boleyn family.
Walpole ostentatiously treats the riots as a bothersome inter-
ruption, easily described and quickly forgotten: "You may like
to know one is alive, dear Sir, after a massacre and the con-
flagration of a capital. . . . I can give you little account of the
origin of this shocking affair. Negligence was certainly its
nurse, and religion only its godmother" (2.223–24). The turbulence in London may be compounded by campaigning in
East Anglia: "I hope your electioneering riotry has not nor will
mix in these tumults" (2.224). From the standpoint of the
scholarly recluse, the nuisance value of both riots and elections
is equivalent. In the concluding section of the letter, Walpole
compares himself and Cole to the inhabitants of Tahiti, whose
island solitude has been destroyed by impertinent intruders:

> *You and I that can amuse ourselves with our books and*
> *papers, feel as much indignation at the turbulent, as they have*
> *scorn for us. It is hard at least that they who disturb nobody,*
> *can have no asylum in which to pursue their innoxious*
> *indolence! Who is secure against Jack Straw and a whirl-*
> *wind? How I abominate Mr Banks and Dr Solander who*
> *routed the poor Otaheitians out of the center of the ocean, and*
> *carried our abominable passions amongst them!*
>
> (2.225)

Walpole the war correspondent is now Walpole the peaceable
islander. The distance between these two roles is perhaps the
best possible measure of a letter-writer who, like "the thin
Camelion fed with Air, receives / The colour of the Thing to
which he cleaves."[23]

---

23. John Dryden, "Of the Pythagorean Philosophy," ll. 616–17, in *Fables Ancient and Modern*. See *The Poems and Fables of John Dryden*, ed. James Kinsley (London: Oxford University Press, 1958, 1962), p. 808.

Part Three

Intimacy Failed and Achieved

5

James Boswell among the "Libertines"

I regretted your last letter was so short. I beg you to write
often and fully. Nothing can oblige me more.
                                        —*Wilkes to Boswell, 22 June 1765*

"**W**HO then shall decline the converse of the pen?"
Not James Boswell, as his surviving correspondence, supplemented by the "Register of Let-
ters," amply attests. *Copia,* however, does not necessarily imply *ingenium:* the forty-two volumes of Horace Walpole's correspondence are misleading in this respect. Before the
discovery of either the Malahide or the Fettercairn papers,
C.B. Tinker declared in no uncertain terms: "He [Boswell] is
not a great letter-writer, for letter-writing to him is seldom an
end in itself. He usually has some secondary purpose in
mind."[1] Tinker's opinion, coming from a scholar with a profound intuitive insight into Boswell's character and literary
genius, cannot be brushed aside. It might be argued that subsequent discoveries cause us to modify or disregard this forthright judgment. Yet the reactions of two subsequent
generations of Boswellians have remained notably muted or
evasive.[2] Their silence tacitly acknowledges what the Yale Ar-
chives document in abundance: the majority of Boswell's let-

---

1. C.B. Tinker, *Young Boswell* (Boston: The Atlantic Monthly Press, 1922),
p. 172.
2. See, for example, *The Correspondence of James Boswell and John Johnston of
Grange,* ed. Ralph S. Walker (New York and Toronto: McGraw-Hill, 1966),
pp. ix, xxix. Also *The Correspondence of James Boswell with Certain Members of
The Club,* ed. Charles N. Fifer (New York and Toronto: McGraw-Hill, 1976),
p. xxii.

ters represent written substitutes for oral communication, the outline of a conversation rather than the conversation itself.

Unlike Virginia Woolf, whose diaries and letters divide the laurels evenly between them, Boswell does not sustain his two enterprises with anything approaching equal commitment. Primary energies are lavished on the daily record, that teeming repository of "the fact imagined." Heir of Richardson and Sterne, he writes to the moment, yet reserves the harvest of the journal largely to himself. Consequently, the reader will search in vain for letters that respond to Temple's injunction ("Throw yourself out upon paper, let me know all the movements of your heart!"), or that exploit to any significant degree the possibilities of the epistolary genre. One misses everywhere a sense of vocation: the majority of Boswell's social letters have been conceived and executed as fillips to friendship, ways of spanning the void with the simplest possible scaffolding.

There are of course notable exceptions to this rule. In a revealing pair of correspondences—one with Henry Herbert, tenth Earl of Pembroke, the other with John Wilkes—Boswell makes a sustained bid for intimacy with two capable, charming, deeply licentious men of affairs.[3] With Pembroke he fails, despite his Lordship's good will and marked talent for epistolary camaraderie; with Wilkes he succeeds, against all the odds. To juxtapose these two correspondences is to understand both the limitations of Boswell's craftsmanship and the strains which threaten the letter-writer's enterprise. Furthermore, his letters to Wilkes bring Boswell momentarily into the company of such as Lady Mary, Cowper, Gray, and Walpole—those who have mastered the principles of epistolary *discordia concors,* the humane art of intimacy.

3. The Boswell-Pembroke correspondence has yet to appear in print. In 1924 C.B. Tinker published what had then been recovered of the Wilkes-Boswell letters, but Tinker's text is unreliable, and his notes are sparse and unhelpful. Since that time the discoveries at Fettercairn House have added considerably to the material now available for study. Both correspondences will eventually be published in the Yale Research Edition, parceled out chronologically in a series of miscellaneous volumes.

On the surface Pembroke and Wilkes have much in common, as men and as correspondents. Both were full-fledged participants in the *vita activa*—members of a social and professional élite, accomplished conversationalists, and successful rakes. Their letters catch a distinctive tone of voice—colloquial, confident, spirited, at ease. They also stake out and cultivate common ground: wine, women, politics, books. The two correspondences could accurately be labeled "libertine," in both senses of the word ("unrestrained in conduct or language"; "characterized by habitual disregard of moral law, especially with regard to the relation of the sexes"). Yet here the similarities end. Quite apart from the testimony of the journal, Boswell's letters communicate and confirm the true spontaneity of his friendship with Wilkes. To our delight, the playful intimacy which governed their personal intercourse translates successfully into epistolary terms. The shared preoccupation with "the noble passion of lust," the sly jokes and innuendos, the easy badinage, all preserve a certain stylized and endearing innocence. Pembroke's bawdy, in contrast, reminds us of an Aretino or a Rochester; it is seldom playful, and often has a cutting edge. To the sympathetic reader, Boswell's correspondences with Wilkes and Pembroke suggest parallel yet contrasting treatments of the same subject—one by Boucher, the other by Bronzino.

I

Unlike the notorious Mr. Wilkes, Lord Pembroke requires a brief introduction. The only child of the ninth Earl by Mary Fitzwilliam, daughter of the fifth Viscount Fitzwilliam of Mt. Merrion, Henry Herbert spent his childhood at Wilton and Pembroke House, Whitehall. He attended first Wandsworth and then Eton, but left college on his father's death in 1750. While on the Grand Tour (1751–55), he was presented to George II, who appointed him cornet in the First Dragoons. In 1756, Pembroke took his seat in the House of Lords, married Lady Elizabeth Spencer, daughter of the third Duke of Marlborough, and was appointed Lord-Lieutenant of Wilt-

shire, Lord of the Bedchamber to the Prince of Wales, and
Major in the First Foot Guards. Lady Pembroke bore him two
children: George, Lord Herbert (1759–1827), and Lady
Charlotte (1773–84). From 1760 to 1762 Pembroke cam-
paigned in Germany, rising to the position of Major-General
in command of the cavalry brigade. In 1764 he was appointed
Colonel of the Royal Dragoons, and in 1767, promoted to the
rank of Lieutenant-General.

Lord Pembroke's two ruling passions were horses and
women. In 1761, he published a treatise on military equita-
tion, fruit of his experience on the Continent, which went
through four editions in the author's lifetime. This popular
manual was followed in 1768 by *Instructions for the Education of
the Cavalry*. Apart from these two published works, the family
correspondence amply documents his consuming interest in
the breeding, training, and riding of horses. Pembroke himself tended to view his dedication to the sexual chase in equi-
ne terms: "I knew the Pretender's Wife at Brussells, and liked
her exceedingly, so well, that I should be happy to endeavor
to prevent the extinction of the Stuart Line, with a view of
mending the breed too, for hitherto it has been a miserable
one."[4] During a long career of vigorous Casanovan activity,
Pembroke outraged public opinion with three particularly
flagrant amours. In 1762, he eloped with Elizabeth Catherine
Hunter, a Maid of Honor and daughter of Thomas Hunter,
an Admiralty lord. The affair proved ideal grist for Horace
Walpole's mill:

> *Lord Pembroke, Earl, lord of the Bedchamber, Major-Gener-*
> *al, possessed of ten thousand pounds a year, master of Wilton,*
> *husband of one of the most beautiful creatures in England,*
> *father of an only son, and himself but eight and twenty, to*
> *enjoy this assemblage of good fortune, is gone off with Miss*
> *Hunter, daughter to one of the lords of the Admiralty, a*
> *handsome girl with a fine person, but silly and in no degree*

---

4. *Henry, Elizabeth and George*, ed. Lord Herbert (London: Jonathan Cape,
1939), pp. 44–45.

*lovely as his own wife, who has the face of a Madonna, and
with all the modesty of that idea, is dotingly fond of him.*[5]

In November of the same year, Kitty Hunter bore Pembroke a son, anagramatically christened "Augustus Retnuh Reebkomp." In 1763, the errant Earl pensioned off his mistress and was reconciled, officially at least, to Lady Pembroke. Then in 1768, while traveling on the Continent, he sired an illegitimate daughter, Caroline Medkaff or Medkalf.[6] The third scandal erupted in 1784, when Pembroke "set off with an opera-girl and left poor Lady Pembroke and his dying daughter, the most amiable, beautiful girl that ever was seen."[7] This liaison lasted until Pembroke's death: when Boswell visited Wilton in 1792 he "felt it strange, and regretted it, that so amiable a man should have contracted such dissolute habits, and at this very time, instead of living respectably with his charming Countess, had Baccelli, the superannuated dancing Courtesan, in a *Cassino* in the neighborhood."[8]

Even between scandals, Pembroke was notoriously unfaithful. Clouds of witnesses abound. According to Horace Walpole, "We are not surprised at any extravagance in his Lordship's morals."[9] Sir Joshua Reynolds spoke severely on the subject: "Never having been accustomed to refuse himself

5. *Horace Walpole's Correspondence*, 42 vols., ed. W.S. Lewis et al. (New Haven: Yale University Press, 1937–83), 22.9–10.

6. *Henry, Elizabeth and George*, p. 41.

7. Margaret Boswell to James Boswell, 29 May 1784, MS. Yale C 439. All quotations from the Boswell Papers are printed with the permission of Yale University and the McGraw-Hill Book Company (William Heinemann Ltd.). Subsequent references to the correspondence appear parenthetically in the text.

8. Journal, 20 Aug. 1792. Citations from Boswell's journal appear parenthetically in the text. Quotations have been transcribed from published sources—either the relevant volumes of the McGraw-Hill trade edition (for journal entries through 28 Sept. 1785) or volume eighteen of the *Private Papers of James Boswell from Malahide Castle in the Collection of Lt-Colonel Ralph Heyward Isham*, ed. Geoffrey Scott and F.A. Pottle (Privately printed, 1928–34), hereafter referred to as the Malahide Papers.

9. *Walpole's Correspondence* 25.497.

anything, he has gone on on all occasions: 'I will have this woman'; but by taking such gratifications he loses what is more valuable: the consequence which he should have in his country from his rank, fortune, and talents" (Journal, 28 Aug. 1785). The most telling comment of all came from Boswell's confidante Margaret Stuart, herself the long-suffering wife of an aristocratic man-about-town: "she restricted somewhat her latitude as to plurality of women, for she found fault with Lord Pembroke for going to other women when it made my Lady very uneasy. '*There*,' said she, 'is the crime—to do what gives another pain'" (Journal, 31 Mar. 1775).

The record looks black: even the editor of Pembroke's family correspondence, Lord Herbert (subsequently sixteenth Earl), tosses *pietas* to the winds and brands his rakish ancestor an "unfaithful, coarse, bad-tempered and restless" man.[10] One is reminded forcibly of Samuel Richardson's heated marginalia, those frantic attempts to tarnish the reputation of Lovelace, who still persists in seducing the readers of *Clarissa* as he beguiles the heroine. For thanks to Pembroke's letters, his undeniable charms continue to turn readers into friends, and to neutralize the censorious reflexes activated by bawdy text or chequered context. At their best, the letters effervesce, capturing the writer's flow of conversation. "In my last I said that asking to hear from you was like asking for Champagne. Whether this Champagne having been in Scotland is improved, like Madeira having been in the East Indies, I shall not say. But, believe me, it has a relish like what one imagines of Nectar or any exquisite liquour of which one has read" (Boswell to Pembroke, 22 Mar. 1775, MS. Yale L 1033). The adage holds true: *le style est l'homme même*—witty, poised, cultured, vivacious; possessed of a more than superficial appreciation for drama, painting, and architecture; passionate yet capable of irony and even self-mockery. To understand Boswell's relationship with Pembroke, we must

10. *Henry, Elizabeth and George*, p. 38.

hold in abeyance the impulse to condemn, and taste the champagne with an unprejudiced palate.

Boswell's correspondence with Pembroke stretches from August 1774 to August 1792—fifty-seven notes and letters in all, twenty-eight from Boswell and twenty-nine from Pembroke. These figures are, however, somewhat misleading. The period of real vitality extends from March 1775 (Boswell tests the water by announcing his plan to visit London that spring, then angles successfully for an invitation to Wilton) to November 1784, when Pembroke's protracted wanderings on the Continent effectively terminate the regular exchange of letters. The correspondence flourishes with greatest vigor during the six years from 1777 to 1783: during that period Boswell could count on finding Pembroke in London, and therefore quicken the relationship in person.

Boswell first met Pembroke in 1768, when the Earl, an eager reader of the *Account of Corsica,* obtained from him a letter of introduction to General Pasquale Paoli. The acquaintanceship was renewed in Edinburgh in 1774: Boswell, warmed by Pembroke's affable manner, "asked the honour of his company to dinner. He agreed to come any day I pleased. I fixed Thursday. I said, 'We Corsicans should meet'" (Journal, 7 Aug. 1774). The dinner proved to be a great success: "everything went on with as much ease and as genteelly as I could wish" (Journal, 11 Aug. 1774). Before returning to London, Pembroke called to ask if Mrs. Boswell had any commissions, and noticing Boswell's bass fiddle standing in a corner, asked: "'Are we brother bassers, as well as brother Corsicans?'" (Journal, 20 Aug. 1774). During the next month, Boswell wrote to Pembroke three times to request his aid in bringing the petition for clemency in the John Reid case to the attention of the King (To Pembroke, 20 Aug., 5 Sept., 22 Sept. 1774, MSS. Yale L 1029–31). Pembroke's letters about the appeal are remarkable for their courtesy and compassion, and testify even at this early stage to a genuine regard for Boswell (From Pembroke, 2 Oct. 1774, MS. Yale C 2195).

Over the next decade Boswell, the proud recipient of an open invitation, breakfasted, dined, and drank convivially with Pembroke during his regular jaunts to London: "My Lord said to me, 'Whenever you are disengaged, you will always find this miserable manger'" (Journal, 21 Apr. 1778). Pembroke entertained Boswell at Wilton, took him to Court, lent him his chariot, discussed raking, Mrs. Rudd, the theatre, and "Beauties *de toute espece*" (To Pembroke, 30 Apr. 1782, MS. Yale L 1048). At all times he paid him the heady compliment of talking "to me of all the fine people as if I had known them as well as he did" (Journal, 3 Apr. 1775). In 1782 Pembroke visited Edinburgh, but Boswell was unable to invite him to "my Romantick place of Auchinleck in Ayrshire" owing to the illness of Mrs. Boswell and the death of Lord Auchinleck (To Pembroke, 3 Feb. 1783, MS. Yale L 1049). From 1784 to 1792, when Boswell once again visited Wilton, they saw each other only briefly and at infrequent intervals. The journal's last account of Pembroke, for all its surface gaiety, strikes a muted elegiac note:

> After having been many years without seeing him except for a few minutes occasionally, I was delighted to find him walking about with me familiarly arm in arm and chatting freely as formerly. I saw that nothing was wanting but opportunity to keep up our gay friendship. But he is, like many others, and those very amiable too, an out of sight out of mind man. . . . When I looked at him, I perceived his figure and gait older. But when he talked, his countenance and manner were as lively as ever. (Journal, 20 Aug. 1792)

Within a year and a half, Pembroke is dead.

The Boswell-Pembroke relationship can be analyzed with confidence precisely because it never reached the stage of true friendship, with a friendship's elusive textures of motive and response. Their correspondence harbors fleeting moments of intimacy, the product of loss or sudden self-revelation: both men experience and transmit their sense of shock at the death of young Lady Eglinton, though Boswell promptly distances emotion in a way which Pembroke apparently finds impossible. The deaths of Topham Beauclerk and David Garrick likewise jolt the correspondents into un-affected communion; in a melancholy letter from Sicily, where Pembroke is searching for distraction after the death of his young daughter, he rejects the comfort of belief in per-sonal immortality and alludes poignantly to the ineffectual charms of travel: "I will say nothing of myself, for I can not run away from myself. Le Chagrin monte en croupe, and sticks close to me" (From Pembroke, 2 Nov. 1784, MS. Yale C 2215). Though they may approach the threshold of intimacy, however, ultimately Boswell and Pembroke stop short, pos-tures hardened into place. It is Boswell who must be held chiefly accountable for this state of arrest: in letter after letter he stresses the Earl's "condescension" in writing to him, a mere Scots advocate.[11] The sense of ease and relative equality which might well have germinated over the span of years is forestalled by formal gestures of deference. Even an epistol-ary friendship, fostered by verbal artifice, cannot take root when one of the partners insists upon reminding the other (and himself) of their discrepancy in rank.

One can trace the source of Pembroke's fascination for Boswell to the Earl's position in the social hierarchy and to his family's illustrious past. The *atavis edite regibus* motif, which surfaces constantly in the letters, also heralds Pembroke's first major appearance on the stage of the journal, and accom-panies his departure from it eighteen years later. Uncertain whether Pembroke will be able to attend the dinner party at James's Court, Boswell suffers the torments of an ambitious host whose noble guest of honor may not appear: "I had a good company besides his Lordship invited; but he being the capital person, I should have been much disappointed if he did not come. My vanity made me very anxious. . . . The com-

11. "While I was quite free and gay with Lord Pembroke, I could not help recollecting how little pretension I in reality had to be so, having been edu-cated narrowly and awkwardly, and though I had been from Scotland roving for a small portion of my life, was now an advocate at Edinburgh" (Journ. 3 Apr. 1775).

pany was: Lord Pembroke (whom I contemplated as the *Herbert,* the master of *Wilton,* etc., and was happy that one of the family of Auchinleck entertained an English nobleman of such rank)" (Journal, 11 Aug. 1774). The same adolescent delight in reflected glory, a carefully cultivated sense of wonder alloyed by self-congratulation, permeates Boswell's description of the second and final trip to Wilton: "it was truly a *sight* to me, a man of *multitudinous imagination,* to behold *my daughters Veronica and Euphemia* sitting with the Earl of Pembroke in his immense drawing room, under the Family Picture of Vandyck, undoubtedly the most capital Work in Portrait painting that the World has to shew. How many *Scotch Lairds* are there whose daughters could have such an honour?" (Journal, 20 Aug. 1792). These two entries, congruent framing images (a Pembroke chez Boswell, three Boswells chez Pembroke), represent a triumph in social engineering, remind us of Boswell's dedication to incarnating the improbable (Samuel Johnson in the Hebrides, Johnson dining amicably with Wilkes), and reenact what Bertrand Bronson has called Boswell's "instinctive ideal," whose first essential ingredient is that "the inner excitement shall be exactly commensurate with the external stimulus."[12] It is precisely the failure to match spirit to event, emotion to setting, that mars the first visit: "In vain did I recollect that I was now at Wilton, that I was with the Earl of Pembroke, that here was the very walk where Sir Philip Sidney composed his *Arcadia.* I was sunk and nonchalant" (Journal, 21 Apr. 1775). Even when Boswell cannot relish to the full the piquancy of the Pembroke connection, his desire to store up epistolary treasures keeps him writing. The summary in the Register of Letters for 10 August 1779 reveals unequivocally this basic motivation: "Earl of Pembroke a lively letter to continue a Correspondence of which I am vain" (MS Yale M 254).

In his more buoyant moments, however, Boswell not only

12. Bertrand Bronson, *Johnson Agonistes and Other Essays* (Berkeley and Los Angeles: University of California Press, 1965), p. 79.

admires but succumbs to Pembroke's allure. Unlike Desmond McCarthy, the fabled Bloomsbury talker whose conversation when recorded fell limp from the pen, Pembroke's unmistakable presence not only molds his correspondence but reaches us through the medium of the journal and the testimony of expert witnesses, chief among them Pasquale Paoli:

> In the morning the General and I talked of Lord Pembroke. I said he never dwelt long enough on any subject. He gives flashes like lightning. They shine, but they are gone before you can see objects by them. Said the General, "He's a fine electric machine. He gives shocks of fire, but it does not continue. It explodes." I said, "He has not much wit but much liveliness. He has a most crystal conversation, but there are not many diamonds in it." Thus did we metaphorize the Earl. (Journal, 22 Apr. 1778)

One remarks with interest that it is Paoli with whom Boswell chooses to "metaphorize" Pembroke: unlike as these two soldiers are, Boswell admires in both a certain "natural" unforced wit, and a relaxed affability which marks the true aristocrat. He defines his ideal in the *Account of Corsica:* "How much superiour is this great man's idea of agreeable conversation to that of professed wits, who are continually straining for smart remarks, and lively repartees. . . . Paoli, though never familiar, has the most perfect ease of behaviour. This is a mark of a real great character. The distance and reserve which some of our modern nobility affect is, because nobility is now little else than a name in comparison of what it was in ancient times."[13]

In the *Journal of a Tour to the Hebrides,* Boswell's praise of Pembroke links the companion with the correspondent:

> This day we were to begin our *equitation,* as I said: for *I* would needs make a word too. It is remarkable, that my noble, and to me most constant friend, the Earl of Pembroke, (who, if there is too much ease on my part, will be pleased to pardon what his

13. *Journal of a Tour to Corsica,* ed. G.B. Hill (London: Thos. de la Rue and Co., 1879), pp. 195, 205.

benevolent, gay, social intercourse, and lively correspondence, have insensibly produced,) has since hit upon the very same word.[14]

The attraction of the letters resides in those very qualities which distinguish the man himself—"fluent vivacity" and "velocity of ideas" (Journal, 21 Apr. 1778). Both Boswell and Pembroke share with the other letter-writers we have been examining the taste for a candid, conversational, "artless" correspondence, which centers on important topics of mutual interest. As Howard Anderson and Irvin Ehrenpreis have noticed, "The letter belongs to a human relationship in a way that is rarely seen in either earlier or more recent periods. Just as the writer's purity of style must act to reveal his character, so the 'substantive' nature of the letter must constitute a link between the correspondents."[15] Pembroke is uniquely placed to skim the cream off of London (be it the latest in sexual scandal, political maneuvering, international news, or literary fashion), and to transmit it to Boswell, languishing in darkest Edinburgh. Pembroke's "enlivening" epistolary champagne is compounded of a heady mixture of ingredients: risqué anecdotes and *double entendre;* a liberal sprinkling of French and Italian phrases, proverbs, and interjections; frequent allusions to Continental writers such as Voltaire and Montesquieu; pungent, uncharitable remarks. Pembroke has little tolerance for those he considers incompetent, pompous, or otherwise ridiculous: "Your friend Dr. Johnson was quite good humoured, and talkative the other night at Lord Lucan's blue stocking. He neither bit, kicked, nor knocked down any body" (From Pembroke, 11 May 1780, MS Yale C 2208). His salty *sermo humilis,* choppy syntax, and associative rather than logical transitions all contribute to the impression that one is listening to a racy, spoken monologue:

14. *Boswell's Life of Johnson,* 6 vols., ed. G.B. Hill, rev. L.F. Powell (Clarendon Press, 1934–50), 5.131. Hereafter referred to as *Life.*
15. *The Familiar Letter in the Eighteenth Century* (Lawrence: University of Kansas Press, 1966), p. 277.

I can not agree with you, My Dear Sir, in thinking it extraordinary, that two Irish men should make one Scotch man drunk. The only account I could get formerly of Stopford from a countryman of his, after a ten years absence, was, that my friend was fit to mount with the Masters. Growling vexation of spirit, and hot climates have, since that time, made a sober man of him. . . . Tell him, pray that I really don't know how to answer his last stupid letter . . . a Lady, a middle aged North Briton, who keeps a house of intrigue in Cleveland Row, Mrs. Chambre, has fallen in love with him, and christened him the handsome Captain. He was a good deal alarmed here with a swelled face, occasioned by a rotten stump—He called it a Palsy, and went up to town, a good deal frightened, for advice, in consequence of which a dentist punched out the tooth root, and the Palsy subsided. Lord William Gordon however swears, that his mouth, far from being horizontal yet, is now as pretty a diagonal, as a man shall see of a summer's day.
(From Pembroke, 12 Mar. 1775, MS. Yale C 2196)

Pembroke's letters may suffer from a lack of polish, yet one could never find them "stricken with sterility," as Strachey did Cowper's. They are not "dried up," but instead overflow with "the juices of life." In them, "the vast and palpitating eighteenth century" presses energetically forward.[16]

There is nonetheless a dark side to Boswell's involvement with Pembroke. A dangerously seductive model, the Earl helped Boswell to justify to himself those irresponsible sexual drives and that debilitating flight from maturity which brought him such unhappiness. Pembroke served as precedent and authority for Boswell's "Asiatick" indulgences, his fantasies of Macheath-like gallantry, and his impulse to escape from the duties of adult life. Boswell was fascinated by the Earl's avid pursuit of pleasure, unimpeded by feelings of guilt or religious scruple. Above all, Boswell's precarious sense of self-discipline was sapped by Pembroke's success: in acting out his libidinous impulses, even when their object

16. Lytton Strachey, *Characters and Commentaries* (New York: Harcourt, Brace and Co., 1933), p. 48.

happened to be a Maid of Honor, he seemed to escape without suffering any lasting setback.

In this instance, at least, Lovelace does *not* get his just deserts. To Boswell's amazement and admiration, Pembroke gallops confidently through life, snatching pleasure at will, while the best Boswell can do in the way of vicarious enjoyment is to accept the loan of his chariot: "It was a delightful vehicle, especially when I recollected it was *The Earl of Pembroke's* (Journal, 21 Apr. 1778). In what ultimately degenerates into a pathetic attempt to match flirtation for flirtation, Boswell adopts in his letters the confident air of a sexual connoisseur: "The last with which your Lordship was pleased to honour me was particularly agreeable from the very high compliment which it paid to my fair countrywoman Lady Eglintoune. It was truly flattering to my taste in the most elegant of all subjects—fine women—to have it confirmed by so excellent a judge as the Earl of Pembroke" (To Pembroke, 20 Oct. 1777, MS. Yale L 1036). As their correspondence dwindles into silence, Boswell, seeking to recover common ground, broaches the same tired subject with a depressingly mechanical air. His last word on the subject of "fine women," the condemnation of Pembroke's liaison with the Italian courtesan, is spoken in the unconvincing guise of the moralist.

The effect of Pembroke's company and example on Boswell's conduct can be inferred from their correspondence, the journal, and from his wife's agitated reaction. On 17 June 1783, Pembroke concludes his letter to Boswell: "I heard a bird sing of Claret, and lost wigs, hats, and watches after we parted in Dover street. These losses did not, I hope, make a pathetick, unsalutory epistle necessary to Mrs. B." (From Pembroke, MS. Yale C 2214). Boswell responds ruefully: "The Bird sung too truly. I am quite ashamed of my coarse intemperance, after a day of elegant felicity. My watch was my only loss in my night walks. Je ne suis pas entré au temple de Cythère. Je me porte bien" (To Pembroke, 29 June 1783, MS. Yale L 1050). The two men refer to an episode which receives

unusually full treatment in the journal, and illustrates all too
clearly the psychological undercurrents of the relationship:

> Then Le Telier's: Lord Pembroke, Lord Herbert, General
> Stopford, Major Skeffington, Dean Marlay. I was in highest
> spirits, and called out, "I am as happy as a prince. I was re-
> solved to be happy, and I *am* happy." But I drank too much
> wine and too fast, and was intoxicated, and talked too openly
> of *myself* and my licentious indulgences, and my wife's good-
> ness. . . . And joked Lord Pembroke about his licentiousness.
> Talked of the great aera to which we looked forward: his
> Lordship's being Lord Lieutenant of Ireland, and how we
> should all have good places. They were all vastly gay too. . . . I
> was not quite at my ease till I had called them all by their
> names: "Stopford," etc., except the lords. I make it a principle
> never to encroach on their rank. . . . All quite in high tavern
> style. We parted, I believe, near ten. . . . I sallied forth shock-
> ingly drunk, and picked up a girl in St. James's Street. Went
> into park; sat on bench and toyed, but happily had sense
> enough left not to run risk. However, when we rose and walk-
> ed along, missed my watch. (Journal, 23 May 1783)

It is all there—the extravagant *Gemütlichkeit* masking a sense
of social inferiority; the tension between the impulse to com-
pete with a famous rake and the need to cultivate a possible
patron; the inappropriate confessions; the guilt and remorse.
Margaret Boswell did not require a contrite letter to intuit,
and to be disturbed by, the consequences of Boswell's continued association with Pembroke (From M. Boswell, 29 May
1784, MS. Yale C 439). One wonders whether, had she lived
to accompany her family in 1792, Mrs. Boswell would have
agreed to take her daughters to Wilton. Another concerned
observer, Sir Joshua Reynolds, lectured Boswell vehemently
on the subject. To judge from a fragmentary passage in the
journal, it seems clear that Boswell had justified his flirtation
with Mrs. Rudd by citing Lord Pembroke's conduct. Reynolds's response was prompt and censorious (Journal, 28
Aug. 1785).

The most obvious reason which drew Boswell to Pembroke
and kept him responsive has been left to the last—the hope of
finding a "place" through the Earl's patronage. As Ralph
Walker has observed: "Boswell's social life was lived partly
among men of place and prominence (cultivated sometimes
because he 'collected' notabilities as another might collect rare
coins, sometimes because by their influence he hoped to further his ambitions). . ."[17] Though it was not made explicit until well into the correspondence, the motive of professional
ambition existed from the outset (To W.J. Temple, 18 Mar.
1775). Boswell first broaches the subject to Pembroke in his
letter of 28 March 1778. Playing with the conceit of "the
Northern Profound," he gingerly extends a rhetorical question into a bid for patronage: "But I wish you could assist me
to keep *above* altogether. I have tolerable parts and more application than most people. Why then should I not be employed in England? . . . I would come to the bar here, had I a
fortune or a place sufficient to support me decently. Your
Lordship will allow me to talk with you a little about this,
when I have the honour and very great pleasure of meeting
you" (To Pembroke, MS. Yale L 1039). The theme becomes
insistent as Boswell bids first for the position of Judge Advocate, and then for that of Solicitor General. All these attempts
come to naught: Pembroke expresses his good will, and even
speaks to Conway on Boswell's behalf, yet stresses his inability
to win even small favors from the powers that be. However,
Boswell continues to harp on the same subject. Prompted to
make an extravagant declaration of devotion, he contrives at
the same time, by invoking a feudal analogy, to suggest that
Pembroke has not fulfilled his lordly obligation:

> *Allow me, My Lord, to take this opportunity of most sincerely
> assuring the Earl of Pembroke, that I constantly feel a very
> grateful sense of his Lordships uniform goodness to me. His
> Lordship has not had an opportunity as yet, to obtain promo-
> tion for me, which I heartily regret, both on his Lordships*

17. Walker, p. xxviii.

account and my own. But he has been pleased to honour me with so many marks of his kind attention which I highly value, that upon the honour of an ancient Scottish Baron, I should rejoice exceedingly to have it in my power to serve him essentially, and should with eagerness exert myself to prove my attachment. . . . It is really hard that I cannot afford to have my winter-residence in London. £500 a year of addition to what I have, would enable me as acts of parliament say. Were your Lordship Lord Lieutenant of Ireland!—I should hope to have the matter settled.

(To Pembroke, 29 June 1783, MS. Yale L 1050)

In 1786, with Pembroke absent on the Continent, Mountstuart indifferent, and his law practice failing, Boswell turns his attention to another earl, more powerful but also more capricious, Lord Lonsdale.

To any reader of the London Journal the Pembroke correspondence transmits an insistent feeling of *déjà vu:* we have encountered this relationship before, enacted by a younger pair of men—twenty-three-year-old Jamie Boswell and Alexander Montgomerie, tenth Earl of Eglinton. In fact one might tentatively suggest that Boswell is seeking to reconstitute the elements of his sprightly companionship with Lord Eglinton, who was responsible for his social and sexual initiation in 1760, and who died tragically in 1769. Like Pembroke, Eglinton was clever but indolent, charming but unreliable, an enthusiastic sportsman and indefatigable rake, a Lord of the Bedchamber who traveled in the "circles of the great, the gay, and the ingenious." The parallels could be multiplied. Indeed, Boswell's portrait of Eglinton captures the essence of the Pembroke we come to know through his correspondence: "My Lord's character is very particular. He is a man of uncommon genius for everything: strong good sense, great quickness of apprehension and liveliness of fancy, with a great deal of humour. . . . He has at the same time a flightiness, a reverie and absence of mind, with a disposition to downright trifling. . . . He is very selfish and deceitful, yet he has much good nature and affection" (Journal, 27 Nov.

1762). Pembroke, like Eglinton before him, symbolizes the seductive pleasures of London—"the bustle and glitter of the metropolis, endless parties, the opportunity to combine gross physical pleasure with the refined intellectual delights of the theatre and of high conversation."[18] Without Pembroke, the experience of London remains incomplete: "Your Lordship's absence from London has been much felt by me. Often have I looked with affection at Pembroke House, with a pleasing recollection of the many happy hours I have been indulgently permitted to pass there, as an easy friend. But I trust there is much good to come yet. For, I have at last *resolved* to transplant myself (To Pembroke, 24 June 1784, MS. Yale L 1052). Sadly, once Boswell has uprooted himself from Scotland, the happy hours, like Pembroke's company itself, elude his grasp.

II

"J'y trouvais le fameux M. Wilkes dans son exile; et malgré ses ecrits mordants contre les Ecossois, nous etions tres bonne Compagnie ensemble" (To Rousseau, 3 Oct. 1765, MS. Yale L 1115). Boswell's lifelong friendship with John Wilkes took shape during three weeks of constant companionship amid the ruins and citrus groves of southern Italy, March 1765. Condemned as an outlaw for seditious and blasphemous libel, Wilkes had followed his mistress of the moment from Paris to Naples, where he resolved to rent a villa and attend to a pair of major literary projects, his History of England and an edition of Charles Churchill's works. Boswell did not encounter Wilkes for the first time in Naples: an introduction at Bonnell Thornton's in London, 23 May 1763, had led to further engagements mentioned in the memoranda but deliberately unrecorded in the journal (for Wilkes was then both bad and dangerous to know). By the time Boswell left for Utrecht, he knew Wilkes well enough to request franks from him ("to astonish a few staunch North-Britons") and to entertain

18. Frederick A. Pottle, *James Boswell: The Earlier Years, 1740–1769* (London: Heinemann, 1966), p. 50.

thoughts of a correspondence. Early in 1765, they overlapped in Turin for one day without actually meeting, then encountered each other by chance in the Customs House at Rome. However, their real intimacy did not develop until the following month, when Boswell, disappointed by the Imperial City and longing for congenial company, followed Wilkes south. Though unfortunately Boswell never wrote up his cryptic notes, the existing record of his wide-ranging conversations with Wilkes has been admirably expanded and analyzed by Robert Warnock[19] and by F.A. Pottle.[20] It documents one of the happiest, most intense experiences of Boswell's life, the seedbed of the ensuing correspondence.

For Boswell, who remembered it for the rest of his life with unshadowed nostalgia, the Neapolitan sojourn coalesced into a magical spot of time, an idyllic moment apart imbued with its own special aura: "The many pleasant hours which we past together at Naples, shall never be lost. The remembrance of them shall inspirit this gloomy mind while I live" (To Wilkes, 22 Apr. 1765, MS. Yale L 1283). Throughout the recovered correspondence, Boswell harks back repeatedly to "the Elysium of Italy": fifteen years after the event, he signs a letter, "Yours as at Naples," and refers to himself later as "an old Vesuvius fellow traveller," "your old classical companion." Though perhaps not to the same degree, Wilkes also looked back with fondness: "You have made me know halcyon days in my exile, and ought not to be surpriz'd at my chearfullness and gaiety, for you inspir'd them" (From Wilkes, 27 Apr. 1765, MS. Yale C 3088). For both men the time together in Italy constituted the imaginative capital of their friendship—a fund of shared experience upon which they could draw in gloomier times, a frame of reference with which to measure the pleasure of the moment, an unfailing source of genial recollection. Amid the sadness and entropy of his final years, Boswell could still rekindle faint memories

19. Robert Warnock, "Boswell and Wilkes in Italy," *ELH* 3 (1936): 257–69.

20. Pottle, pp. 207–8.

of the "tempo felice": "It was however truly pleasant to me to see John Wilkes enjoying life as I have seen him do in Italy, six and twenty years ago" (Journal, 16 Nov. 1792).

It was at all times a decidedly improbable friendship: Whig vs. Tory, free-thinker vs. High Church *dévot*, Englishman vs. Scotsman. A confrontation lurked in every letter: while celebrating Wilkes's charms and attainments, Boswell at the same time zealously repudiated the demagogue's politics and the agnostic's flippant irreverence. As Boswell himself emphasized, in an acute definition of his alchemical talents as man and correspondent:

> *I have no small pride in being able to write to you with this gay goodhumour for I do in my conscience beleive you to be an ennemy to the true Old British constitution, and to the order and happiness of Society. That is to say I believe you to be a very Whig and a very Libertine. But Philosophy can annalyse human Nature, and from every Man of parts can extract a certain quantity of good. Dare I affirm that I have found Chearfullness knowledge wit and generosity even in Mr. Wilkes. I suppose few Crucibles are so happily constructed as mine: and I imagine that I have a remarkable talent for finding the gold in your Honours Composition.*
> (To Wilkes, 22 Apr. 1765, MS. Yale L 1283)

Boswell never let the attractive side of Wilkes blind him to those traits he deemed repugnant. In Professor Pottle's opinion, "His affection for Wilkes is another striking case—perhaps the most striking that could be adduced—of his power of combining sympathy with adverse moral judgement."[21] It was unattractive ambition, and not earnest indignation, that almost killed the friendship: during the period of the tumultuous Middlesex controversy, Boswell played the prudent young lawyer, and cautiously kept his distance, refusing to greet Wilkes or to visit him in jail, much less to correspond with him. It says much for Wilkes, and the cohesive force of memory, that the two were able in large measure to recapture

21. Pottle, p. 208.

their previous intimacy once the jailed outlaw had attained respectability.

Except when the association threatened to jeopardize his career, Boswell reveled in his dealings with Wilkes, who attracted him for a number of interlocking reasons. The collector's instinct for catching the attention of celebrities and documenting the privileged relationship helps to explain certain features of the correspondence—the request that Wilkes's letters be signed, and sealed "in such a manner that I may not tear a word in opening them"; the sprightly tone and provocative content, designed to elicit "lively sallies from *a Lord Mayor of London*" (To Wilkes, 26 May 1775, MS. Yale L 1291). Wilkes often obliged by replying "as if in repartee." Indeed Boswell informed Wilkes frankly that he was preserving his letters "in my Cabinet": as Geoffrey Scott observed, "he foresaw that his intercourse with famous men could be re-enacted, after his death, not only in the great *Life*, but in his correspondence. He stored their letters; he made copies of his own.[22]

First Wilkes's notoriety as ministerial gadfly, then his celebrity as Mayor and M.P. fascinated Boswell and aroused his trophy-hunting impulses; Wilkes's blithe spirits and wit converted an admirer into a boon companion. Throughout the journal, letters, and *Life*, "gay" is Wilkes's distinguishing epithet. As C.B. Tinker deduced from a fraction of the evidence now before us: "it was the gaiety of Wilkes that appealed essentially to Boswell. It was clear to him that Wilkes, with all his eminence, never forgot to 'shine,' never forgot that social intercourse with the world of wit was the goal of human endeavour."[23] At the beginning of their friendship, as at the end, Wilkes's "perpetual gayety" never ceased to astonish Boswell, whose own emotions tended to fluctuate violently from hour to hour. Boswell's reaction on the Grand Tour holds true for subsequent meetings: "He is as gay in his Exile,

22. Malahide Papers 1.1.
23. Tinker, p. 69.

as when he used to make Aylesbury ring with his jovial mirth.
. . . Wilkes is a most extraordinary Man. He has constant flow
of health and spirits, and is allmost the only instance of a man
of genius who enjoys continual happiness in this strange
World" (To John Johnston, 11 May 1765, MS. Yale L 753).
Hampered by his own unreliable "flow of spirits," Boswell en-
vied both the constancy and the intensity of Wilkes's buoyant
temperament. As he explored the paradox of Wilkes in a letter to Rousseau, Boswell penetrated beyond the superficial
antitheses which shocked Gibbon,[24] to expose perhaps the
most profound reason for his interest in Wilkes:

> *C'est un Homme qui a beaucoup pensé sans etre sombre, et qui
> a fait beaucoup de mal sans etre Scelerat. Ses Sallies vives et
> males sur les objets moraux me remuoient assez agreablement
> l'Esprit, et m'elargirent mon Prospect, en me convaincant que
> Dieu pouvoit créer une ame totalement tranquille et gaye,
> nonobstant la reflection allarmante qu'on doit mourir.*
> (To Rousseau, 3 Oct. 1765, MS. Yale L 1115)

Wilkes, an "infidel" like Hume, embraced life without needing to believe in immortality. For Boswell, on the other hand,
as for Samuel Johnson, even the prospect of eternal damnation was preferable to that of annihilation.[25]

The other quasi-formulaic epithet bestowed upon Wilkes,
"classical," identifies a second compelling accomplishment—
the scholarship which culminated, late in Wilkes's life, in editions of Catullus and Theophrastus. When Boswell refers to
Wilkes as "my classical companion," he is simultaneously al-
luding to their time in "Parthenope," "hac regione classica,"
and paying tribute to a fund of knowledge that far surpasses
his own (To Wilkes, 2 Mar. 1765, MS. Yale L 1281; *Life* 5.339,
n. 5). Wilkes's learning is not inert: wit leavens the mastery of
classical texts and is fueled by it. Wilkes, Boswell feels, represents that rare combination—a gentleman, a *bon vivant*, and a

24. See *Memoirs of the Life of Edward Gibbon*, ed. G.B. Hill (London: Methuen and Co., 1900), p. 301.
25. See W.J. Bate, *Samuel Johnson* (New York and London: Harcourt
Brace Jovanovich, 1977), p. 451–52.

scholar, whose company ministers to melancholy at all hours. In fact Boswell honors Wilkes for those traits he holds in common with Johnson: "classical learning, modern literature, wit, and humour, and ready repartee" (*Life* 3.79).

An additional factor enriches the friendship—Boswell's feeling of gratitude for Wilkes's kindness, generosity, and encouragement at moments of stress, self-doubt, or high emotion. Wilkes comforted Boswell when he learned of his mother's death, entertained him in London at his mistress's establishment in Kensington Gore, and lent him money. More important from our perspective, he had faith in Boswell's unusual literary genius. In Italy, Wilkes urged Boswell to "Publish what you have by you"; he assured Boswell that "Posterity shall do justice to him as an excellent author"; and after the publication of the *Life*, he "was clear for my publishing my travels" (Memoranda, 18 Feb. 1765; From Wilkes, 22 June 1765; Journal, 3 Jan. 1793). In an age which valued the general, the public, and the reticent—in art as in life—Wilkes confirmed Boswell's bent for self-revelation, exploration, and celebration: "he was the first person who ever assessed Boswell's peculiar gift correctly and encouraged him to exploit it. . . . Long before any one else, he recognized that Boswell's letters and journal were significant art, not the mere exercises that Boswell himself considered them."[26]

The correspondence between Wilkes and Boswell was conceived and conducted as a sparring match, a duel of wits between affectionate opponents who rarely overstepped the implicit bounds of civilized repartee:

> *I am so far from being disgusted at your freedom with me, that it quite charms me. I regretted your last letter was so short. I beg you to write often and fully. Nothing can oblige me more. You are an enthusiast in your way for your King, as you say, and your religion. The French always call'd me an enthusiast for liberty. We have both the* vivida vis, *which marks us.*
>
> (From Wilkes, 22 June 1765, MS. Yale C 3089)

26. Pottle, pp. 208–9.

The quotation from Lucretius ("Ergo vivida vis animi per-
vicit," *De rerum natura* 1.72) highlights the salient feature of
the exchange, its tone of controlled raillery, proper to "men
of wit and humour." Yet while the letters may remind us at
times of the published correspondence with the Hon. Andrew Erskine, they are, it should be added immediately, more
poised, more mature; their lightheartedness never sinks to
puerile imitations of *Tristram Shandy*. Unlike the calculated
badinage of the Erskine collection, these letters, truly "easy,"
"desultory," and "ingenious," display "a pretty vein of
Jocularity" blessedly undilated by youthful preciosity.[27]

The two chief subjects of humor are religion and politics;
Scotland and Scotsmen run a distant third. From the outset
Boswell warns Wilkes to tread softly, lest his own deeply felt
convictions be bruised: "I glory in being an enthusiast for my
King and for my Religion, and I scorn the least appearance of
dissimulation. As the gay John Wilkes you are most pleasing
to me, and I shall be glad to hear from you often. Let serious
matters be out of the question, and you and I perfectly har-
monise" (To Wilkes, 15 June 1765, MS. Yale L 1285). When
Wilkes ignores or forgets the limits of mockery, as in his letter
of 5 March 1779, the reaction is swift and sharp:

> *The last letter which you wrote to me was full of wit and
> pleasantry, for which I thank you. But when I found you
> saying that "you were sorry there was not another rebellion in
> Scotland as you* hoped *for another Culloden" I was* really
> shocked. . . . *Your boast is humanity. You should not then
> even* in sport *throw a* firebrand *which may scorch a freind.
> I desire and expect a pleasing apology from you . . .*
> (To Wilkes, 23 Mar. 1779, MS. Yale L 1294)

Boswell mingles direct reproof with an indirect use of classical
and biblical allusion, and in doing so exemplifies the proper
mode of appeasement—a return to the rules of the epistolary
game. In contrast to these two treacherous topics, jokes

27. *Boswell's Correspondence with the Honourable Andrew Erskine*, ed. G.B. Hill
(London: Thos. de la Rue, 1879), pp. 14, 40.

against Scotsmen were docilely received. Boswell bears with patience if not good humor all the shafts Wilkes can shoot. Boswell's attitude is best formulated in his account of the Wilkes-Johnson dinner, at which the two erstwhile adversaries join in abusing the Scots: "All these quick and lively sallies were said sportively, quite in jest, and with a smile, which showed that he meant only wit" (*Life* 3.77). The subject of Culloden, however, is no laughing matter.

Wilkes in all his varied guises (libertine, classicist, gay politician, affectionate friend) calls forth from Boswell one of his finest letters, which deploys literary allusion to carry the burden of meaning, to create a shared world of value, and to forge a bond of cultural and personal solidarity:

> *I ought to have written to you long ago to make an apology for having carried your* Sopha *with me to Scotland. The truth is that I was so dissipated while in London, that I had not leisure to finish the perusal of even that* short enchanting *performance; so it accompanied me home. Surely one may well apply to Crebillon's writings* part *at least of Cicero's elegant panegyrick on polite learning.* Haec studia adolescentiam agunt *with a vengeance; I am not so clear as to* senectutem oblectant. *Your own experience proves to you* delectant domi, non impediunt foris. *Nobody will deny* pernoctant nobiscum, *and that they* peregrinantur *I can bear witness; for without egatism in talking of myself, I remember you studied with as much keeness at Rome and Naples when you was outlawed, as any man could do. I hope to be in London next month, and shall then faithfully restore your* Sopha. *We must contrive to meet oftener than we did last spring, and to drink something more animating than Chocolade; though indeed you and I have such spirits that we scarcely require any thing to increase our vivacity.*

(To Wilkes, 27 Feb. 1779, MS. Yale L 1293)

Unlike many of Boswell's more diffuse letters, this one distills the essence of a friendship: its private subtext emerges from and responds to a unique community of two. Without straining for effect, Boswell adroitly steers his course between the facetious and the stilted. On the surface, the letter concerns the loan of a book, recent events in Scotland, the publication of Wilkes's speeches; its true subject is the friendship itself. The first paragraph juxtaposes Crébillon *fils* to Cicero—a deft yoking of opposites (erotic French *conte* vs. lofty defense of literature) equivalent in the epistolary sphere to the bringing together of Wilkes and Johnson, the contemporary and the classical, the rake and the moralist. Boswell dashes off a witty exercise in mock exegesis: Cicero's "elegant panegyrick" is glossed with deliberate irreverence, to tease Wilkes but also to compliment him on his eclectic taste and distinctive blend of dissipation and scholarship. The fact that in the process a famous passage from the *Pro Archia* is trivialized and even misinterpreted is itself part of the joke.

This game of impudent juxtaposition extends through the final sentence: "We must make a point of having the dinner with Lord Mountstuart, we three only, which was agreed to almost two years ago." Lord Bute's heir and the archpatriot of Middlesex—the expressed wish for such an explosive conjunction of personalities typifies Boswell's strategy in epistolary art as well as social life. He had succeeded once, at Dilly's in 1776; why not try again? Meanwhile, the suggestion dovetails brilliantly with the overall pattern of barbed intimacy.

As this letter demonstrates, Boswell could on occasion put into practice the doctrine of decorum: style and substance are cleverly adjusted to the recipient. High spirits, a sense of ease and assurance, an appreciative audience—all inspire a polished and subtle response. At its most adroit and expansive the Wilkes-Boswell correspondence calls to mind the letters between Mme de Sévigné and Bussy Rabutin—worldly, mocking, and affectionate in turn, spirited, spontaneous, inflected by the cadences of the speaking voice. Both men would have agreed with their seventeenth-century predecessors, that "la lettre est art de s'accorder à autrui. . . . de tenir compte du relatif, c'est-à-dire des nuances des rapports entre correspondants."[28] Above all, their letters transmit "la présence vivante de celui qui écrit."[29] Such a "présence vivante"—all the more compelling for its "art de s'accorder à autrui"—is likewise the signal achievement of the correspondence to which we turn next.

28. Roger Duchêne, *Mme de Sévigné et la Lettre d'Amour* (Paris: Bordas, 1970), p. 109.

29. Duchêne, p. 74.

6

Samuel Johnson and Mrs. Thrale: The "Little Language" of the Public Moralist

> Dr. Johnson wrote a long letter to Mrs. Thrale. I wondered to
> see him write so much so easily.
> —*James Boswell*, Tour to the Hebrides, 25 *August 1773*

LIKE the Lady of Shalott's mirror, epistolary language subdues the outside world; like her loom, it also weaves a private meaning. Yet the major letter-writers of the eighteenth century did not inhabit a solitary palace of art: men and women of letters, they perfected a public voice and the ability to perform in a spotlighted arena. Almost without exception, the mask of the forum prepares us to some degree for the face of the closet. The gap between private features and public persona is least obtrusive in the case of Lady Mary and Boswell. Cowper occupies a middle ground: he neither retreats completely behind the mask nor incurs the risk of continuous self-revelation. The remarkable divergence between Thomas Gray's "official" poetic and "unofficial" epistolary manner prompted Matthew Arnold's interpretation of "he never spoke out." It is the Johnson of the letters to Hester Thrale who exemplifies the far end of the spectrum, the widest possible divorce between *ex cathedra* and *sub rosa* selves.

That the lineaments of the private correspondent differ in essentials from the face of the Rambler was to no one more apparent than to contemporary readers, who had come to equate Johnson with the grave, sonorous, judicial presence implicit in his public oeuvre. Thus the appearance of Mrs.

Piozzi's edition of 1788 jolted many who thought they knew the sage into cautious revaluation. In an anonymous review of the collection, Arthur Murphy, who had introduced Johnson to the Thrales in 1765, formulated the contrast in these terms:

> His letters to Mrs. Thrale are continued [after the death of Henry Thrale] with unremitting attention, and they are often in the language of the heart, full of esteem for her talents, admiration of her wit, and the sincerest gratitude for all her kindness. . . . We here see Dr. Johnson, as it were, behind the curtain, and not preparing to figure on the stage; retired from the eye of the world, and not knowing that what he was then doing would ever be brought to light. We see him in his undress; that is, the undress of his mind, which, unlike that of his body, was never slovenly.[1]

Even Cowper and Walpole, two of Johnson's habitual detractors, grudgingly altered their opinion. After encountering the portrait of Johnson *en pantoufle,* Cowper wrote to Lady Hesketh: "If I remember right, the Letters of Johnson [to Mrs. Thrale] pleased me chiefly on this account, that though on all other occasions he wrote like nobody, in his Letters he expresses himself somewhat in the stile of other folks. For I hate Triplets in Prose, and can hardly think even *His* good sense sufficient counterpoise for his affectation."[2] Horace Walpole "thought Johnson a more amiable character after reading his Letters to Mrs. Thrale"—"but," Boswell is quick to add, "[he] never was one of the true admirers of that great man."[3]

Murphy, Cowper, and Walpole were all reacting to the absence of what, for want of a better term, we may call the Ramblerian voice. Johnson's letters usually resemble a moral

---

1. *Monthly Review* 78 (1788): 325–26.
2. *The Letters and Prose Writings of William Cowper,* 4 vols. to date, ed. James King and Charles Ryskamp (Oxford: Clarendon Press, 1979–), 3.190–91.
3. *Boswell's Life of Johnson,* 6 vols., ed. G.B. Hill, rev. L.F. Powell (Oxford: Clarendon Press, 1935–50), 4.314. All subsequent references to the *Life* will be to this edition.

essay that has been cursorily adjusted to the identity of the recipient. By contrast, only a handful of the letters to Mrs. Thrale adopt the public mode of address. The majority wield a concise, down-to-earth, vigorously colloquial style, akin to the language of the *Lives of the Poets* yet even more fluid and relaxed. This private epistolary style is terse rather than expansive; it relies on simple and compound structures; it exhibits a decided preference for paratactic rather than hypotactic constructions. Nothing could be further from the stock conception of Johnsonese than this lively paragraph embedded in a letter from Ashbourne: "You talk of pine-apples and venison. Pine-apples it is sure we have none; but venison, no forester that lived under the green-wood-tree ever had more frequently upon his table. We fry, and roast, and bake, and devour in every form."[4] The Johnson who pictures and reports himself devouring venison à la Friar Tuck has discarded his *gravitas* for something closer to cap and bells.

What circumstances, emotional as well as material, sparked the vigor and the gaiety of the letters to Mrs. Thrale? The precise nature of the relationship eludes ready-made categories. From James Boswell to Katharine Balderston, the jokes, insinuations, raised eyebrows, quizzical glances, and murky clinical diagnoses have multiplied in a void.[5] Despite the peculiar French letter (307.1) and the sinister padlock, it must be emphasized that nothing close to convincing testimony of

4. *The Letters of Samuel Johnson, with Mrs. Thrale's Genuine Letters to Him*, 3 vols., ed. R.W. Chapman (Oxford: Clarendon Press, 1952), 2.206–7. All subsequent references appear parenthetically in the text.

5. A representative cross section includes the following: James Boswell, "Ode by Dr. Samuel Johnson to Mrs. Thrale upon Their Supposed Approaching Nuptials," in *Boswell: Laird of Auchinleck, 1778–1782*, ed. Joseph W. Reed and Frederick A. Pottle (New York: McGraw-Hill, 1977), pp. 319–21. T.B. Macaulay, "Samuel Johnson," *The Works of Lord Macaulay: Essays and Biographies* (New York: Longmans, Green and Co., 1898), 4.476. Thomas Hitchcock, *Unhappy Loves of Men of Genius* (New York: Harper and Brothers, 1891), chap. 2. Sir Samuel Scott, "Dr. Johnson and Mrs. Thrale," *Nineteenth Century* 116 (1934): 308–18. Katharine C. Balderston, "Johnson's Vile Melancholy," in *The Age of Johnson*, ed. F.W. Hilles (New Haven: Yale University Press, 1949), pp. 3–14. For the most lucid verdict, see James L. Clifford, *Hester Lynch Piozzi* (Oxford: Clarendon Press, 1941), pp. 206–7.

overtly masochistic rituals has been found.[6] What seems most probable is that the two people involved were themselves never inclined to analyze a complex, ultimately volatile mixture of emotions. We therefore must rest content with their own explicit commentary on this *amitié amoureuse*. However complicated, even disturbing, we find Johnson's affection for Mrs. Thrale, he himself never hesitated to stress the intensity of his attachment.

Quite early in their friendship, Johnson wrote to apologize for the failure to send a letter promptly (a lapse entirely characteristic of his other correspondences, but quite unusual in this one): "If my omission has given you any uneasiness, I have the mortification of paining that mind which I would most wish to please" (211). In an undated journal entry, Mrs. Thrale recorded: "[Spe]aking once of His friendly affection for me, [he s]aid kindly, I do certainly love you better [tha]n any human Being I ever saw—better I th[ink] than even poor dear Bathurst . . ."[7] In June 1783, as the ties of friendship began to unravel, Johnson concluded an account of his recent stroke with a pathetic plea: "I have loved you with virtuous affection, I have honoured You with sincere Esteem. Let not all our endearment be forgotten, but let me have in this great distress your pity and your prayers" (850). Later that same year, alarmed by Mrs. Thrale's apparently unmotivated withdrawal of intimacy, he stressed the continued importance of her letters: "Since you have written to me with the attention and tenderness of ancient time your letters give me a great part of the pleasure which a life of solitude admits" (900). Finally, the cry of protest at her second marriage summarizes his perception of their now-vanished bond. A painful sequence of preterites rings the knell of passing friendship as it epitomizes what once had been: "I, who have loved you, esteemed you, reverenced you, and served you, I who long thought you the first of human kind" (970).

6. Walter Jackson Bate, *Samuel Johnson* (New York and London: Harcourt Brace Jovanovich, 1977), pp. 439–41.
7. Quoted in Clifford, p. 88.

In her "Recollections of Dr. Johnson," Frances Reynolds corroborates these fervent testimonials: "On the praises of Mrs. Thrale he used to dwell with a peculiar delight, a paternal fondness, expressive of conscious exultation in being so intimately acquainted with her."[8] This "conscious exultation" was reciprocated, if not matched, by Hester Thrale, who apostrophized Johnson in her journal: "Friend, Father, Guardian, Confident!"[9] W.K. Wimsatt aptly sums up the relationship as it flowered during the decade and a half from 1765 to 1780: "An impressive woman, a woman in most respects unusually gifted, enjoys unusually intimate, tender, and mutually benevolent relations with an extraordinary man."[10]

In light of Johnson's emotional investment in their relationship, it is highly significant that, after the final rupture with Mrs. Thrale, he burned all the letters at his immediate disposal. The gesture symbolized both the angry termination and the melancholy commemoration of a friendship somehow incarnate in the documents themselves. Johnson laid claim to total immolation, of letters as well as memories, in an angry outburst to Fanny Burney: "I drive her quite from my mind. If I meet with one of her letters, I burn it instantly. I have burnt all I can find. I never speak of her, and I desire never to hear of her more. I drive her, as I said, wholly from my mind."[11] Despite the dramatic gesture of closure, however, Johnson could not eradicate his tenderness for the memorials of friendship: as R.W. Chapman has deduced, he did preserve Mrs. Thrale's surviving letters from the general destruction that took place shortly before his death.[12]

The intimacies of the Johnson-Thrale correspondence

8. *Johnsonian Miscellanies*, ed. G.B. Hill (Oxford: Clarendon Press, 1897), 2.272.

9. *Thraliana*, ed. Katherine C. Balderston (Oxford: Clarendon Press, 1942), 1.528 (1 Feb. 1782).

10. W.K. Wimsatt, "Images of Samuel Johnson," *ELH* 41 (1974): 363–64.

11. *Diary and Letters of Madame D'Arblay*, ed. Charlotte Barrett (London: Chatto and Windus, 1876), 1.576.

12. Chapman, 3.298.

were rooted in the domestic world of Streatham Park, the Thrale's principal residence. Johnson, who became an adopted member of the family, called the place "home" (330)—a word charged with the magnetic currents of security, stability, pleasure, and even joy. In striking contrast to the dark and cramped house off Fleet Street, where he dined on a roast from the local cook house, singed his wig with impunity, slept in dirty linen, and dodged a flock of quarrelsome inmates, Streatham offered a welcome sphere of total care.

A set of symbolic polarities informs and enriches the letters to the mistress of Streatham: garden versus city, involvement versus isolation, feast versus famine. Other visitors commented on the charms of the estate; to Susan Burney, for example, it suggested an Edenic peaceable kingdom: "As a *place,* it surpassed all my expectations. The avenue to the house, plantations, etc. are beautiful; worthy of the charming inhabitants. It is a little Paradise, I think. Cattle, poultry, dogs, all running freely about, without annoying each other."[13] But for Johnson alone the Streatham environment offered an escape from physical dilapidation and mental torment. In this "little Paradise" he could slough off the old man, recovering for himself a state of inner peace and communal harmony. And Hester Thrale made the metamorphosis possible. In addition to her social roles as wife, mother, and presiding hostess, she came to occupy the central place in Johnson's private cosmos—at once keeper of the garden, beneficent tutelary deity, and mother/lover Eve.

To be away from Mrs. Thrale and the Streatham milieu was to be exiled from the focus, the center. One constant theme runs through all Johnson's letters to his "mistress": "Do not let separation make us forget one another" (684). He was never in any danger of forgetting her, but might not the opposite prove true? Absent from home, "as you and mistress allow me to call it" (330), Johnson missed many physical comforts (Anna Seward cynically refers to his "cupboard love" for Mrs. Thrale[14]). But primarily he longed for her company and her conversation: "I wish I had you in an Evening, and I wish I had you in a morning, and I wish I could have a little talk, and see a little frolick" (686). Allied to the theme of absence and longing is the subject of governance: "Do you think that after all this roving you shall be able to manage me again? . . . Pray keep strictly to your character of governess" (267, 287). Though expressed in a jocular tone, these references to management and control help us to recognize the most important opportunity Streatham provided: absolution from responsibility, temporary relief from the burden of guilty self-absorption, a precious chance "to give vent to the imagination, and discharge the mind of its own flatulencies" (194).

At Streatham, with Hester Thrale, Johnson escapes from freedom: "When we get together again but when alas will that be? you can manage me, and spare me the solicitude of managing myself" (686). W.J. Bate interprets such wishes as evidence for a "strong element of infantilism" in Johnson's psychological makeup; such regressive symptoms, Bate claims, are "always potentially present in individuals subject to constant 'superego' demand . . ."[15] One need not have recourse to Freud, however, to recognize the basic need for maternal support: "I wish to live a while under your care and protection" (383).

The care and protection Johnson found with the Thrales launched, sustained, and filled his letters. Paradoxically—given his cries of unhappiness from London, Oxford, Lichfield, and Ashbourne—separation could almost be desired, since it intensified rather than thwarted Johnson's love: "Pray contrive a multitude of good things for us to do when we meet, something that may *hold all together*. Though if any thing makes *me* love you more, it is going from you" (752).

14. Anna Seward, *Letters* (Edinburgh: A. Constable and Co., 1811), 2.103.
15. Bate, p. 387.

This recognition guides his vocation as letter writer. Distance creates unhappiness; unhappiness purifies emotion; emotion breeds letters; letters crystallize love. It is important to recognize that Johnson's letters are singularly free of the harsh, deprecating, or surly remarks recorded in Mrs. Piozzi's *Anecdotes*. Only by mail could the impurities of physical presence be filtered out.

Within the context of his total oeuvre, Johnson's letters to Mrs. Thrale are unique in style, texture, and emotional intensity. Both in quantity and in quality, they also contradict two of his most fervently expressed opinions—the painful drudgery of composition and the inherent "fallacy and sophistication" of "epistolary intercourse." On the first of these two subjects, Johnson held forth repeatedly. To cite but two examples: "I allow you may have pleasure from writing, after it is over, if you have written well; but you don't go willingly to it again"; "Composition is, for the most part, an effort of slow diligence and steady perseverance, to which the mind is dragged by necessity or resolution, and from which the attention is every moment starting to more delightful amusements."[16] Clearly the writer whose surviving letters to Mrs. Thrale number about 350 was not shackled by duty or spurred by necessity. As he confessed to her, with a typical impulse toward generalization: "on my part, I find it very pleasing to write; and what is pleasing is very willingly continued" (283). The high literary standard, varied subject matter, and technical inventiveness of the letters—qualities we shall be documenting in detail—all attest to the sincerity of this declaration.

Johnson's *jeu d'esprit* of 27 October 1777 has most often been taken to anticipate, in the guise of mocking obliquity and satirical inversion, the forthright strictures on "the great epistolick art" advanced in the central section of his *Life of Pope:*

16. *Life* 4.219; *Adventurer* No. 138, *The Idler* and *The Adventurer*, ed. W.J. Bate, John M. Bullitt, and L.F. Powell (New Haven and London: Yale University Press, 1963), p. 494.

In a Man's Letters you know, Madam, his soul lies naked, his letters are only the mirrour of his breast, whatever passes within him is shown undisguised in its natural process. Nothing is inverted, nothing distorted, you see systems in their elements, you discover actions in their motives.

Of this great truth sounded by the knowing to the ignorant, and so echoed by the ignorant to the knowing, what evidence have you now before you. Is not my soul laid open in these veracious pages? do not you see me reduced to my first principles? This is the pleasure of corresponding with a friend, where doubt and distrust have no place, and everything is said as it is thought. The original Idea is laid down in its simple purity, and all the supervenient conceptions, are spread over it stratum super stratum, as they happen to be formed. These are the letters by which souls are united, and by which Minds naturally in unison move each other as they are moved themselves. I know, dearest Lady, that in the perusal of this such is the consanguinity of our intellects, you will be touched as I am touched. I have indeed concealed nothing from you, nor do I expect ever to repent of having thus opened my heart.

(559)

The teasing tone of this letter, with its mock-serious absolutes ("whatever passes . . . is shown undisguised," "Nothing is inverted, nothing distorted"), its inflated rhetorical questions ("Is not my soul laid open in these veracious pages? do not you see me reduced to my first principles?"), its sprinkling of philosophical jargon ("original Idea," "supervenient conceptions," "stratum super stratum"), and its heaving erotic-pathetic diction ("his soul lies naked, his letters are only the mirrour of his breast"), all appear at first reading to suggest that Johnson actually believed the opposite to be true. Thus R.W. Chapman in his note on the letter refers us to the *Life of Pope* for a statement of Johnson's "serious views."[17] Nevertheless, a careful comparison of these two general discussions with each other and with Johnson's actual practice will reveal that both sets of remarks are fraught with slippery tonal ambiguities and theoretical inconsistencies.

17. Chapman, 2.228, n. 2.

As a philosophical empiricist and a watchful Christian moralist, Johnson continually insisted upon fallen man's frightening capacity for self-deception. Any blithe assertion that human beings are naturally good or innately capable of social beneficence provoked a scornful reaction. Thus in the letter to Mrs. Thrale he satirizes two foolish *idées reçues*—that man can know "whatever passes within him . . . undisguised in its natural process"; and that souls, to use appropriate Pauline language, can in this life see face to face. In the middle of a paragraph loaded with false or wildly exaggerated claims, Johnson inserts one serious observation: "This is the pleasure of corresponding with a friend, where doubt and distrust have no place, and everything is said as it is thought." All due allowance must be made for an element of teasing distortion, designed in this instance to bring the observation tonally into line with the commonplace untruths surrounding it. At the same time, we should not hesitate to recognize the degree to which Johnson's practice in the letters to Mrs. Thrale bears out the wisdom of this statement. "Doubt and distrust" truly "have no place," at least in the years of unblemished friendship. Insofar as he is capable of knowing and facing it, Johnson expresses the truth of his emotions without reserve. As Arthur Murphy recognized, he speaks "the language of the heart."

Just as the playful critique of Letter 559 pulls in two directions at once, so the strictures on letter-writing in the *Life of Pope* do not entail an absolute rejection of the genre's potential to foster intimate self-revelation. The apparent extremity of Johnson's opinion here should be attributed to his reaction against the sentimental "cant" of Pope's much-vaunted candor:[18]

> Of his social qualities, if an estimate be made from his Letters, an opinion too favourable cannot easily be formed; they

18. So in the preface to his volume of letters (1737), Pope claimed that they revealed his "real sentiments, as they flowed warm from the heart, and fresh from the occasion, without the least thought that ever the world should be a witness to them." Quoted in Samuel Johnson, *Lives of the English Poets*, ed. G.B. Hill (Oxford: Clarendon Press, 1905), 3.207, n. 1.

exhibit a perpetual and unclouded effulgence of general benevolence and particular fondness. There is nothing but liber-
ality, gratitude, constancy, and tenderness. It has been so long
said as to be commonly believed that the true characters of
men may be found in their letters, and that he who writes to
his friend lays his heart open before him. But the truth is that
such were simple friendships of the *Golden Age,* and are now
the friendships only of children.[19]

Johnson emphatically disbelieved—and with good reason—
such protestations as Pope's to Caryll: "my style, like my soul,
appears in its natural undress before my friend."[20] In the
first part of his commentary, he dismisses Pope's claim that
his letters form "a Window in the bosom."[21] He then turns his
attention to their alleged stylistic "undress": "If the Letters of
Pope are considered merely as compositions they seem to be
premeditated and artificial. It is one thing to write because
there is something which the mind wishes to discharge, and
another to solicit the imagination because ceremony or vanity
requires something to be written."[22] Perhaps the most effective critique of the dual claims to unmediated truth and stylistic negligence comes in another letter to Mrs. Thrale,
composed just after he had begun serious reading for the *Life
of Pope:* "Now you think yourself the first Writer in the world
for a letter about nothing. Can you write such a letter as this?
So miscellaneous, with such noble disdain of regularity, like
Shakespeare's works, such graceful negligence of transition
like the ancient enthusiasts. The pure voice of nature and of
friendship" (657). Johnson rejects all "enthusiastic" claims for

19. *Lives of the English Poets* 3.206–7.
20. *The Correspondence of Alexander Pope,* ed. George Sherburn (Oxford:
Clarendon Press, 1956), 1.155. Compare the verdict of James A. Winn in *A
Window in the Bosom: The Letters of Alexander Pope:* "Pope obviously did not
show 'his Heart to all the world'; the window he made in his bosom in his
published letters was carefully constructed to reveal only a few aspects of his
mind, selected and polished for public display" (Hamden: Archon Books,
1977, p. 200).
21. *Correspondence of Alexander Pope* 2.23.
22. *Lives of the English Poets* 3.208.

the familiar letter, yet shows what the genre can accomplish in the very act of deflating its votaries.

The key to Johnson's practice and his achievement in the letters to Hester Thrale is his conception of them as a form of intimate conversation. With the exception of several moral essays-in-miniature (e.g., 204, 338, 465), he attempts on most occasions to recreate the warm inconsequentiality, the private allusiveness, and the darting fragmentations of candid oral discourse. Just before the final rupture in mid-1784, Johnson asked sadly: "Shall we ever exchange confidence by the fireside again?" (938). "Fireside confidence" aptly describes the way in which he viewed their correspondence. Inconsistent as it may seem, given his taste for combative display in conversation, Johnson set a high value on the private *tête-à-tête*. In *Rambler* No. 89 he commends "that interchange of thoughts which is practised in free and easy conversation; where suspicion is banished by experience, and emulation by benevolence; where every man speaks with no other restraint than unwillingness to offend, and hears with no other disposition than desire to be pleased."[23] In writing to Mrs. Thrale, Johnson attempts to duplicate the salient features of such an "interchange of thoughts," to banish from his letters the attributes of "ceremony" and "vanity" he had criticized in Pope.[24]

Johnson loved "to hear . . . my Mistress talk" (554); he also loved to receive "talking" letters: "Such tattle as filled your last sweet Letter prevents one great inconvenience of absence, that of returning home a stranger and an enquirer. . . . Continue therefore to write all that You would say" (537). He encouraged her to speak openly, freely, and at length, just as if she were presiding over the teapot late at night in the parlor at Streatham: "If you go with Mrs. D—, do not forget me amidst the luxuries of absolute dominion, but let me have kind letters full of yourself, of your own hopes and your own

---

23. *Rambler* No. 89. See *The Rambler*, ed. W.J. Bate and Albrecht B. Strauss (New Haven: Yale University Press, 1969), 2.108.

24. "That is the happiest conversation where there is no competition, no vanity, but a calm quiet interchange of sentiments" (*Life* 2.359).

fears and your own thoughts, and then go where you will" (407). Here and elsewhere Johnson asks for a certain kind of letter, which he in turn is prepared to supply: "I never said with Dr Dodd that *I love to prattle upon paper*, but I have prattled now till the paper will not hold much more, than my good wishes, which I sincerely send you" (583). The essential function of such "prattle" is well defined in a letter that complains of Sophy Thrale's failure to write: "Incommunicative taciturnity neither imparts nor invites friendship, but reposes on a stubborn sufficiency self-centered, and neglects the interchange of that social officiousness by which we are habitually endeared to one another" (906). Throughout the full span of the correspondence, Johnson defines both explicitly (in direct invitations such as that quoted above, No. 407) and tacitly (by consistently writing a certain kind of letter) his personal ideal for "epistolary intercourse."

The underlying conversational model for the Johnson-Thrale correspondence manifests itself in several ways. The single most obvious feature to be derived from the exemplar of fireside confidence is an all-pervasive stress on significant particulars. In Johnson's theory of biography, details if properly selected play an important part in the revelation of character; by witnessing to inner vices and virtues, the walk of a Cataline or the punctuality of a Melancthon furthers the biographer's moral program. The didactic thrust of biography is missing from the familiar letter—yet here too particulars can advance the understanding of character, and in doing so promote the goal of emotional reciprocity. The best possible gloss on Johnson's commitment to significant detail in the familiar letter comes, appropriately enough, from Madame de Sévigné: "Mandez-moi bien de vos nouvelles. Je vous écris en détail, car nous aimons ce style, qui est celui de l'amitié."[25]

Of course the specificity of Johnson's letters often reflects a pragmatic interest in the fortunes of the Thrale brewery, po-

25. Madame de Sévigné, *Correspondance*, ed. Roger Duchêne (Paris: Gallimard, 1972–78), 3.952 (To Coulanges, 1 Dec. 1690).

litical maneuvers in Southwark, the children's health, improvements at Streatham, or the latest medical reports. More often, however, the emphasis on "trifles" helps to communicate a total identification with the pleasures and pains of his adopted family. "Surely my heart is with you in your whole System of Life" (300). Curiosity becomes a form of desire: "Never imagine that your letters are long, they are always too short for my curiosity, I do not know that I was ever content with a single perusal" (308). Johnson-in-exile yearns to capture the very texture of life at Streatham. He also wishes to sustain, even to deepen, his relationship with Hester Thrale: "You have had two or three of my letters to answer, and I hope you will be copious and distinct, and tell me a great deal of your mind; a dear little mind it is, and I hope always to love it better, as I know it more" (401). By responding to her bulletins, and by sending his own, Johnson promotes that sharing of experience which not only bridges a physical gap, but also turns absence into a rarified form of presence.

Johnson's letters consist frequently of a patchwork of specific details, queries, and comments. Nothing is too minute to be related or glossed:

Last night I came safe to Lichfield; this day I was visited by Mrs. Cobb. This afternoon I went to Mrs. Aston, where I found Miss T——, and waited on her home. Miss T——wears spectacles, and can hardly climb the stiles. I was not tired at all, either last night or to-day. Miss Porter is very kind to me. Her dogs and cats are all well.

In all this there is nothing very memorable, but sands form the mountain. *I hope to hear from Streatham of a greater event, that a new being is born that shall in time write such letters as this, and that another being is safe that she may continue to write such. She can indeed do many other things; she can add to the pleasure of many lives, and among others to that of Her most obedient and Most humble servant.*

(252)

In substance this letter communicates one of Johnson's favorite themes: "The variations of life consist of little things.

Important innovations are soon heard, and easily understood. Men that meet to talk of Physicks or Metaphysicks, or law or history may be immediately acquainted. We look at each other in silence only for want of petty talk upon slight occurrences" (537). In Letter 252, the style, a radically simplified version of Johnson's *sermo humilis*, points the message: a cluster of simple declarative sentences composed primarily of monosyllables adheres grain by grain, just as "sands form the mountain." The total effect is not lifeless or condescending, for Johnson infuses his terse reportage with deadpan humor and affectionate concern.

In a letter containing a similar paucity of information Johnson communicates his sympathetic presence with even greater success. The factual content is severely limited: along with a letter from Hester Thrale he has received a peevish missive from Miss Langton, who complains of a fractured courtesy; Johnson's rheumatism continues to give trouble but his nights have been restful; "Our two last fawns are well; but one of our swans is sick" (262). Johnson gives the letter shape and point by framing his chronicle with two gnomic truths: "Sweet meat and sour sauce. . . . Life, says Foresight, is chequer-work." Thus each subsection, inconsequential in its own right, serves to illustrate a general truth, down to the balanced halves of the prevailing compound sentence structure: "the rheumatism has taken away some of my courage: but last night I slept well." Furthermore, Johnson succeeds in drawing out the humorous element in Miss Langton's behavior by placing her remarks in a ludicrously inappropriate historical perspective: "There was formerly in France a *cour de l'amour;* but I fancy nobody was ever summoned before it after three-score: yet in this court, if it now subsisted, I seem likely to be nonsuited." By contextualizing the minutiae of Ashbourne's humdrum routine, Johnson turns life into art—administering solace to himself and delight to his reader.

Not only does Johnson manipulate detail to achieve a conversational density, sweep, and relevance; he also cultivates a distinctive brand of sly, po-faced irony. This vein of laconic humor depends for its effect on an ear attuned to the rhythms and inflections of speech, and on a mind quick to respond to half-buried allusions. Mrs. Thrale—and Mrs. Thrale alone of Johnson's correspondents—provided just such an audience: she could be relied upon to hear the actual voice of the letter-writer speaking his sentences as they were being read. Therefore Johnson could know that his quiet jokes would not misfire for lack of a trained, receptive audience. It would seem inevitable that we—Johnson's unsuspected readers, his intimates at two centuries' remove—are bound to miss many of those same shades of ironic intent. Fortunately Mrs. Piozzi's marginalia allow us at most points to decode the irony—though she herself, no great mistress of economical humor, often underestimates the ability of other readers to detect comic twists and stratagems.

During one of his regular visits with Dr. Taylor at Ashbourne, Johnson undertook an excursion to Chatsworth, one of the principal country houses of England and a major touristic port of call. The following day he sent a terse report to Mrs. Thrale:

> *I was yesterday at Chatsworth. It is a very fine house. I wish you had been with me to see it, for then, as we are apt to want matter of talk, we should have gained something new to talk on. They complimented me with playing the fountains, and opening the cascade. But I am of my friend's opinion, that when one has seen the Ocean, cascades are but little things.*
>
> (288)

The brevity and the seeming placidity of Johnson's response to the great mansion themselves generate part of the dry humor of this paragraph. To limit oneself to saying about Chatsworth, "It is a very fine house," is roughly equivalent to describing St. Paul's Cathedral as "a very fine church." Johnson deliberately abstains from the sort of rhapsodic commentary with which Boswell embroiders his account of their joint visit to another grand country house, Keddleston Hall:

> I was struck with the magnificence of the building; and the extensive park, with the finest verdure, covered with deer, and cattle, and sheep, delighted me. The number of old oaks, of an immense size, filled me with a sort of respectful admiration: for one of them sixty pounds was offered. The excellent smooth gravel roads; the large piece of water formed by his Lordship from some small brooks, with a handsome barge upon it; the venerable Gothick church, now the family chapel, just by the house; in short, the grand group of objects agitated and distended my mind in a most agreeable manner.[26]

This is Boswellian enthusiasm with a vengeance. Johnson by contrast distrusted and avoided enthusiasm in every sphere, from religion to landscape gardening. His deliberate *nil admirari* posture recalls a pungent remark delivered to Boswell during the Keddleston visit: " 'One should think (said I) that the proprietor of all this *must* be happy.'—'Nay, Sir, (said Johnson,) all this excludes but one evil—poverty.' "[27]

Next to the third sentence ("as we are apt to want matter of talk, we should have gained something new to talk on") Mrs. Piozzi jotted "Ironical." The reader of Johnson's letters does not really need this interpretative clue. But he does require the assistance she provides in deciphering the humor of the final sentence: "A Joke on Percy now Bishop of Dromore." Mrs. Piozzi explained this allusion in a letter to Richard Duppa: "In one of these [Percy's letters to his wife] he said 'I am enjoying the fall of a murmuring Stream . . . but to you who reside close to the roaring Ocean, such scenery would be insipid'. *This* our Doctor laughed at, as ridiculous Affectation."[28] Thanks to her commentary, the allusive thrust of the remark emerges from obscurity. Yet this passage is more complex than a mere "Joke on Percy." In the word "compli-

26. *Life* 3.160.
27. *Life* 3.160.
28. Quoted by Chapman, 1.288, nn. 2, 3.

mented" Johnson directs Hester's response to, and signals his appreciation of, the faintly ludicrous element in the situation itself. The notion that he should be entertained (let alone honored) by the display of mechanical gadgets, themselves simulating natural phenomena for which he cared very little, seemed at one level quite droll—just as it seemed laughable to Boswell that their Highland guide should seek to entertain Johnson by whistling at wild goats.[29] On another level, such compliments and contrivances, though they must not be over-valued, should not be unduly scorned. "There is nothing, Sir, too little for so little a creature as man."[30]

In the run of letters describing daily life at Ashbourne, Johnson perfected the laconic, tongue-in-cheek style of delivery that marks his Chatsworth bulletin. The material was not readily susceptible to comic treatment: it consisted of Dr. Taylor's incessant tinkering with his spacious grounds and his equally engrossing agricultural experiments. A Parson Trulliber figure, Taylor displayed to all who knew him a mercantile orientation and an "incurably veterinary cast of . . . mind."[31] Johnson's friends often wondered how he could like this man, let alone visit him year after year, advise him on health and preferment, and write many of his sermons. Not only did Johnson's steadfast friendship with the worldly clergyman puzzle Boswell in particular ("I wondered at their preserving such an intimacy"),[32] it must also have seemed more than a little improbable to Johnson himself. When pressed for an explanation he resorted to a line from Ecclesiasticus: "Sir, I love him; but I do not love him more; my regard for him does not increase. As it is said in the Apocrypha, 'his talk is of bullocks . . .'"[33] Recourse to quotation allowed Johnson to defuse his ambivalent, potentially discor-

29. *Journal of a Tour to the Hebrides*, ed. Frederick A. Pottle and Charles H. Bennett (New York: Viking Press, 1936), p. 110.
30. *Life* 1.433.
31. John Wain, *Samuel Johnson* (New York: Viking Press, 1975), p. 296.
32. *Life* 3.180.
33. *Life* 3.181.

dant feelings through wit—to make a joke, hint his disapproval, yet remain loyal all the same.

To achieve similar ends in his Ashbourne letters, Johnson
devised over the course of several years a special ironic
"turn," which side-stepped overt criticism yet expressed, however obliquely, an unmistakable negative judgment:

> *I have seen the great Bull, and very great he is. I have seen
> likewise his heir apparent, who promises to inherit all the bulk
> and all the virtues of his Sire. I have seen the Man who
> offered an hundred guineas for the young Bull while he was
> yet little better than a Calf. Matlock I am afraid I shall not
> see, but I purpose to see Dovedale, and after all this seeing I
> hope to see You.*

(237)

The repetition of key words, the use of indirect quotation, the
reliance on anaphora, the grandiose genealogical terminology: these devices parody Taylor's speech and mock the
obsession with animal husbandry. Without breaking his stride
Johnson pivots in the final sentence to his own plans, then
contrives an affectionate cadence with which to end the letter.

One year later, back in the Midlands, the Ashbourne idiom
is resumed: "There has been a man Here to day to take a
farm after some talk he went to see the Bull, and said that he
had seen a bigger. Do you think he is likely to get the farm?"
(258). Johnson offers in this one short paragraph a masterpiece of compressed ironic narrative. We hear three voices:
the truculent clergyman-farmer, the blundering tenant, and
the shrewd observer. A story is told and an attitude expressed
with the utmost economy of means. The sly question ("Do
you think he is likely to get the farm?") invites Mrs. Thrale
into the scene while simultaneously detaching her from it; together with the observer-narrator, she can relish the human
comedy, predict the conclusion to the rural vignette, yet preserve a mocking detachment. In a later Ashbourne letter an
equivalent blend of sympathetic identification with ironic distance is achieved by the repetition of one word, "our": "Our

Bulls and Cows are all well, but we yet hate the man that had seen a bigger Bull. Our Deer have died, but many are left. Our waterfal at the garden makes a great roaring this wet weather" (282).

As the Ashbourne visits multiply, however, Johnson abandons the posture of involvement for a different kind of strategy:

> Dr *Taylor desires always to have his compliments sent. He is, in his usual way very busy,—getting a Bull to his cows and a Dog to his bitches. His waterfall runs very well. Old Shakespeare is dead and he wants to buy another horse for his mares. He is one of those who finds every hour* something new to wish or to enjoy.
>
> (553)

A bald catalogue of his activities turns Dr. Taylor into a species of professional panderer, who fills his days with arrangements for lucrative copulation. The allusion to Dryden's couplet from *Absalom and Achitophel* ("Blest madman, who could every hour employ / With something new to wish or to enjoy") cuts in two ways: Taylor's occupation is foolish, yet he is genuinely "blest" in possessing a benign way to fill the vacuity of life.

Admittedly this particular brand of humor, what we might call Johnson's "Ashbourne voice," is an acquired taste. It is subtle, oblique, and dry; it depends on minute adjustments of pace and tone; it can merge without warning into, or dart briefly out from, a central core of *gravitas*.[34] More immediately accessible is another special effect, the built-in complimentary close. This device, which R.W. Chapman labels "the syntactical conclusion," makes its appearance in the very first surviving

---

34. ". . . of the talent of humour he had an almost enviable portion. To describe the nature of this faculty, as he was wont to display it in his hours of mirth and relaxation, I must say, that it was ever of that arch and dry kind, which lies concealed under the appearance of gravity . . ." See Sir John Hawkins, *The Life of Samuel Johnson, LL.D.* (London: J. Buckland, 1787), p. 386.

letter to Mrs. Thrale: "Do not blame me for a delay by which I must suffer so much, and by which I suffer alone. If you cannot think I am good, pray think I am mending, and that in time I may deserve to be, Dear Madam, Your most obedient and most humble servant" (172). As Chapman observes, Johnson uses this device "with great facility and felicity," and nowhere more so than in the letters to Hester Thrale.[35] In fact it becomes something of a private trademark: out of 200-odd syntactical conclusions in all of Johnson's surviving letters, sixty-three have been counted in those to Mrs. Thrale, as against thirteen in those to Boswell, for example.[36] It also provides a barometer with which to measure Johnson's emotional weather: he almost never employs the device when afflicted by *mens turbata,* as the diary entries describe various kinds of inner disturbance.

This built-in close can be quite perfunctory ("Pray write to Dear Madam Your most obedient and most humble Servant" 408); but even when short, it is usually carefully turned: "The days grow short, and we have frosts; but I am in all weathers, Madam, Your most humble Servant" (557). A literary device peculiar to the letter-form, it is ideally suited to the expression of gallantry—whether serious, playful, gently mocking, or even wistful in tone.[37] The lighthearted mood tends to predominate, invited by the special character of the technique itself, which resembles a dancer's graceful pirouette: "Though I am going to dine with Lady Craven, I am Madam Your most humble servant" (659); "I hope on Monday to be your slave in the morning, and Mrs. Smith's in the Evening, and then fall again to my true Mistress, and be the rest of the week, Madam, Your most obedient . . ." (350).

---

35. R.W. Chapman, "The Formal Parts of Johnson's Letters," in *Essays on the Eighteenth Century* (Oxford: Clarendon Press, 1945), p. 152.

36. In his famous letter to Lord Chesterfield, Johnson inverts the posture of gallantry suggested by the syntactical conclusion: he turns the formula into a weapon, twisting the knife with one last flourish of icy *politesse.*

37. Chapman, p. 152.

Nonetheless, Johnson becomes adept at imbuing the playful with serious undertones, as in this letter from the Midlands:

> *Mr. Seward left Lichfield yesterday, I am afraid, not much mended by his opium. He purposes to wait on you. and if envy could do much mischief, he would have much to dread, since he will have the pleasure of seeing you sooner than, Dear Madam, Your most obliged and most humble Servant . . .*
>
> (266)

As the friendship with Hester begins to dwindle after Henry Thrale's death, Johnson struggles to reassert the unclouded intimacy of years past. His epistolary conclusions encapsulate the struggle: their form preserves the gallant framework erected in the old days, their contents are curdled by an unmistakable pathos: "Do not let Mr. Piozzi nor any body else put me quite out of your head, and do not think that any body will love you like Your, etc." (778). Measured against the sprightly flourishes of previous letters, these final examples turn compliment into supplication: "Let me have your kindness and your prayers and think on me, as on a man who for a very great portion of Your life, has done You all the good he could, and desires still to be considered as, Madam, Your most humble servant" (858). The gallant Johnson of the 1770s is here reduced to conjuring up the spectre of days and letters gone by, "the attention and tenderness of ancient time" (900). Sadly, these desperate efforts at emotional resurrection are doomed to failure.

The appeal of Johnson's experiments with traditional epistolary formulas and the pyrotechnics of compliment is matched by an attractive talent for self-mockery. Like the deadpan ironies of Ashbourne and the manipulation of colloquial detail, this thawing into reflexive parody both witnesses and contributes to the uniquely conversational mood of the Thrale letters. To a degree unparalleled elsewhere, Johnson demonstrates that he can take *himself* lightly. On occasion he will mock his penchant for quoting hackneyed apothegms:

"At Lichfield I found little to please me. One more of my few
school fellows is dead, upon which I might make a new reflection, and say Mors omnibus communis" (260). He can make
fun of one of his deep-seated character traits, the habit of
doing everything by extremes:[38]

> *You are afraid, you say, lest I extenuate myself too fast, and*
> *are an enemy to Violence, but did you never hear nor read,*
> *dear Madam, that every Man has his genius, and that the*
> *great rule by which all excellence is attained, and all success*
> *procured is, to follow genius, and have you not observed in*
> *all our conversations that my genius is always in extremes,*
> *that I am very noisy, or very silent; very gloomy, or very*
> *merry; very sour or very kind? and would you have me cross*
> *my genius when it leads me sometimes to voracity and some-*
> *times to abstinence?*
>
> (686)

At times Johnson also parodies the procedure that underlies
many of his moral essays, an inexorable broadening out from
particular human phenomena to melancholy general truths:

> *Mr. Grene the Apothecary has found a book which tells who*
> *paid levies in our parish, and how much they paid, above an*
> *hundred years ago. Do you not think we study this book hard?*
> *Nothing is like going to the bottom of things. Many families*
> *that paid the parish rates are now extinct, like the race of*
> *Hercules. Pulvis et umbra sumus. What is nearest us, touches*
> *us most. The passions rise higher at domestick than at imperial*
> *tragedies. I am not wholly unaffected by the revolutions of*
> *Sadler street, nor can forbear to mourn a little when old*
> *names vanish, and new come into their place.*
>
> (233)

This passage also contains a telegraphic moral epitome, as if
Johnson were trying to compress the maximum number of

---

38. "Every thing about his character and manners was forcible and violent; there never was any moderation; many a day did he fast, many a year
did he refrain from wine; but when he did eat, it was voraciously; when he
did drink wine, it was copiously. He could practise abstinence, but not tem-
perance" (*Life* 4.72).

home truths into the minimum possible space: "Pulvis et umbra sumus. What is nearest, touches us most. The passions rise higher at domestick than at imperial tragedies." As Mrs. Thrale could be expected to recognize, these shorthand references collapse the bulk of his public teaching into jumbled clichés.

In a series of four letters on the pseudo-Venetian regatta of 1775, Johnson tries his hand at extended self-parody. The result is surprisingly deft—considerably more so, in fact, than the imitations of "Johnsonese" excerpted by Boswell in the *Life*. Johnson seizes the occasion to mimic all of his salient traits as moral preacher: the sententious aphorisms, the sweeping generalizations; the periodicity, Latinity, doublets and antitheses. Indeed he shapes in microcosm several *Rambler* essays, whose context and stylistic exaggeration insure a comic effect:

> *You will see a show with philosophick superiority, and therefore may see it safely. It is easy to talk of sitting at home contented when others are seeking or making shows. But not to have been where it is supposed, and seldom supposed falsely, that all would go if they could; To be able ‹to› say nothing when every one is talking; to have no opinion when every one is judging; to hear exclamations of rapture without power to depress; to listen to falsehoods without right to contradict, is, after all, a state of temporary inferiority, in ‹which› the mind is rather hardened by stubborness, than supported by fortitude. If the world be worth winning let us enjoy it, if it is to be despised let us despise it by conviction. But the world is not to be despised but as it is compared with something better. Company is in itself better than solitude and pleasure better than indolence. Ex nihilo nihil fit, says the moral as well as natural philosopher.*

> (409)

With glee Johnson tangles the reader in convoluted syntactic coils while puncturing his own "philosophick superiority." The delightful sequence of mini-essays on the regatta ends with a command that, if carried out by the letter-writer, would rob him of subjects for moral discourse and thereby of a public identity. A "syntactical conclusion" helps to bring down the rocket in a shower of sparks:[39]

> *It is the good of publick life that it supplies agreeable topicks and general conversation. Therefore wherever you are, and whatever you see, talk not of the Punick war; nor of the depravity of human nature; nor of the slender motives of human actions; nor of the difficulty of finding employment or pleasure; but talk, and talk, and talk of the regatta, and keep the rest for, dearest Madam, Your, etc.*

(414)

The capacity to embellish and to communicate meaning by means of literary allusion further distinguishes Johnson's letters to Mrs. Thrale from those to his other correspondents.[40] Like the techniques we have just been considering, Johnson's generous allusiveness transforms a potentially unilateral sequence of gestures into a genuine dialogue. Mrs. Thrale's alert response to a wide range of material is anticipated, taken for granted, and even woven into the shape of the letter, which thereby becomes a shared enterprise rather than a detached soliloquy. Furthermore, the uninhibited practice of fragmentary quotation cannot help but flatter the recipient: it pays an unusual tribute to Mrs. Thrale's learning in an age when very few women had won access to the masculine world of *literae humaniores*. Finally, the prevalence of allusion defines a community of interest apart from—though to a degree contiguous with—the domestic concerns of London or Streatham. In certain letters Johnson imaginatively places himself and his correspondent in the library instead of the salon, the nursery, the counting house, or the dining room.

---

39. "When Johnson rises to an epistolary setpiece we may suspect irony— and, sure enough, the rocket presently explodes and comes down in a shower of sparks." See Mary Lascelles, review of Chapman's *Letters*, *Review of English Studies* 5 (1954): 93.

40. "In his letters to his other friends these quotations and allusions are as rare as in those to her they are abundant." See *Letters of Samuel Johnson*, ed. G.B. Hill (Oxford: Clarendon Press, 1892), 1.xii.

Johnson's practice extends from a single allusion, dropped almost in passing, through whole paragraphs fraught with literary reference, to letters whose entire fabric consists of interlocking quotations. Single phrases or lines can point an argument or heighten an emotion, as in this example of anguished protest at Hester Thrale's indifference:

> *How this will be received by You I know not, I hope You will sympathise with me, but perhaps*
>
> *My Mistress gracious, mild, and good,*
> *Cries, Is he dumb? 'tis time he shou'd.*
>
> *But can this be possible, I hope it cannot.*
>
> (850)

The couplet associates Mrs. Thrale with the group of putative friends who chorus hypocritically in the cynical refrains of "Verses on the Death of Dr. Swift." Johnson can also make humorous use of brief allusions: "I shall charge you with having lingred away in expectation and disappointment, two months which are both physically and morally considered as analogous to the fervid and vigorous part of human life . . . two months which, as Doodle says, you never saw before, and which, as la Bruyere says, you shall never see again" (266). The totally unexpected juxtaposition of *Tom Thumb* to La Bruyère sends up a momentary flare of burlesque. The joke resides in the banality, the superfluity, and the incongruity both of the quotations and the act of quotation. A similar incongruity, this time between the epic microcosm of the *Aeneid* and the domestic microcosm of life at Lichfield, is exploited in this embellishment of a day's routine: "I could tell you about Lucy's two cats, and Brill her brother's old dog, who is gone deaf, but the day would fail me. Suadentque cadentia sidera somnum. So said Aeneas but I have not yet had my dinner" (408).

Johnson only realizes the full potential of literary allusion, however, in letters preoccupied with themes of distance, separation, and longing. In time of stress or deep emotion, the technique of linked quotation offers a major advantage, particularly to a man of Johnson's temperament: it allows him to express the full depths of feeling while preserving control, to transmit direct messages by indirection. Since Hester Thrale can be relied upon not only to recognize the source but also the context of a quotation, Johnson can with decorous brevity speak volumes—and speak *through* volumes, appropriating the words of other men to convey his own emotions. Though he would not have relished the comparison, in this respect Johnson resembles no one so much as Thomas Gray.

Two short letters (Nos. 552 and 191) largely depend upon such a web of allusion to articulate their emotional subtext. In the longer of the two (552), Johnson writes from Ashbourne to Streatham, where Mrs. Thrale is about to leave for a seaside excursion. The tone is mixed; the serious as well as the comic dimension of the letter depends upon an informed interpretation of the references to Shakespeare and to Virgil:

> And so, here is this post without a letter. I am old, I am old, says Sir John Falstaff. 'Take heed, my dear, youth flies apace.' You will be wanting a letter sometime. I wish I were with you, but I cannot come yet.—
>
>   *Glacies et frigora Rheni*
> *Me sine sola vides. Ah! ne te frigora laedant*
> *Ah tibi ne glacies teneras secet aspera plantas! Ecl. x.*
>
> I wish you well; B‹urney› and all, and shall be glad to know your adventures. Do not however think wholly to escape me, you will, I hope, see me at Brighthelmston. Dare you answer me as Brutus answered his evil genius? I know not when I shall write again now you are going to the world's end. *Extra anni solisque vias*, where the post will be a long time in reaching you. I shall notwithstanding all distance continue to think on you, and to please myself with the hope of being once again Madam, Your most humble servant . . .

Johnson whimsically redirects the lines from Virgil, especially the quotation from Eclogue 10, part of Gallus's lament for his absent Lycoris:

Alpinas a! dura, nives et frigora Rheni
me sine sola vides. a! te ne frigora laedant!
a! tibi ne teneras glacies secet aspera plantas![41]

Instead of sliding about perilously in the mountains, Mrs.
Thrale will be bathing comfortably in the ocean. Brighton is
not "the world's end"—or Philippi, for that matter. Yet
humor is not unmixed with sadness: Johnson's hyperbolic
pose holds loneliness at arm's length without subduing it.

This sense of loneliness, even of foreboding, emerges with
greater force from Falstaff's line (2 *Henry IV*, 2.4). It seems
probable that Johnson intends to remind Hester Thrale of
the conversation between Falstaff and Doll Tearsheet:

Fal. Thou dost give me flattering busses.
Dol. By my troth, I kiss thee with a most constant heart.
Fal. I am old, I am old.
Dol. I love thee better than I love e'er a scurvy young boy of
         them all.
Fal. What stuff wilt have a kirtle of? I shall receive money
         o'Thursday. Shalt have a cap tomorrow. A merry song,
         come. It grows late; we'll to bed. Thou'lt forget me when
         I am gone.

It would be dangerous to press the parallels too far. But to
anyone who knows the history of the Johnson-Thrale friendship, the uncanny relevance of this exchange will be apparent.
With the benefit of hindsight, we respond to poignant dramatic ironies that Johnson cannot fully have intended. Nevertheless, in a letter that cites three accurate literary
predictions, the presence of a genuinely prophetic cast of
thought cannot be ignored.

The second letter (191) voices a darker mood. Its spine
consists of three thematically connected quotations: from

41. ". . . art gazing, ah, heartless one! on Alpine snows and the frost-
bound Rhine, apart from me, all alone. Ah, may the frosts not harm thee!
Ah, may not the jagged ice cut thy tender feet!" (trans. H.R. Fairclough, Loeb
Classical Library).

Ovid's *Tristia* (1.1), Virgil's *Aeneid* (6.425), and Ovid's *Heroides* (1.2):

> You are returned, I suppose, from Brighthelmstone, and
> this letter will be read at Streatham.—*Sine me, liber, ibis in
> urbem.*
> I have felt in this place something like the shackles of des-
> tiny. There has not been one day of pleasure, and yet I cannot
> get away. But when I do come, I perhaps shall not be easily
> persuaded to pass again to the other side of Styx, to venture
> myself on the irremeable road. I long to see you, and all those
> of whom the sight is included in seeing you. *Nil mihi rescribas;*
> for though I have no right to say *Ispa veni*, I hope that *ipse
> veniam*. Be pleased to make my compliments.

In part this triad assimilates Lichfield, where Johnson was staying with Lucy Porter, to a mythological realm, a classical place of banishment—Pontus, Hades, Ithaca. In fact Johnson begins a letter, written from Lichfield one week later, "I hope soon to return from exile" (192.1). Furthermore, in light of the reference to *Aeneid* 6, one should note that Johnson believed the name of his self-appointed place of exile to mean "field of the dead."[42]

The first quotation, from Ovid's *Tristia*, implicitly compares the letter-writer to the forlorn poet, who longs for Rome and the company of his friends while languishing by the Black Sea. Strictly speaking the line is not appropriate, for Johnson in the city is writing to Hester Thrale in the country. However, he intends to evoke a tone and a dramatic situation—that of a voice crying in the wilderness. A similar inten-

---

42. In his final letter to Mrs. Thrale, 8 July 1784, Johnson alludes with special poignancy to the same line: "When Queen Mary took the resolution of sheltering herself in England, the Archbishop of St. Andrew's attempting to dissuade her, attended on her journey and when they came to the *irremeable stream* that separated the two kingdoms, walked by her side into the water, in the middle of which he seized her bridle, and with earnestness proportioned to her danger and his own affection, pressed her to return" (972, my italics). Virgil's "irremeabilis unda" (6.425) is of course the Styx, which Johnson himself was soon to cross. See Mary Lascelles, "Johnson's Last Allusion to Mary Queen of Scots," *Review of English Studies* 8 (1957): 32–37.

tion holds true for the second Ovidian reference, adapted
from the beginning of *Heroides* 1, Penelope's apostrophe to
Ulysses:

> Haec tua Penelope lento tibi mittit, Ulixe;
>   nil mihi rescribas attinet: ipse veni! . . .
> non ego deserto iacuissem frigida lecto,
>   nec quererer tardos ire relicta dies;
> nec mihi quaerenti spatiosam fallere noctem
>   lassaret viduas pendula tela manus.[43]

Once again a literal application of these lines would not be
appropriate, for Penelope at home is speaking to Ulysses in
exile. Yet here as well Johnson wishes to present himself as
the forsaken lover, "cold in my deserted bed," for whom the
days and nights hang heavy. Lichfield without Hester is
Ithaca without Ulysses; for that reason, Streatham has become the focus of longing.

Johnson employs all of his favorite devices—literary allusion, parody, sly irony, intimate detail—to create in certain
letters a tonal montage, the epistolary equivalent to a conversation with a close friend, which can pass rapidly through a
spectrum of moods and attitudes precisely because speaker
and addressee know each other so well. One such letter announces Johnson's arrival for the annual visit with Dr. Taylor:

> *Last Saturday I came to Ashbourn; the dangers or the plea-*
> *sures of the journey I have at present no disposition to recount.*
> *Else might I paint the beauties of my native plain, might I tell*
> *of 'the smiles of Nature and the charms of art', else might I*
> *relate how I crossed the Staffordshire Canal one of the great*
> *efforts of human labour and human contrivance, which from*
> *the bridge on which I viewed it, passed away on either side,*
> *and loses itself in distant regions uniting waters that Nature*

---

43. "These words your Penelope sends to you, O Ulysses, slow of return
that you are; writing back is pointless: come yourself! . . . Then had I not lain
cold in my deserted bed, nor would now be left alone complaining of slowly
passing days; nor would the hanging web be wearying now my widowed
hands as I seek to beguile the hours of spacious night" (trans. Grant Shower-
man, rev. G.P. Goold, Loeb Classical Library).

had divided, and dividing lands which Nature had united. I might tell how these reflections fermented in my mind till the chaise stopped at Ashbourne, at Ashbourne in the Peak. Let not the barren name of the peak terrify you; I have never wanted Strawberries and cream. The great Bull has no disease but age. I hope in time to be like the great Bull; and hope you will be like him too a hundred years hence.

In the mean time, dearest Madam, you have many dangers to pass. I hope the danger of this year is now over, and you are safe in Bed with a pretty little Stranger in the cradle. I hope you do not think me indifferent about you, and therefore will take care to have me informed.

(254)

The shape of the letter might be diagrammed as an inverted pyramid: it narrows down from broadly based generalities to pointed expressions of sympathy and concern. The first paragraph reduces mock-epic elevation to humble domesticity, the high style to the low, elegant pastoral to colloquial georgic. It begins by invoking the stately world of Addison's "A Letter from Italy" and hinting a contrast, via the rhetorical figure of *occupatio,* with "the beauties of my native plain": "Else might I . . . might I . . . else might I . . ." It ends with references to ripe fruit and flourishing livestock.

The letter as a whole rotates on a tripod of wordplay, by means of which the second paragraph, which seems to introduce an entirely new subject, actually returns to the themes of the first. Johnson announces his safe arrival, then asks about the arrival of the new baby; he recounts his travels and alludes to her travails; he describes "the great efforts of human labour," then hopes "you are safe in Bed with a pretty little Stranger in the cradle." The letter begins with the "dangers" of Johnson's journey and concludes with a wish that "the danger of this year is now over." Surely this witty monologue and others equally adroit, though they do not flaunt their technical accomplishment, go far toward disproving Mary Lascelles's verdict on Johnson's achievement: "Judged by the standards of their age, these are not letters of art."[44]

44. Lascelles, review, p. 93.

To read Johnson's letters to Hester Thrale is to perceive certain striking parallels with an earlier master of intimacy—a letter-writer of equivalent literary eminence, public reticence, and private self-revelation. Throughout their correspondence Johnson and Mrs. Thrale seem to be recapitulating with more than subliminal awareness the emotional drama and stylistic maneuvers of Swift's *Journal to Stella*. Both partners articulate significant lines of connection, actual and potential. Johnson is the first to do so: early in the correspondence he couches a parallel in the guise of an anti-Swiftian jibe. The jibe itself forms part of a teasing yet deeply felt compliment:

> *Now I know you want to be forgetting me, but I do not want to be forgotten, and would rather send you letters like* Presto's, *than suffer myself to slip out of your memory. That I should forget you there is no danger, for I have time enough to think both by night and day, and he that has leisure for any thing that is not present, always turns his mind to that which he likes best.*
>
> (214)

The tone of the reference to "letters like *Presto's*" is difficult to interpret: it is disparaging but not dismissive. Johnson tacitly acknowledges that Swift's letters, or letters like Swift's—for all their whimsy, unabashed egotism, and arch informality—do serve their primary purpose, to make vividly present the memory of the correspondent. The second sentence further implies that Johnson as letter-writer shares a basic goal with Swift—the perpetuation and intensification of a deeply affectionate tie. Johnson's reference to the *Journal* in his *Life of Swift* demonstrates a similar ambivalence: "Whether these diurnal trifles were properly exposed to eyes which had never received any pleasure from the presence of the Dean, may be reasonably doubted. They have, however, some odd attraction."[45]

Mrs. Thrale, on the other hand, appears to take uncomplicated pleasure in the similitude. An entry from *Thraliana*

45. *Lives of the English Poets* 3.23.

compares her own witticisms favorably to Stella's: "I do not think my bons Mots like Stella's the best among those of my Friends, but I think Stella's very paltry ones; and much wonder at the moderate degree of Excellence with which Dr Swift was contented to make a Bustle with my Namesake Miss *Hester* Johnson."[46] Casting herself in the role of latter-day Stella, she invites Johnson to play the corresponding part of the Dean. He accepts the invitation and produces impromptu verses of Swiftian "easiness and gaiety":[47]

> On other occasion I can boast verses from Dr. Johnson.—As I went into his room the morning of my birth-day once, and said to him, Nobody sends me any verses now, because I am five-and-thirty years old; and Stella was fed with them till forty-six, I remember. My being just recovered from illness and confinement will account for the manner in which he burst out suddenly . . .[48]

The Swift-Stella prototype, which reminds Mrs. Thrale of Pope's relationship with Martha Blount, also figures prominently in a reflective passage from *Thraliana*, dated 1 May 1779:

> It appears to me that no Man can live his Life quite thro', without being at *some* period of it under the Dominion of *some* Woman—Wife Mistress or Friend.—
>
> Pope & Swift, were softened by the Smiles of Patty Blount & Stella; & our stern Philosopher Johnson trusted me about the Years 1767 or 1768—I know not which just now—with a Secret far dearer to him than his Life: such however is his nobleness, & such his partiality, that I sincerely believe he has never since that Day regretted his Confidence, or ever looked with less kind Affection on her who had him in her Power.[49]

This entry has been much quoted by biographers seeking to puzzle out the nature of Johnson's "Secret." No one has yet

46. *Thraliana* 1.156.
47. *Lives of the English Poets* 3.65.
48. *Johnsonian Miscellanies* 1.259.
49. *Thraliana* 1.384–85.

asked what the passage tells us about Mrs. Thrale's perception of their bond, how that perception influenced her practice as letter-writer, and how her practice guided Johnson's own. In an important marginal gloss she adds the example of Sterne's *Journal to Eliza* to those of Swift and Pope: "Sterne's attachment to Mrs Draper was another of the odd Things of this kind—Their Letters printed under the Names of Yorick & Eliza are a proof of his strong Admiration."[50] Not only are Mrs. Thrale's comparisons just; they also reflect a penetrating intuition of Johnson's motives and methods in his letters to her. She acts here as her own interpreter, creating a direct line of biographical and literary affiliation. It is the basis of that affiliation that needs to be examined.

The emotional constitution of the two friendships is almost identical: an older man relaxes to an unprecedented degree in the company of a much younger woman, who can be treated (by reason of her age and sex) as a pupil, but also conversed with (because of her intelligence, wit, and wide reading) as an equal. In both cases, the man comes to count the woman as his closest friend. Irvin Ehrenpreis describes Esther Johnson as Swift's "dearest, most intimate companion," who "had nursed him through his diseases, presided at his entertainments, heard out his daily complaints, and had thrown a motherly screen between his uneasy nature and the haze of annoyances which beset him."[51] The protective intimacy of this unique companionship explains the *Journal to Stella:*

> They knew each other in and out; the good and the bad, the deep and the trivial; so that without effort or concealment he could use those precious moments late at night or the first thing on waking to pour out upon her the whole story of his day, with its charities and meannesses, its affections and ambitions and despairs, as though he were thinking aloud.[52]

50. *Thraliana* 1.384, n. 3.
51. Irvin Ehrenpreis, *The Personality of Jonathan Swift* (London: Methuen and Co., 1958), pp. 18, 25.
52. Virginia Woolf, *The Second Common Reader* (London: Hogarth Press, [1932] 1974), p. 69.

Johnson's epistolary ideal, as we have seen, is that of fireside confidence; the same goal conditions the letters to Esther Johnson.

Swift writes to "MD" at ease: early in the morning or late at night, swaddled in bedclothes or huddled in a dressing gown. Physical relaxation promotes stylistic undress: thus Swift "prattles" by letter. "So I'll rise, and bid you farewel; yet I'm loth to do so, because there is a great bit of paper yet to talk upon"; "No, faith, you are just here upon this little paper, and therefore I see and talk with you every evening constantly, and sometimes in the morning . . ."[53] In reading the *Journal* we overhear one side of an ongoing dialogue:

> *Well, 'tis now almost twelve . . . and now I am got to bed.*
> *Well, and what have you to say to Presto now he is a-bed?*
> *Come now, let us hear your speeches. No, 'tis a lie, I an't*
> *sleepy yet. Let us sit up a little longer, and talk. Well, where*
> *have you been to-day, that you are but just this minute come*
> *home in a coach? What have you lost? Pay the coachman,*
> *Stella. No, faith, not I, he'll grumble.—What new acquain-*
> *tance have you got? come, let us hear.*[54]

Swift like Johnson juggles subjects and tones, approximating on paper the shifting rhythms, half-voiced associations, and abrupt juxtapositions of oral exchange. Both men piece together a mosaic of epigrams, proverbs, endearments, precepts, and domestic minutiae—of health and diet, purchases and parcels, excursions and confrontations, dreams and idle thoughts:

> *We are now all impatient for the queen's speech, what she will*
> *say about removing the ministry, &c. I have got a cold, and I*

---

53. Jonathan Swift, *Journal to Stella*, ed. Harold Williams (Oxford: Clarendon Press, 1948), 1.153, 232, Cf. *Journal to Stella* 1.53: "Oh Lord, here's but a trifle of my letter written yet; what shall Presto do for prittle prattle to entertain MD?" For a thorough discussion of Swift's conversational model, see Frederick N. Smith, "Dramatic Elements in Swift's *Journal to Stella*," *Eighteenth-Century Studies* 1 (1968): 332–52. Also Archibald C. Elias, "Jonathan Swift and Letter-writing: The Natural and the Playful in His Personal Correspondence," (Ph.D. diss. Yale University, 1973), chap. 2.

54. *Journal to Stella* 1.112.

*don't know how; but got it I have, and am hoarse: I don't
know whether it will grow better or worse. What's that to you?
I won't answer your letter to-night. I'll keep you a little longer
in suspence: I can't send it. Your mother's cakes are very good,
and one of them serves me for a breakfast, and so I'll go sleep
like a good boy.*[55]

Through Jamesian "solidity of specification," Swift as well as
Johnson invites his reader to become a vicarious participant,
whose intuited responses pattern the letter as it is being
written.

The most obvious expression of Swift's relaxed, conversational approach—his desire to make the familiar letter as familiar as possible—is the famous "little language." Johnson
also uses nicknames and diminutives, such as "My Mistress,"
"little Mama," "funny little thing," "this little Dog."[56] In both
instances the vocabulary of the nursery, the schoolroom, and
the inner closet not only fosters tonal intimacy, it also evades
the latent demands of sexuality by veiling the erotic in the
fraternal.[57] W.J. Bate's discussion of Johnson's "infantilism"
in the French letter applies more cogently to Swift's practice
in the *Journal.* As Ehrenpreis has pointed out, Swift projects
himself as "an innocent child with Mrs. Johnson as a tolerant
mother," or treats her "as an erring child with himself as a
fatherly mentor . . ."[58] Both Swift and Johnson expect to be
masters while asking to be mastered: "Ah, why don't you go
down to Clogher nautinautinauti-deargirls; I dare not say
nauti without dear: O, faith, you govern me."[59] In creating
for their correspondents the identity of mother/lover, they
take refuge in a fantasy of guiltless ambivalence.

55. *Journal to Stella* 1.105.
56. Nos. 264.3, 623, 197.
57. Many of William James's letters to his sister Alice are similarly flir-
tatious within a "safe" fraternal context. Jean Strouse describes them as "self-
absorbed and seductive": "He addressed courtly, playful letters to her as
'You lovely babe,' 'Charmante Jeune Fille,' 'Perfidious child!' and 'Cherie
Charmante de Bal.'" See *Alice James: A Biography* (New York: Bantam Books,
1982), pp. 55–56, 107.
58. Irvin Ehrenpreis, *Dr. Swift* (Cambridge: Harvard University Press,
1967), pp. 658–59.
59. *Journal to Stella* 1.124.

Just as Mrs. Thrale is closely bound up in Johnson's mind with Streatham Park, so thoughts of Stella mingle with dreams of Laracor. Both men, when in exile from the *locus amoenus*, think of their respective correspondents as the keeper of a personal Arcadia. This vision of a secret garden and its tutelary spirit carries a positive symbolic charge: it implies strong, enduring loyalties, simple pleasures, and temporary absolution from responsibility. The city, by contrast, is associated with politics, illness, and hypocrisy. Ironically, for both Johnson and Swift life in London alone could bring lasting contentment; yet these devoted city-dwellers long for the pastoral spot where the cherished correspondent dwells. Lonely and ill, Johnson reports wistfully from Bolt Court: "I am writing over the little garden. The poplars, which I have just now watered, grow kindly; they may expect not to be neglected for they came from Streatham" (839.1). The following month, still beset by sickness and "the black Dog" of melancholy, he ends a letter mired in the present with a glance backward to the verdant past: "I have however watered the garden both yesterday and to day, just as I watered the laurel in the Island" (857). In Swift's letters the Laracor cameos, like Johnson's references to Streatham, emblematize the absent person whose memory permeates a distant place:

> *The duke of Argyle is gone; and whether he has my memorial, I know not, till I see Dr. Arbuthnott, to whom I gave it. That hard name belongs to a Scotch doctor, an acquaintance of the duke's and me; Stella can't pronounce it. Oh, that we were at Laracor this fine day! the willows begin to peep, and the quicks to bud. My dream's out: I was a-dreamed last night that I eat ripe cherries.—And now they begin to catch the pikes, and will shortly the trouts (pox on these ministers), and I would fain know whether the floods were ever so high as to get over the holly bank or the river walk; if so, then all my pikes are gone; but I hope not. Why don't you ask Parvisol these things, sirrahs? And then my canal, and trouts, and whether the bottom be fine and clear?*[60]

60. *Journal to Stella* 1.219–20.

If Hester Thrale is the Mistress of Streatham, then Esther Johnson is the *genius loci* of Laracor: ". . . and so I bid my dearest MD farewel till to-night. I heartily wish myself with them, as hope saved. My willows, and quicksets, and trees will be finely improved, I hope, this year."[61]

In their letters (to Hester, to Esther) these two men of public affairs discover an unsuspected private self and a language with which to define it. "T'other I," in Swift's phrase—the Rambler, the Examiner—is banished from the intimate matrix they shape with such meticulous care. Johnson's valedictory summation of his friendship aptly describes the mission he shares with Swift:

> *To those that have lived long together every thing heard and every thing seen recals some pleasure communicated, or some benefit confered, some petty quarrel or some slight endearment. Esteem of great powers or amiable qualities newly discovered may embroider a day or a week, but a friendship of twenty years is interwoven with the texture of life.*

(900)

To capture the texture of a friendship, and to weave their letters into it, is the task both men successfully accomplish.

61. *Journal to Stella* 2.484.

Index

Index